PASTORAL MINISTRY
FOR THE NEXT GENERATION

"We will tell the next generation the praiseworthy deeds of the Lord . . .
That the generation to come may know them . . ."
(Psalm 78:4, 6).

Jere L. Phillips, PhD

innovo
PUBLISHING

Collierville, Tennessee

Published by
Innovo Publishing, LLC
www.innovopublishing.com
1-888-546-2111

Providing Full-Service Publishing Services for
Christian Authors, Artists & Organizations: Hardbacks, Paperbacks,
eBooks, Audiobooks, Music & Film

PASTORAL MINISTRY FOR THE NEXT GENERATION

Unless otherwise noted, all Scripture is taken from the King James Version of the Holy Bible.
Some references to "thee" have been modernized.

Library of Congress Control Number: 2014956413
ISBN 13: 978-1-61314-995-9

Cover Design & Interior Layout: Innovo Publishing, LLC

Printed in the United States of America
U.S. Printing History

First Edition: December 2014

ENDORSEMENTS

"There are few callings as momentous and weighty as God's call of a pastor to the gospel ministry. The task of pastoral ministry demands deliberation and instruction, and in *Pastoral Ministry for the Next Generation*, Jere Phillips provides both. This text is a great read for those looking to count the cost prior to their call and those trying to follow Christ in shepherding His flock."

—**Ed Stetzer, president of LifeWay Research Division, editor of edstetzer.com, and lead pastor of Grace Church in Hendersonville, TN**

"Jere Phillips knows ministry, not only as a professor, but as one who has been on the frontlines of church leadership. In *Pastoral Ministry for the Next Generation*, he brings his insights to bear on the challenges and opportunities ministers will face in our rapidly changing culture. The book will be valuable not only for beginning ministers, but for veterans who are facing a changing ministry landscape."

—**Michael Duduit, executive editor, *Preaching* magazine; dean and professor of Christian Ministry, College of Christian Studies, Anderson University, Anderson, SC**

"To serve Jesus, the Great Shepherd, as a pastor who oversees His flock is an unspeakable joy and blessing. Since 1983, I have served as a senior pastor in Southern Baptist churches. I know the ups and downs, the joys and sorrows, of being a pastor. I also recognize a valuable resource for pastors and the churches they serve. Dr. Jere Phillips' new book, *Pastoral Ministry for the Next Generation*, is such a resource. I have known and respected the author for many years. Any pastor, new or seasoned, will benefit greatly from the wisdom offered in his writings. I wholeheartedly recommend this work."

—**Steve Gaines, PhD, senior pastor, Bellevue Baptist Church, Memphis, TN**

"Jere Phillips knows the ministry of the pastor. He has been a pastor and knows firsthand the many responsibilities pastors face. For many years, he has been teaching preachers at Mid-America Baptist Theological Seminary in Cordova, Tennessee. He has kept up with the trends and practices of pastoral ministry and preaching during those years. I do not know anyone who brings more wisdom and practical experience to the table than Dr. Phillips. This book will be a blessing to any pastor of any age. I encourage all pastors to read it and heed it!"

—**Dr. Bob Pitman, evangelist, Muscle Shoals, AL**

"Dr. Jere Phillip's latest book, *Pastoral Ministry for the Next Generation*, is a tremendous resource for pastors. He draws from experience gained from his personal pastoral ministry, denominational service, and his current role as seminary professor to speak to the very heart of pastoral ministry. You will not only appreciate the breadth of his experience when you read this book, but you will also appreciate the freshness of the vision he casts for pastoral ministry that not only will encourage pastors but will serve [as] a valuable tool to help equip them for the challenging and changing dynamics of pastoring a church in the twenty-first century. I found the book to be thoroughly biblical, refreshingly practical, and spiritually edifying. Dr. Phillips has a gift to speak with clarity to both the heart and the mind of pastors. This book is a resource that any pastor would find helpful."

—**Charles Fowler, senior pastor, Germantown Baptist Church, Germantown, TN**

"Dr. Phillips' approach to pastoral ministry spans the generations. His years of practice as a pastor, staff member, and denominational servant developed in him experience and wisdom applicable for all types of churches. His years of teaching and mentoring pastors have enabled him to keep up with the latest developments and maintain a freshness to his approach. The practical steps found in his book have guided me in my ministry as part of God's shaping me to be His man. *Pastoral Ministry for the Next Generation* is the go-to manual for every newly called minister of the gospel (and many 'old hands' as well)."

—**Pastor Jim Collier, Kirby Woods Baptist Church, Memphis, TN**

To those great pastors God placed in my life . . .

Robert Orr, who was there at my salvation, baptism, and call to ministry
Fred Wood, who taught the love of writing
J. D. Grey, who taught how to lead
Ken Story, who taught the value of churchmanship
Adrian Rogers, who taught the love of preaching
D. L. Lowrie, who taught prayer and loyalty
Gary Watkins, who taught what it means to have a shepherd's heart

Also dedicated to those great pastors of the next generation, the future church awaits
your spiritual leadership under the guidance of Jesus Christ,
that great Shepherd of the sheep.

CONTENTS

Introduction: Timeless, Yet Timely

Chapter 1—Ministry in the New Millennium 13

Chapter 2—The Biblical Basis for Pastoral Ministry 21

Presbuteros—Elder
The Spiritually Mature Man of God

Chapter 3—The Man of God 29

Chapter 4—Receiving the Three Calls of Christ. 39

Chapter 5—God's Call to a Place. 51

Chapter 6—The Minister's Family 67

Poimen—Shepherd
The Shepherding Pastor

Chapter 7—Being a Good Shepherd. 75

Chapter 8—Beginning Well 81

Chapter 9—Pastoral Care: Knowing and Caring for the Flock 93

Chapter 10—What Do You Do When Someone Dies? 103

Chapter 11—Pastoral Counseling Ministry 123

Chapter 12—Marriage in a New Millennium 137

Chapter 13—Conducting Church Ordinances 157

Chapter 14—Feeding the Flock: Your Teaching and Preaching Ministry 163

Chapter 15—Biblical Worship in a Contemporary World 195

Chapter 16—Fulfilling The Great Commission: Leading Evangelism and Missions. . .205

Chapter 17—Developing the Flock: Assimilating New Members/Making Disciples . . .215

Chapter 18—Working with Deacons 221

Episcopos—Bishop
Servant Leadership and Administration

Chapter 19—The Pastor's Oversight: Being a Spiritual Leader 233

Chapter 20—Time Management: Leading Yourself 241

Chapter 21—Developing a Ministry Team: Working with Ministry Staff and Laypersons . .249

Chapter 22—Planning for Ministry: Discovering and Implementing God's Vision 261

Chapter 23—Organizing Ministry: Budget and Calendar Preparation 269

Chapter 24—Getting Along with People: Preventing and Resolving Conflict 277

Chapter 25—Principles of Organizational Communication 291

Chapter 26—Managing Legal and Business Issues. 297

Chapter 27—Cooperating with Your Denomination. 305

Chapter 28—Ending Well. 311

Introduction

TIMELESS, YET TIMELY

Pastoral ministry is timeless. Certain aspects of this life and work endure through all generations until the Lord returns. People need to be saved and grow as disciples of Christ. Churches need someone who will love them and lead them, someone who will feed them faithfully with the Word, someone who will guide them into knowing God's truth and living truth daily, and someone who will equip them for ministry and enable them to reach people throughout the world for Jesus.

Yet, the milieu of ministry constantly changes. People expect their ministers to baptize them, marry them, and bury them, but marriage in today's culture involves questions for next generation ministers that their grandfathers never imagined. Next-Gen ministry requires thoughtful processing of biblical foundations and contemporary applications.

This book provides a biblically based, future-focused approach. It is written for young pastors but can help ministers of any generation (especially new pastors). At the same time, the source and subject of all ministries are neither the culture of the people, nor the craftsmanship of the pastor. Rather, whatever we are and all that we do emerges from the calling and purpose of Christ Jesus our Lord.

You may find a few flourishes of poignant prose in these pages, but I do not write to impress you with literary skill. I want to equip you for effective ministry. Consequently, this book may be the most practical work you read this year. It does not float into the theoretical stratosphere; it stays down to earth where you and I, and the people of our churches, live.

I've written not only out of forty-five years of ministry experience but from constant study of and interaction with young preachers. Decades of serving local churches taught me not only the practical application of pastoral ministry but the love of pastoral service. Service in denominational life put me in contact with pastors of all ages, but I especially sought out younger pastors, particularly as church planters. Teaching young pastors keeps me fresh and forces me to stay up with the upcoming generations of ministers. Their eagerness to be effective as missional instruments in God's hand has inspired and challenged me. I may have learned more from them over the years than they have from me, but I pray it evened out somewhere along the way.

Being a minister in any generation has its rewards and its problems, but Next-Gen pastors are eager to engage the culture with the Gospel. You want to be Transformers, not in the sense of Optimus Prime, but with just as much power. Not handcuffed to tradition, you may chafe a bit when forced to bridge the canyons of culture between the Builders, Boomers, Bridgers, and Millennials. Many younger ministers bypass the traditional route of serving smaller, older churches and go straight to church planting in order to avoid spending time and energy changing existing congregational mores.

Frankly, that trend concerns me, and it should disturb you. We definitely need more church planters, but if younger pastors reject existing churches and refuse to invest their energies in cultivating churches for generations to come, we will see thousands of churches closing over the next decades.

Much of the frustration younger ministers express relates to the difficulty in creating change. Some of your emotions revolve around a sense that your education did not prepare you for the practicalities of ministry. Prayerfully, this book will address both issues. As a seminary professor, I believe in training people for the real work they will engage in churches, mission fields, and other ministries. As this book is used in the classroom, it serves equally in the hands of an active pastor trying to improve his skills.

Keep in mind that not all tradition is bad, nor is all change good. Maintaining every vestige of tradition as monuments to the past creates ecclesiastical museums of dying churches. At the same time, change for change's sake risks launching a self-perpetuating hamster wheel of frustration, lacking substantive foundations for the future. The wise Next-Gen leader will learn how to consolidate the gains of the past without jeopardizing the possibilities of the future.

While you will find a section on creating change, the entire book has a tone of transformation. It builds on firm foundations of successful, practical ministry in the myriads of ministerial functions, but hopefully it takes you to the next level in each discipline. Transformational ministry seldom happens suddenly; it usually occurs over time in incremental growth. The best way to transform churches is to reform the pastor. This book will equip you as God's instrument of biblical change for His church.

As you engage the tools for implementing effective ministry, please do not fall prey to the error that believes skills substitute for spiritual dynamic. You need to know how to accomplish the various tasks of ministry, but tools alone do not empower you for the task; they merely help you do it. Empowerment comes from God. His Holy Spirit, instrumental in your call to ministry, enables you for the ministry. It is God in us both "to will and to do His good pleasure" (Philippians 2:13).

Ministry is a spiritual enterprise. While you may accomplish a certain level of success using human mechanisms, anything of eternal consequence requires divine initiative. Only as you minister in the power of God's Spirit can you expect results that exalt the Lord Jesus Christ through His Bride, the Church.

What a wondrous calling that is! Considering the earthen vessels He has to work with, can we really comprehend the majestic grace necessary for God to use us? To be employed by God in service to His people should humble us and motivate us to give our all in fulfillment of His purpose.

Amazed by His mercy and grace in saving us and using us, we have no room for complaining of the conditions, harping about the hardships, or pouting over the problems. Whatever we encounter in the way of difficulties, remember they are "light affliction which is but for a moment, (it) works for us a far more exceeding and eternal weight of glory;" (2 Corinthians 4:17).

Every day, we should thank God for the high privilege of being under-shepherds of His flock. Let us take the example of the Good Shepherd and embrace His love for the people. With grateful hearts, may we minister for His glory and their good.

Chapter 1

MINISTRY IN THE NEW MILLENNIUM

"We will tell the next generation the praiseworthy deeds of the Lord . . .
That the generation to come may know them . . ." (Psalm 78:4, 6).

Ministry in any age challenges pastors to bring ageless biblical truth to bear on people living in a contemporary culture. The new millennium consummated a change process that enculturated postmodern philosophy, secularized societies, and hedonistic lifestyles. Most people do not wake up and contemplate postmodernism over their breakfast cereal, but this philosophy inundates education, music and entertainment, government, and business. Postmodernism denies absolute, biblical truth and insists on seeing every assertion as relative to individual perspective. We do not need to expose the fallacies of deconstruction and post-structuralism to be effective, but we must understand the effects these concepts have on the average person.

As a result, society has become increasingly secularized with more people than ever claiming "none" when asked about their religious preference. Western culture presses believers to restrain their religious expression when outside their homes or churches. Christianity, especially conservative Evangelicalism, has become increasingly isolated, as it advocates biblical positions on issues such as abortion and homosexuality.

People think differently as a result of decades of unbiblical influences. This observation is not limited to the younger generations. People of all ages have adopted a mindset that militates against a Christian culture. Interview persons on any street in America and you will encounter people who believe the Bible is a nice book but not the truth on which they should build their lives. They think Jesus was a wise teacher but not the Son of God. They love the idea of a nebulous spirituality but reject the framework of the Church and dismiss it as just another organized religion.

Into this setting, the Next-Generation pastor must carry the standard of Christ and lovingly, but firmly, plant it among a people who have turned their hearts from God. To be faithful to the One Who called you to His service and to be effective in ministry among new Millennials, you will need a clear comprehension of the people around you and the type of ministry you have been given.

A Biblical Ministry

One size does not fit all. Next-Gen ministers serve in wide variations of culture, background, expectations, and possibilities. For example, a minister's location influences his choice of certain ministry tools to one degree or another. However, even within a geographic region, churches and people differ greatly. You may minister in a Southern state, but is the church a new congregation or an established one? Is it urban or rural? Are the people younger or older? Are they multiethnic or homogeneous? What socio-economic groups make up the congregation? Is the church small, medium, or large? What values do the people and pastor hold? How much leadership equity has the minister built up with this group?

The Bible provides durable principles to guide ministers through the maze of ministry options. Ministers may be tempted to imitate successful methods of other pastors, but pragmatism must bow to Biblicism if we are to fulfill God's mandate.

To be fully equipped for ministry in any generation, God's servants must be completely committed to God, utterly dependent on God's Spirit, constantly immersed in God's Word, faithfully devoted to God's people, and fearlessly engaged in God's mission. You must understand the times in which you live but must not surrender your souls to the cultural whims of the day.

We begin with Scripture. God uses His Word, empowered as well as inspired by His Spirit, to equip His ministers. "All Scripture is given by inspiration of God, and is profitable for doctrine, for reproof, for correction, for instruction in righteousness: *That the man of God may be perfect (complete), thoroughly furnished unto all good works*" (2 Timothy 3:16–17, emphasis added).

God has provided all we need to serve Him. He gives salvation through Christ, empowerment by the Holy Spirit, and equipping via His inspired Word. Paul affirmed the profitability of Scripture for doctrine (sound belief), reproof (confrontation of sin), correction (pointing to a return to the right path), and instruction in righteousness (teaching for correct future behavior) (2 Timothy 3:16). However, the purpose of this profitable, divinely inspired Word is to equip the man of God for godly service (2 Timothy 3:17).

> To be fully equipped for ministry in any generation, God's servants must be completely committed to God, utterly dependent on God's Spirit, constantly immersed in God's Word, faithfully devoted to God's people, and fearlessly engaged in God's mission.

This book seeks to help Next-Generation ministers apply biblical principles of pastoral ministry in your contemporary setting without compromise to either. The only foundation for future ministry rests in the timeless truths of God's Word. Ministers do not have to make the Bible relevant; it already is. Our eternal God speaks to all generations.

An Authentic Ministry

Next-Gen ministers value authenticity, desiring to be real and genuine, absent from any hint of hypocrisy. One study showed that 100 percent of churches deemed effective at reaching younger adults held authenticity as one of their key values. One college minister observed that most students reject religious views not so much on the basis of philosophical constructs as in reaction to parents who may have correct theological beliefs but do not live out those beliefs in actuality.[1]

Next-Gen pastor Stephen Furtick listed authenticity as a prime trait of ministers who will reach the coming generations.[2] When asked what advice he might give a young preacher, Dr. Charles Swindoll included, "Be real . . . Be who you are. Don't let a day pass when you played a role."[3]

Authentic ministry comes from who you are, not simply through what you do. To fulfill God's call to serve His church, a pastor not only masters certain skills, he must become God's minister—a task God initiates and consummates. God shapes willing servants into good ministers of Jesus Christ to serve His Body—the Church (1 Timothy 4:6). Paul reminds us: "For we are his workmanship, created in Christ Jesus unto good works, which God has before ordained that we should walk in them" (Ephesians 2:10). Unless we are willing to undergo the Master's makeover, we cannot function effectively as His ministers. Godly pastors cooperate with Him in the process of transformation.

Paul called his son in the ministry a "man of God" (1 Timothy 6:11). That little preposition—*of*—carries a dual meaning: to come *from* God and to belong *to* God. Ministers are made by Him and, thus, belong to Him. Authentic ministry involves allowing God to make you into His minister. He then equips you to actualize His ministry.

Christian leaders and individual believers must come to grips with who they are in Christ. Without the insecure need to create a façade of religious respectability, authentic Christians genuinely live out the Christ-life through the power of the Holy Spirit.

Authenticity is not new. Every generation of ministers, from biblical days onward, have strived to be genuine. Hypocrisy has never been a virtue of the Church. However, being authentic does not excuse unbiblical theology, nor should it justify using rough language in a feeble attempt at being relevant to a secularized culture. Some ministers fall prey to what Brett McCracken calls "the dangerous pursuit of 'cool.'"[4] Trying to appeal to a secularized generation, they try to look and sound a certain way. A few preachers go so far as to use curse words in the pulpit or join the boys for a beer at the local pub. Such behavior does not commend a minister to any generation.

Genuinely authentic ministers are servants of a holy God who practice what they preach; word and deed are consistent with Christlikeness. While Paul became all things to all men that by any means he might win some, he maintained the consistency of who he was as a man in Christ. He did not compromise his convictions or his credibility in order to accommodate the Greek philosophers at Mars Hill. Instead, he showed the reality of Christ by his example as much as by his arguments.

These pages will help you cooperate with the Lord in *becoming* so you might be successful in *doing*. Certainly, no book can substitute for the Holy Spirit's interaction with the human spirit. At best, your reading serves as a guide while you discover from God's Word how He wants to work in and through your life to touch the lives of His people.

A Missional Ministry

Many young pastors want their churches to be missional. They build their mission, organization, and ministry around intentional outreach to unreached people. They react against the tendency of many traditional churches that focus on ministry to their members. While most churches give financially to support missionaries and often conduct outreach forays into the local community, a high percentage of the programming, budget allotment, and ministerial time is expended for the benefit of the congregation.

Missional pastors have a passion for reaching the lost. They believe the Church exists to fulfill Jesus' Great Commission and define their personal ministry by equipping and motivating believers to transform their communities through the Gospel.

Next-Generation pastors disagree as to how one impacts the unchurched. Many identify people's primary need as spiritual—they need to be born again through the redemptive work of Christ's atonement on the cross. Others broaden their view to include social ministry and social justice within the meaning of redemption.

Some young pastors have followed a nonbiblical way toward the goal of being missional. They sacrifice orthodoxy for orthopraxy. Orthopraxy focuses on right behavior as opposed to concern about right belief (orthodoxy). Often, they are more concerned about the church identifying with and reaching the current culture than remaining true to the church's biblical foundations. However, one cannot engage in enduring missiology without valid theology that emerges from faithful exposition of God's Word.

Divorcing biblical fidelity from effective ecclesiology denies the integrated validity of both. God blesses His Word. If a minister tries to ignore biblical truth for a narrative that tickles the ear of an unchurched person, he may reach the person, but for what? If the Gospel he preaches is something other than focused on Jesus Christ, Son of God and Savior of sinners, it no longer remains Good News.

Next-Gen pastors who are faithful to Scripture will be missional by nature. Jesus' commands and example involved compassionate ministry to the entire person. Yet, He noted the difference between people who came to Him not because they wanted to follow Him but because they received free bread. Jesus met people's physical needs, but encouraged them not to seek "the meat which perishes, but for that meat which endures unto everlasting life, which the Son of man shall give unto you . . ." (John 6:26–27).

Perhaps a singular aspect of being a true missional church is determining what directs decision making. Ed Stetzer notes, "Being missional means moving intentionally beyond our church preferences, making missional decisions rather than preferential decisions. . . . The most effective comeback churches will be those that intentionally think like missionaries in their context."[5]

An Applied Ministry

Social ministry is one means by which many missional pastors try to reach people in their generation. They see ministry to the poor as basic Applied Christianity. Social ministry is not a dirty word. Both testaments encourage, even mandate, aid to the poor, the widow, the orphan, and the "stranger in your gates" (noncitizens) (Exodus 22:21–23; Deuteronomy 24:14–22).

Some older ministers identify social ministry with the social gospel, a movement that substituted an emphasis on social justice in place of evangelism. On the other hand, younger ministers may overlook the danger of seeing compassionate application of Christian love as an end rather than a means.

The New Testament is replete with examples of Jesus and the early Church as they compassionately met physical needs. However, the result was not merely that people were healed and helped but that people might have faith in the Great Physician. Instead of engaging in a generational conflict over whether or not the Church should engage in social ministry, both groups should return to the biblical example of giving a cup of cold water *in Jesus' name* (Mark 9:41).

> *Being missional and being biblical are not mutually exclusive. One cannot be effectively missional without being biblical and one cannot be truly biblical without being missional.*

Some of the greatest evangelistic results have come from ministries that touch hurting lives with physical assistance, which opens the door for sharing the Gospel of Christ. At the former Home Mission Board of the Southern Baptist Convention, some of the most successful evangelistic results came from missionaries associated with the Church and Community Ministry Division (social ministries with an evangelistic purpose). In Africa, an international missionary who baptized thousands of converts was an agricultural worker. In Memphis, one of the most conservative churches in America, Bellevue Baptist, has reached thousands of people for Christ through its Impact Memphis ministries, combining social action and evangelistic purpose.

Being missional and being biblical are not mutually exclusive. One cannot be effectively missional without being biblical and one cannot be truly biblical without being missional. The Gospel is not the exclusive property of congregants. The Gospel transforms Christians into missionaries who share the Jesus Who changed their lives so others might know Him too.

Next-Gen missional pastors would benefit from a study of the long history of evangelical social ministry by traditional Christians in every generation. Who built hospitals across the nation? Who provided the hunger relief funds for the tsunami victims in Indonesia, cleaned up after hurricanes and tornadoes around the world, or cooked most of the meals for the Red Cross after major disasters? The answer to each involves evangelical believers who apply their Christian faith to minister to the entire person with a view of bringing each one to Christ.

A Team Ministry

Leadership experts often describe the loneliness of leadership. Making decisions affecting people often requires leaders to keep others (even close associates) at a distance. They fear relationships can cause poor decisions based on friendship rather than facts.

Spiritual leaders should not fall prey to secular fears. Jesus brought His disciples close to Him. While He spent some time alone in prayer, He often took disciples with Him so they learned to pray. He involved them in ministry, preparing them to take over when He returned to heaven.

Next-Generation leaders embrace Jesus' methods. They like teams. Church planters typically develop a team of leaders to expand the work. Pastors develop a team of ministers and lay leaders to help develop and implement vision. Some Next-Gen preachers use sermon seminars to engage others in developing ideas for preaching—a few in polishing the sermon itself, many more in exploring ways to communicate the message God has given the pastor.

Certainly, ministers must have time alone with God. The pastor has the ultimate responsibility for getting a word from God to feed and lead the flock. Tough decisions mean the buck still stops at his desk. Yet, in many aspects of ministry from A–administration to W–worship planning, a team approach finds its way into the Next-Gen pastor's leadership style.

A Multigenerational Ministry

Following the Genesis principle of reproduction "each after his own kind," succeeding generations of ministers tend primarily to touch people of their own age group. Many Next-Gen church planters focus on reaching young families because of the natural networks and interests built around their own families.

However, the reality of congregational life involves multigenerational cultures. Each church, even new church plants, contains several different generational cultures. They speak diverse languages, have dissimilar values, dress differently, think differently, and often have difficulty communicating with each other on the depth levels of spirituality, ethics, principles, and beliefs.[6]

Much has been written about the distinct characteristics of the various American generations, such as the Builders, the Boomers, the Busters, Generation X (also called the Bridgers), and the Millennials (also called Generation Y, or the Mosaics). Generations have been categorized by influences, values, and buying patterns. However, most approaches to understanding the generations have been limited to considerations within peer groups or interactions between them. Not much help has been offered to the pastor who must minister across the ages to every generation at once.

The different generations influence not only the culture around the church, but also produce distinct cultures and subcultures within the church. Some congregations have ignored the changes and subsequently dwindled in size to fit the one or two demographical groups that have control of the church. Others have focused only on musical taste and found themselves embroiled in worship wars that tore apart the fabric of fellowship.

On the other hand, many Next-Gen pastors embrace a multigenerational approach to ministry advocated by leaders like Voddie Baucham, who complains the average church not only segregates itself racially, but generationally. True, Bible-study classes and age-group ministries tend to follow developmental growth patterns. However, many traditional churches tend to go further, separating families by various church ministries and hindering natural multigenerational influences. Baucham urges churches to reintegrate families within and around church ministries, thus incorporating the biblical strengths of each.[7]

Both Moses and Paul placed responsibility for spiritual nurture within the family. Through Moses, God instructed the people of Israel to pass on His commandments and statutes to each

> *Next-Gen ministers must develop skills in reaching across generational cultures to embrace the entire congregation.*

succeeding generation by talking about His Word in the normal contexts of family life (Deuteronomy 6:7, 11:19). Paul taught fathers to bring their children up "in the nurture and admonition of the Lord" (Ephesians 6:4). Next-Gen ministers must develop skills in reaching across generational cultures to embrace the entire congregation. Reggie Joiner argues for blending church and multigenerational family ministry by intentionally working together to impact children and youth for Christ.[8]

Ministry in the new millennium encompasses new challenges and opportunities. Strategies and methods must change as each generation launches forth into the future, but the basic Gospel comprising the essence of our ministry remains constant. With unswerving commitment to Christ and His Word, Next-Gen ministers can find exciting applications to reach every generation for Jesus.

Chapter 2

THE BIBLICAL BASIS FOR PASTORAL MINISTRY

"'And I will set up shepherds over them which shall feed them: and they shall fear no more, nor be dismayed, neither shall they be lacking,' says the LORD" (Jeremiah 23:4).

What do you call someone who preaches to a congregation, cares for people in sickness and in health, oversees the administration of church organizations, shares spiritual advice with individuals and couples, helps grieving families bury their loved ones, supervises a staff of workers, and trains people in the skills needed to perform their tasks?

Preacher or Prophet?
Chaplain?
Bishop or Elder?
Counselor?
Undertaker?
Administrator?
Coach?

One word comes to mind—*pastor*. Why do so many people have a problem with that term? After all these years in ministry, I still love it when someone calls me "pastor." Many ministers believe this title is outdated, as few people relate to the concept of a shepherd in the Information Age.

Beyond the label, a more basic debate swirls around the issue of a minister's multiple roles.

- Some ministers want simply to preach. (Someone else can take care of all that "people stuff.")
- Others want to be the Chief Executive Officer and run the organization. (Someone else can take care of all that "people stuff.")
- A few want to be teaching elders, focusing on the meat and potatoes of the Word in hour-long feasts. (Someone else can take care of all that "people stuff.")

Yet, the people stuff is why the church needs the minister in the first place. Yes, pastors need to feed the people through preaching and teaching. Yes, they must lead the people, whether through direct administration or by delegated authority. Still, they can do neither if they do not know and care for the people.

Since precepts of Scripture are culturally universal and contemporarily relevant, a study of the biblical bases of pastoral ministry offers some direction. The Bible uses three words to describe the person we simply call pastor: *poimen*, literally "shepherd" but often translated as "pastor"; *presbuteros*, from which we get the word *elder*; and *episcopos*, rendered as "bishop" or "overseer."

Each term encompasses numerous roles and tasks of pastoral ministry. A pastor's job is huge; no one word can describe it adequately. Consider basic aspects of each term:

1. Shepherd

Is shepherding an outmoded idea? Not at all. In biblical days, other models existed that could have described the role of congregational leader. If God wanted to emphasize the pastor's administrative role, He could have called a Sanhedrin to lead His church. Israel had more than its share of successful business or political leaders, but Jesus did not name CEOs or kings to pastor the church. Why not use familiar words like *priest* or *prophet*? Yet, Old and New Testaments constantly refer to the minister as shepherd.

This term says more about the minister's heart than his duties. The pastor may care for God's people in many different ways. As a church grows, he may not be able to call every person by name, visit every home each month, or heal all wounds personally. Yet, if he does not have the heart of a shepherd, his ministry will degenerate into an insensitive mode of administration.

In both testaments, prophets and apostles used the term *shepherd* to describe individuals tasked with the care of God's people. Granted, Old Testament employment of *shepherd* may refer to kings and rulers, but such use further emphasizes God's desire that the people who lead His people be good shepherds.

In the New Testament, *poimen* (translated shepherd) almost always refers to the pastor. When Paul listed God's gifts to the Church, he used *poimen* to identify the pastor (Ephesians 4:11). Peter called Jesus Christ the *archipoimen*—the Chief Shepherd (1 Peter 5:4).

> *The Good Shepherd knows the sheep, leads the sheep, feeds the sheep, guides the sheep, and protects the sheep—even if it means laying down his life.*

Jesus Himself claimed the title Good Shepherd (*kalos poimen*) (John 10:11). The Good Shepherd knows the sheep, leads the sheep, feeds the sheep, guides the sheep, and protects the sheep—even if it means laying down his life. Jesus could have said He was the High Priest of the Congregation, which He was. He could have said He was the Chief Cornerstone of the

Church, which He was. However, He chose the metaphor of Good Shepherd not simply because it was a familiar term, but because it expressed His heart. The man who would lead Jesus' church would do well to follow Jesus' model.

Consider these scriptural admonitions to the shepherds:

- Jeremiah 23:4, "And I will set up **shepherds** over them which shall feed them: and they shall fear no more, nor be dismayed, neither shall they be lacking, says the LORD."
- Psalm 80:1, "Give ear, O **Shepherd** of Israel, you that leads Joseph like a flock; you that dwells between the cherubim, shine forth."
- Isaiah 40:11, "He shall feed his flock like a **shepherd**: he shall gather the lambs with his arm, and carry them in his bosom, and shall gently lead those that are with young."
- Mark 6:34, "And Jesus, when he came out, saw much people, and was moved with compassion toward them, because they were as sheep not having a **shepherd**: and he began to teach them many things."
- John 10:11, "I am the good **shepherd**: the good **shepherd** gives his life for the sheep."
- John 10:14, "I am the good **shepherd**, and know my sheep, and am known of mine."

These passages are representative of the shepherd theme found throughout Scripture. God affirms the leaders of His congregational flock as good shepherds who love the people.

At the same time, God warns ministers who misuse the office of shepherd for selfish purposes:

- Jeremiah 50:6, "My people have been lost sheep: their **shepherds** have caused them to go astray, they have turned them away on the mountains: they have gone from mountain to hill, they have forgotten their resting place."
- Ezekiel 34:2, "Son of man, prophesy against the **shepherds** of Israel, prophesy, and say unto them, Thus says the Lord GOD unto the **shepherds**; Woe be to the **shepherds** of Israel that do feed themselves! Should not the **shepherds** feed the flocks?"
- Ezekiel 34:8–10, "As I live, says the Lord GOD, surely because my flock became a prey, and my flock became meat to every beast of the field, because there was no shepherd, neither did my **shepherds** search for my flock, but the **shepherds** fed themselves, and fed not

my flock Therefore, O **shepherds**, hear the word of the LORD; Thus says the Lord GOD; Behold, I am against the **shepherds**; and I will require my flock at their hand, and cause them to cease from feeding the flock; neither shall the **shepherds** feed themselves anymore; for I will deliver my flock from their mouth, that they may not be meat for them."

- John 10:12, "But he that is a hireling, and not the **shepherd**, whose own the sheep are not, sees the wolf coming, and leaves the sheep, and flees: and the wolf catches them, and scatters the sheep."

God gives us the shepherd model not for methodology, but for motivation. Next-Gen ministers have means of caring for people that biblical shepherds never imagined. Yet, their hearts must have the same sacrificial tenderness toward people. God has entrusted them to our care. If we ignore or abuse this heavenly stewardship, the Chief Shepherd Himself will call us to account.

2. Elder

Another word used for pastor is *elder*. The Old Testament use of *elder* often refers either to one's age or to specialized roles held by leaders of the congregational nation of Israel. The New Testament frequently uses the term not only to refer to age or leadership but also to indicate the position of pastor. Some pastors may be older and experienced, but Timothy's tenure as pastor demonstrates that a young, but spiritually mature, man might also serve well (1 Timothy 4:12).

So what should we understand the biblical term *elder* to mean? First, it was a common term that the Jewish Christians of the early Church could understand to describe the congregational leader. Second, and more importantly, it referred to the spiritual maturity expected of a leader of God's people. A quick perusal of the minister's qualifications demonstrates the spiritual reputation required to be a pastor.

The pastor/elder is one of two offices in the New Testament Church: pastor and deacon. Nowhere does Scripture refer to three offices of the church: pastor, deacon, and elder. The Bible may refer to bishops and deacons or to elders and deacons, but never to bishops, elders, and deacons in the same context. One issue on which we can agree is the term *elder* refers to a pastor. If a rose by any other name smells as sweet (thank you, Will Shakespeare), a pastor by any other name is still a pastor.

3. Bishop

Also called overseer, from the term *episcopos*, the bishop was not someone who supervises other pastors but rather was concerned with leading the people of God. While some people like the title because it carries a connotation of authority, the New Testament concept of bishop reflected responsibilities more than rights. In Paul's letters to Timothy and Titus, Paul used the term *bishop* when describing the leadership as well as character of a pastor. Paul also wrote to the bishops and deacons in Philippians 1:1, clearly meaning the pastors and deacons.

Biblical pastors are servant leaders. Jesus taught the disciples that the greatest should be the servant, not the master, of all (Mark 9:35). He washed their feet at the last Passover as a living object lesson of humility and servanthood (John 13:1–18.) Paul instructed young Pastor Timothy to be the Lord's servant (2 Timothy 2:24).

> *Biblical pastors are servant leaders. Jesus taught the disciples that the greatest should be the servant, not the master, of all.*

The concept of being a bishop, or overseer, describes the pastor's responsibility to lead God's people responsibly. Certainly, the term contains an element of administration. However, the minister who yearns to lead the church should wisely observe the method of the first pastors (the apostles). Peter spurned the administration of benevolence ministry and led the church to choose qualified, responsible men to whom administration might be delegated (Acts 6).

Spiritual leadership does not mean the pastor is the CEO but that he has the primary role of spiritual guidance according to biblical examples. (By the way, since Peter presented the idea to the whole congregation and it "seemed good to them," the creation of deacons appears to be a prime example of congregational involvement in church decision making.)

Three in One: An honest view of Scripture concludes the three words (elder, shepherd, and bishop/overseer) are interchangeably descriptive of the pastor. In Acts 20, Luke employed all three words in the same passage. Paul called the *presbuteroi* (elders) of the church at Ephesus together and urged them to take heed to themselves and to the flock (*poimnio*) of God. He reminded them that God had made them overseers (*episcopous*) and, thus, they were to feed (*poimainein*) the church.

Peter also wrote to the elders (*presbuterous*), claiming himself to be an elder, and admonished them to feed (*poimanate*) the flock (*poimnion*), taking oversight (*episkopountes*) in love, not constraint. Lest we continue to think that being an overseer means to exercise lordship, Peter admonished the pastors to lead by example and not as lords over possessions. His letter serves as another reminder that being a bishop is a responsibility to serve, not a right to rule (1 Peter 5:1–3).

This book is organized around these three terms for *pastor*. The section on *presbuteros* (elder) focuses not on church government but on the idea of the pastor's spiritual maturity, his call to ministry, and his spiritual formation. The second section, built around *poimen* (shepherd), contains chapters dedicated to methods of pastoral care, including starting a new ministry, preaching, worship planning, counseling, conducting weddings and funerals, visitation in homes and hospitals, conducting baptism and the Lord's Supper, personal and corporate evangelism, and disciple making.

The final section deals with the concept of *episcopos* (being a leader/bishop/overseer). It concentrates on various leadership functions, including personal and corporate leadership development, budget and calendar formation, financial management, working with deacons and committees, leading business meetings, resolving conflict, communication methods (including using technology to multiply ministry), and handling legal issues such as incorporation and constitution/bylaws.

The concluding section helps ministers understand how to end a ministry well. You will learn how to know when to leave a church or ministry, how to handle forced termination, and how to end a ministry so the church and the Lord might say, "Well done, good and faithful servant."

PRESBUTEROS—ELDER

The Spiritually Mature Man of God

Chapter 3

THE MAN OF GOD

"But thou, o man of God . . ." (1 Timothy 6:11).

People can find inspirational communicators, personal counselors, organizational leaders, and comforting advisors outside the church. The key distinction of a pastor is that he is known as a man of God. A minister may have many admirable skills, but unless he bears the mark of God in his life, he will not succeed in the long term as a pastor.

How does a young pastor become accepted as an elder—a spiritually mature man of God qualified to lead a congregation? By becoming known as a man of God. Paul encouraged his son-in-the-ministry, Timothy, "Let no man despise your youth; but be an example of the believers, in word, in conversation, in charity, in spirit, in faith, in purity" (1Timothy 4:12). Wise ministers realize they do not gain respect as a pastor simply by holding a position, attaining a certain age, or achieving a level of experience.

Next-Gen pastors earn a following by being an example of what a believer should be. Notice the areas in which Paul urged Timothy to take heed:

- **In Word**—While verses 13 and 14 indicate Timothy should give attention to preaching and teaching the Word of God, this particular admonition refers to Timothy's manner of speaking. Godly ministers guard their tongues. Scripture is full of instructions about how God's people should speak and not speak. Young men of God do not talk foolishly, nor do they employ coarse language privately or from the pulpit (Ephesians 5:4). Sadly, some role models influencing Next-Gen preachers include pastors who use inappropriate language, even while proclaiming God's Holy Word. These men may have many admirable, successful qualities, but they are not examples "in Word."
- **In Conversation (manner of life)**—Young ministers gain the respect of their congregations and communities by maintaining lifestyles worthy of emulation. Paul was able to encourage people to follow him because his life was modeled after Christ (1 Corinthians

11:1). Paul advised Pastor Titus to encourage younger men to display a pattern of good works based on pure doctrine, with seriousness and sincerity (Titus 2:7). Like good soldiers, ministers of any age discipline themselves that they may endure the difficulties inherent in pastoral work (2 Timothy 2:3).

- **In Charity (love)**—Love the Lord and love the people. Sounds simple enough. However, some people are not very loveable. Being an example of what a believer should be means loving everyone, in action as well as in word. The only way we can do that is to love God supremely. His love, then, flows through us to each person we encounter.
- **In Spirit**—Our spirit, that is our attitudes, should emulate Christ, beginning with humility (Philippians 2:5–8). People will forgive a poor sermon from time to time. They may overlook faults and failures. They will not endure a leader whose heart is hard, whose attitude is arrogant, or whose spirit is selfish. Let Christ's mind be in us, a spirit of humble service and servant leadership.
- **In Faith**—We cannot simply preach about faith; we must live it. We are not only saved by faith, we live by faith (Galatians 3:11). How can we teach people to trust God when we rely so much on the flesh? People need to see us trusting God and demonstrating our faith in daily life.
- **In Purity**—Younger ministers do not have a monopoly on temptation. Still, Paul warned his preacher-son: "Flee also youthful lusts: but follow righteousness, faith, charity, peace, with them that call on the Lord out of a pure heart" (2 Timothy 2:22). In an Internet-dominated culture, people can access lust-oriented material with a click of the mouse. Perhaps the number one gateway to moral disaster in ministry is the accessibility to pornography.

I've had numerous young ministers seek counseling because their marriages and their ministries were failing due to the lack of moral discipline and personal purity. Keep close to Jesus and stay pure in heart and body. You cannot be a man of God and a slave to the world. Your ministry must incarnate godliness in ministry.

Incarnational Ministry

One must be before one can do. Too often, pastors rush to master the competencies of ministry before gaining the character necessary to be a minister. Being a *presbuteros* (elder) requires spiritual characteristics of personhood that honor God and command the respect of God's people. Such qualities derive from one's intimate interaction and union with Christ. George Barna asserts, "Unless you are intensely devoted to continually cultivating your relationship with Christ, people have no valid reason to follow you and you have no business striving to lead God's people."[1]

Moses bore many titles, but the greatest was "man of God" (Deuteronomy 33:1; Joshua 4:6). Prophets, like Samuel, were known as men of God (1 Samuel 9:6). Shemaiah the prophet had the courage to rebuke Rehoboam because he was a man of God (1 Kings 12:22). An unknown man of God warned Jeroboam of God's impending judgment (1 Kings 13:1). Elijah and his successor, Elisha, were recognized as men of God (1 Kings 17:24; 2 Kings 5:8). David not only was a man after God's heart and king over Israel, but in spite of his failures he was a man of God (Nehemiah 12:24). Paul addressed his protégé, Timothy, as a man of God (1 Timothy 6:11).

Being a man of God in any generation requires at least four concurrent commitments:

1. **Residing in communion with Christ.** The disciples lacked formal religious training but were recognized as having been with Jesus (Acts 4:13). Jesus chose the Twelve to be with Him before sending them forth to preach (Mark 3:14). Without constantly abiding in Christ, we cannot bear spiritual fruit—in ministry or in life (John 15:4).

2. **Representing the character of Christ.** People expect ministers to exhibit the character qualities of Christ. Men of God should rely on the power of the Holy Spirit to reproduce Christ's character in their lives. If the pastor sins, he not only debases himself and his ministry, but he profanes the name of Christ whom he represents.

3. **Receiving the three calls of Christ.** Becoming a man of God begins with God's call. Jesus reminded His disciples, "You have not chosen me, but I have chosen you" (John 15:16). The man of God in vocational Christian service receives three calls: God's call to salvation, His call to ministry, and His call to specific places of service.

4. **Responding to the commission of Christ.** A man of God embraces His mission. One's purpose in life centers on Christ's commission. The man with a heart for God finds satisfaction from co-laboring with the Lord in fulfilling God's goals.

While the Call and Commission of Christ will be expanded in subsequent chapters, consider for a moment implications of the first two commitments:

A Man in Christ: Residing in Communion with Christ

The man of God is first *a man in Christ*. Paul's self-perception centered on his union with Christ. He taught that the believer is a new creation in Christ (2 Corinthians 5:17). Throughout Paul's epistles, "a man in Christ" and "Christ in you" interchangeably portrayed the essence of a Christian's being. Paul believed, through conversion, a person truly was no longer the person he was prior to conversion but was a new being in Christ.

The Holy Spirit immerses us *in Christ* at salvation (1 Corinthians 12:13; Galatians 3:27). At the same time, Jesus taught the necessity of our continually abiding in Him (John 15:5). Only Christ makes abiding in Him possible through His Spirit, but He requires our cooperation. Empowered by the Spirit, we must intentionally cultivate our communion *with Him* from the position of resting *in Him*.

> Only Christ makes abiding in Him possible through His Spirit, but He requires our cooperation. Empowered by the Spirit, we must intentionally cultivate our communion with Him from the position of resting in Him.

Communion with Christ is foundational to effective ministry. A minister is uniquely accountable as to the possession of this quality or the lack of it. Lyman Abbott said, "Just as men do not seek a doctor to find what he knows about anatomy, but to make them well, even so men seek a minister not to find what he knows about theology, but to receive from him healing and ministry which can only come from one who has a personal spiritual vitality and can convey that vitality to others."[2]

The source of vital spirituality comes from Christ Himself as He indwells the believer. He is the vine; we are merely branches. Any lasting results of our ministry comes from abiding in Him. As Jesus' disciples engaged in turning the world upside down (or right side up!), they lacked education, wealth, and power. Their effectiveness resulted from their identification and communion with Christ. Luke recalled, "Now when they saw the boldness of Peter and John, and perceived that they were unlearned and ignorant men, they marveled; and they took knowledge of them, that they had been with Jesus" (Acts 4:13).

Without constantly abiding in Christ, we not only fail to produce spiritual fruit, we open ourselves up to spiritual attacks. In one of my most tragic memories, I recall a preacher who fell into immorality. Blessed with astonishing success early in his ministry, his diminished effectiveness had been evident for several years, but no one knew why. When the news of his extramarital romance became public knowledge, we were shocked and bewildered. How could someone who had been so strong in the faith, who was so mighty in the pulpit, who had had such a passion for souls, come to this end? He had ceased having regular communion with Christ, and, consequently, lost his inner spiritual dynamic. In that weakness, he fell to the vulnerability of the flesh.

Paul also wrestled with the flesh, although not in the same way as our above-mentioned friend. He cried to God for relief and called himself a "wretched man" in the midst of spiritual crisis (Romans 7:24–25). In that struggle, Paul found a truth that not only helped him to know what to do but empowered him to do it. Victory came by abiding in Christ. Paul's discovery applies to every believer as we live each day in constant communion with our Lord.

If being *in Christ* is basic to the behavior of the average Christian, how much more true is that for the minister? Levitical law demanded a greater sacrifice for the sin of priests than for the error of common men (Compare Leviticus 4:3, 22–23, and 27–29). Jesus' parable demonstrated "to whom much is given, much shall be required" (Luke 12:48). Paul gave different degrees of qualification for persons who would be deacons and pastors, indicating that higher expectations existed for men who oversaw the flock of God (1 Timothy 3:1–15). James urged believers to be careful in seeking to be teachers because of the greater accountability for people in leadership (James 3:1).

William Taylor said, "If we would kindle the flame of piety in the hearts of others, we must take the live coals with which we do so from the burning altar of our own spirit."[3]

A Man in Christ: Representing the Character of Christ

Being *in Christ* results in demonstrating the nature of Christ through our lives. No one can produce godly character by exerting the flesh; Christlikeness can only come from abiding in Christ. His Holy Spirit produces fruit corresponding to His character (Galatians 5:22–23). Ministers who claim to be heralds of God must insure their lives bear the image of the One they serve.

Holiness—Sanctification

The most fundamental quality of divine character is holiness. Moses was awed by the majestic holiness of the Lord (Exodus 15:11). The mother of Samuel blessed God saying, "There is no one holy like the Lord" (1 Samuel 2:2). The psalmist wrote often of the

> *Ministers who claim to be heralds of God must insure their lives bear the image of the One they serve.*

righteousness, blamelessness, and holiness of the Most High (Psalm 11:7, 18:30, 47:8). Isaiah was allowed to view the heavenly throne and to hear the proclamation of the seraphim: "Holy, Holy, Holy is the Lord" (Isaiah 6:3). John the Beloved also was caught up in a vision of glory and heard that same shout: "Holy, Holy, Holy is the Lord God, the Almighty, who was and who is and who is to come" (Revelation 4:8).

Jesus, God the Son, shares that quality of holiness. His disciples called Him "the Holy and Righteous One" (Acts 3:14). Even the demonic opposition acknowledged

Christ to be the "Holy One of God" (Mark 1:24). Followers of Jesus are expected to reflect the same qualities of the One Who indwells them. He said, "Be ye therefore perfect, even as your Father which is in heaven is perfect" (Matthew 5:48). Peter quoted the Father's admonition for believers to "be holy for I am holy" (1 Peter 1:16).

The person called to be a minister of the Most High is primarily a person *in Christ* and, as such, should reflect the character of the Indweller. Without maintaining personal holiness *in Christ,* the Christian minister not only is unable to fulfill his role as minister but also leaves himself vulnerable to the onslaught of the enemy and the accusation of the world.

Humility—Servanthood

Some ministers want to be the sole authority in charge of everything and everyone. Christ spoke with great authority, but He alone is sovereign. At best, pastors are undershepherds, bearing not a right, but a responsibility for the flock of God. Peter warned elders to not to act as overlords but to lead their people willingly as examples (1 Peter 5:2–3). Jesus demonstrated the humility of a servant-leader by submitting Himself totally to the will of the Father all the way to the cross (Philippians 2:3ff).

The early disciples struggled with personal egos. They often debated who would be the greatest among them. Jesus reminded them that the desire for superiority was a trait of unbelievers. He expected better of them (Luke 22:24–25). At the Last Supper, Jesus provided an object lesson in servant-spiritedness as He laid aside His garments and washed the disciples' feet (John 13:1–14).

We servants are not above our Master (John 13:16). If Jesus led with a spirit of humility, His ministers should assume His attitude of humility and approach ministry as an act of loving and sacrificial service.

Love—Sacrifice

God is love (1 John 4:16). Whoever abides in Christ and Christ in him will love by virtue of a loving God indwelling him through His Spirit. Even when we cannot love in our flesh, the Holy Spirit produces love as the fruit of God in us. People are not impressed with our skills, knowledge, or academic pedigree; they are moved by God's love flowing through us.

Francis Chan admits he had difficulty relating to the idea of a loving heavenly Father because of the distant relationship he had with his own father. His idea of God was fearsome, someone to be obeyed but Whose care was not intimate or personal. Francis experienced a major change in his appreciation of God's love when he became a father himself. His love for his daughter and her love for him introduced an entirely different understanding of God's love. He wrote, "Through this experience, I came to understand that my desire for my children is only a faint echo of God's great love for me and for every person He made. I am just an earthly, sinful father, and I love my kids so much it hurts. How could I not trust a heavenly, perfect Father who loves me infinitely more than I will ever love my kids?"[4]

John called himself "the disciple whom Jesus loved" not because Christ loved him more than the others (John 13:23, 19:26); John was simply overwhelmed by the fact that Jesus loved him at all. In his first pastoral letter, John described God's love in many ways. **Consider three qualities of godly love**:

- **Godly love is sacrificial.** "In this was manifested the love of God toward us because that God sent his only begotten Son into the world, that we might live through him" (1 John 4:9). Worldly love looks to gain something from others; godly love seeks to give. God so loved us He gave His Son (John 3:16). Jesus did not feel like a martyr in this great gift but willingly gave Himself for us. In doing so, the Good Shepherd provided an example for every pastor (John 10:11).
- **Godly love is unconditional.** "Herein is love, not that we loved God, but that he loved us, and sent his Son to be the propitiation for our sins" (1 John 4:10). Often, we place a premium on love. We love people who love us, or we care for people who are nice and lovable. Even in ministry, we are tempted to spend our time with people who like us and who are good to us. However, Jesus did not place conditions on His love, but "while we were yet sinners, Christ died for us" (Romans 5:8).
- **Godly love is reciprocal.** Ministers are made to be channels of God's love and grace. We are not the end-users of God's ministry. Because we receive God's love, we become conduits carrying His love to everyone around us. "Beloved, if God so loved us, we ought also to love one another" (1 John 4:11).

Certainly more aspects of Christ's character should find their way into the minister's life, but these three—holiness, humility, and love—are especially vital. Blessed is the man of God of whom the people say, "When we see our pastor, we think of Jesus."

Developing Communion and Character through Spiritual Formation

"Till Christ be formed in you" (Galatians 4:19).

God's original purpose for humankind is to reflect His image. "So God created man in his own image, in the image of God he created him; male and female he created them" (Genesis 1:27). Tasks, such as the work of stewardship over creation, came later. The Westminster Confession concerning the chief end of man (loving God and enjoying Him forever) is irrelevant without accepting the primary goal of revealing God and His glory.

Sin, which corrupted human life at the Fall, did not alter God's intention. Through Jesus, God wills that believers be restored to their original purpose. God wants us to be re-formed into the image of His Son. "For whom he did foreknow, he also did predestinate to be conformed to the image of his Son," (Romans 8:29).

At salvation, the indwelling of God through His Holy Spirit regenerates the human spirit and introduces the potential again to fulfill the divine intention. However, the process of sanctification is a cooperative effort of yielding to God's Spirit as He shapes our character in the image of God's Son. "But we all, with open face beholding as in a glass the glory of the Lord, are changed into the same image from glory to glory, even as by the Spirit of the Lord" (2 Corinthians 3:18).

This process is not always swift or easy, solely due to human unwillingness to surrender aspects of life to the Lord. Paul struggled with the Galatian Christians who started the Christian journey by faith, only to be sidetracked by self-centered legalists. He cried out, "My little children, of whom I travail in birth again until Christ be formed in you . . ." (Galatians 4:19).

Communion Is Derived from Love

One quality of Next-Gen ministers that I've appreciated is their deep love for Jesus. When we love someone, we want to be with that person. Whether in person or via telephone, text, or social media, we desire contact and interaction. Communion with Christ is quality time in His presence, soaking up every word He speaks, sharing with Him our deepest thoughts and feelings, and following obediently as He leads.

The beginning of spiritual transformation is the love of Christ. Divine love for Christ results from receiving the divine love of Christ. It is His love. "We love Him because He first loved us" (1 John 4:19). We could never love Jesus without receiving and responding to His love for us.

Not ironically, the more time we spend with Christ, the more we desire to be with Him. Ours should be the prayer of David, a man after God's own heart: "As a deer longs for flowing streams, so longs my soul for thee, O God. My soul thirsts for God, for the Living God" (Psalm 42:1–2).

Communion with Christ Involves Communication

The more you are with someone you love, the deeper you communicate, resulting in truly knowing that person. As we speak with Christ in prayer and hear Him speak to us through His Word, we not only understand Him, but we also find ourselves drawn closer to Him. As we commune with Him through prayer and the Word, we find the Spirit working to fashion Christ's character within us.

Communicate with Prayer

We pray because Jesus prayed. That's pretty extraordinary. God the Son was one with God the Father, yet being found in human form He prayed constantly. He prayed privately (Matthew 14:23) and He prayed openly (John 11:41–43). He expressed Himself freely, as we see no more plainly than during His passion in the Garden of Gethsemane prior to the crucifixion (Matthew 26:36–44). He prayed specifically for others and for Himself (John 17; Luke 23:33–34). Today, He still prays, ever making intercession for you and me (Hebrews 7:25). Jesus taught His disciples to pray (Luke 11:1–4), and throughout Scripture He continues to teach His disciples today to pray.

Without prayer, no one can truly commune with Christ, much less serve Him effectively. Communing prayer takes time and effort. It goes deep into the soul and presses to the heart of God. That great prophet of prayer, E. M. Bounds reminds us, "Much with God alone is the secret of knowing Him and of influence with Him. He yields to the persistency of a faith that knows Him. He bestows His richest gifts upon those who declare their desire for and appreciation of those gifts by the constancy as well as earnestness of their importunity."[5]

Hear God Communicate Through the Word

Even more than speaking to God, communion and communication involves hearing from God. God spoke to the prophets and patriarchs directly. He communicates with us through His Word. We can never really know God unless we invest significant time in Scripture.

The Bible is relevant in every generation because it was written not merely by the hands of ancient men in a distant culture but by the direction and inspiration of Eternal God. Observe what the Word says about itself: "All scripture is given by inspiration of God, and is profitable for doctrine, for reproof, for correction, for instruction in righteousness: That the man of God may be perfect, thoroughly furnished unto all good works" (2 Timothy 3:16–17).

Scripture did not originate in the mind of human writers but was inspired by God—"God-breathed." Peter reminded early believers, "For the prophecy came not in old time by the will of man: but holy men of God spoke as they were moved by the Holy Ghost" (2 Peter 1:21).

Scripture is profitable for:

- **Doctrine**—teaching God's will and ways
- **Reproof**—convicting, exposing, rebuking whenever we depart from the Lord

- **Correction**—restoration of our hearts and lives: "Wherewithal shall a young man cleanse his way? by taking heed thereto according to Your word" (Psalms 119:9).
- **Instruction in righteousness**—teaching us to live in the ways of God

However, the text does not stop there. The ultimate result of the Word is that the man/woman of God may be perfect (mature, complete), fully equipped for all good works.

Make a Daily Appointment with God

One of the most helpful ways to develop a consistent communion with Christ is to make an appointment with Him each day, an appointment with Jesus just like an appointment with anyone else, but with a much higher priority. Yes, we should experience a constant communion with God throughout the day, praying without ceasing (1 Thessalonians 5:17). Still, having a regular appointment with God will help develop consistency in our time with Him.

The biggest challenge to having a consistent quiet time is thinking about it as a quiet time rather than a daily appointment with Jesus. The goal is not to add to the "to do" list but to enjoy a relationship with One Who loves you. "God is faithful, through whom you were called into fellowship with His Son, Jesus Christ, our Lord" (1 Corinthians 1:9).

While consistency is helpful in developing a consistent communion with Christ, having a variety of times and approaches will also encourage you to keep your communion fresh and authentic.

Whatever your method, give yourself to communion with Christ; only through Him can your life or ministry be truly worthwhile. Being in Christ, we "live and move and have our being" encompassed by our Lord Who is our life (Acts 17:28; Colossians 3:4).

Chapter 4

RECEIVING THE THREE CALLS OF CHRIST

"Before I formed you in the belly I knew you; and before you came forth out of the womb I sanctified thee, and I ordained you a prophet to the nations" (Jeremiah 1:5).

Few people wake up one day and say over their cornflakes, "I think I'll be a minister." Pastoral ministry is not simply a vocation, although you may earn your living serving a church, mission, or other Christian ministry. Pastoral ministry is a calling.

Some ministers struggle with the concept of God's call. While leading a graduate level seminar for ministers in Australia, I discovered many of the students admitted they had no concept of a call. A leading pastor in the United States confessed he never felt called to ministry but merely volunteered. Through the years of pastorates, denominational service, and seminary teaching, I have counseled countless young men and women who questioned whether they were genuinely called by God into vocational Christian service. Does someone need a sense of divine prompting before entering ministry?

I believe a biblical minister answers not just one, but three calls. The first call—to salvation—lasts for eternity. The second call—to vocational ministry—is intended for a lifetime (although a minister can disqualify himself). The third call—to specific places of service—will come in a series throughout one's ministry.

Like love and marriage, unless you respond to these calls in proper order, you may experience a lot of heartache and cause much harm. A few people end up in ministry almost accidentally. Fred was a wonderful layman in his church. He was a deacon, a Sunday School teacher, and even led music on occasion. His small church often struggled with finding pastors. They could not pay enough money for a full-time minister and few jobs were available to support a bivocational pastor. Following the departure of the last pastor, the church asked Fred to fill in and share a few devotional thoughts in the place of a sermon. Fred used his teaching experience to take care of the pulpit responsibilities, thinking it would be for only a few weeks.

Good Example

Months passed as the church found the situation comfortable and affordable. Fred would not let the church pay him since he had a nice income from his business. Finally, the other men said, "Fred, you just need to become the pastor." So he did. He never felt a call to the work. He never underwent training or sought education to improve his knowledge or skills. He just approached this task like he did in his business ventures. The problem was, church is not a business and Fred, the pastor, was much more controlling than Fred, the deacon, who filled in temporarily. Inevitable conflict between Fred and his former friends finally forced him to leave the church. His brief foray into ministry harmed him and his family and left spiritually wounded parishioners in its wake.

You can use this book to learn information and gain skills that will help you serve ably in pastoral ministry. However, if you have not responded to the three calls of God, perhaps you need to reconsider your father-in-law's offer of a job in his company.

The Call to Salvation

God wants you to be saved. Some theologians question whether God wants everyone to be saved. Suffice it to say, God is "not willing that any should perish, but that all should come to repentance" (2 Peter 3:9). Unfortunately, not all people will respond to God's grace through Christ. Through the years, I have witnessed seminary students and experienced ministers realize they were baptized as children but had not come to a saving knowledge of Christ. With great joy, they confessed their need and received Jesus as Savior and Lord.

The fact that you are reading this book indicates you are either a minister or are feeling called to ministry. An unregenerate clergy gave birth to many evils both before and after the Reformation. Because people became clergy without becoming Christian, they did not care about the Bible or sound doctrine or a regenerate church. They loved position, power, prestige, possessions, and pleasure. If you would be a "good minister of Jesus Christ," (1 Timothy 4:6), be sure you have a personal relationship with Jesus Christ as Lord and Savior.

Be a saved preacher, Youth Minister, missionary, Minister of Music, Recreation Director, or

> *Exercise:* Write out your testimony in no more than two pages. If you can't do that, perhaps you need to find a spiritual adviser and work through some issues. The point is not whether you have a testimony that could fill a book. The point is that you can see past all the peripherals of your experience and clearly identify when you became aware of your need for a Savior, how you came to repent of sin and believe that Jesus is God's Son and that He died for you and rose again, and how you received Him by faith.
> When you have finished, read it aloud to yourself. Next, find a friend or family member and read it aloud to him or her. Finally, start sharing your testimony with at least one person every day. You will find many who respond by wanting to take those three steps with you.

whatever it is that God has called you to be. For that matter, if you don't have the call to ministry, be a saved lawyer, doctor, dentist, ditch digger, butcher, baker, or Indian chief. God wants everyone to be saved, regardless of vocational calling.

If you have not responded to God's call to salvation, this might be a good time to do just that. How? As God's Spirit convicts you of sin, you must repent, believe on Jesus Christ (God's Son Who died for our sins and rose again), and receive Jesus as Savior and Lord. After all, those three little steps are the foundations of salvation. Scripture says, "Repent and be converted that your sins might be blotted out" (Acts 3:19). Scripture says, "Believe on the Lord Jesus Christ and you will be saved . . ." (Acts 16:31). Scripture says, "But to as many as received Him (Jesus) to them He gave the power (authority) to become sons (and daughters) of God, even to as many as believed on His name" (John 1:12).

Putting the words into a prayer might sound something like this: "Lord Jesus, I am a sinner. I repent, I am sorry for my sin, and I turn from sin to follow You. I believe that You are God's Son, that You died on the cross for me, and that God raised You from the dead. I receive You as my Lord and Savior. Thank You for saving me. Help me to live for You from this day forward. In Your name, I pray. Amen."

The prayer does not save you. God does that. However, His promise is that if you repent, place your faith in Jesus' death and resurrection, and receive Jesus as Lord and Savior, you will be saved—by God's grace through your faith (Acts 3:19; John 1:12, 3:16; Ephesians 2:8–10). This gift of God is yours. Thank Him again, even if you've been saved for years; it's a nice thing to do.

The Call to Vocational Ministry

". . . Who hath saved us, and called us with an holy calling, not according to our works, but according to his own purpose and grace, which was given us in Christ Jesus before the world began, . . ." (2 Timothy 1:9).

Writing to his son in the ministry, Paul reflected upon God's grace. God not only had saved him, but God called him "with a holy calling." This holy calling to ministry came subsequent to salvation. While all believers are called to minister in various ways, this calling was special. It involved a vocational expression of ministry.

Although Paul served in some churches bivocationally, supporting himself through tent making, he considered himself a minister, not a maker of tents. God's call was clear and compelling: to proclaim Christ's Good News throughout the world. Paul's version of the call involved missionary work as a church planter. Timothy's call was as a pastor. Both men received the same "holy calling."

God does not call everyone to vocational ministry, yet God does call every believer to ministry. The apostle Paul noted that vocational ministers equip the saints

Exercise: What's your story? Take a few minutes and write about your experience with THE CALL. Nailing down your testimony of responding to God's call now will help you when the inevitable struggles in ministry come later.
If you haven't already done so, share your story with your wife and children. They need to know your heart. If God is calling you, He is calling your family. Scripture says, "The two shall be one." If God calls you and you are married, He calls you both. If He calls you and you have children, He calls you all. Be sure to allow God time to work in their lives as he has worked in yours. A family unified in THE CALL will persevere through all the challenges of THE WORK.

(all believers) for the work of the ministry. The New Testament Church is blessed by ministering saints in service to the King. Still, God issues a special call to some of His saints. "And He gave some to be prophets, and some apostles and some evangelists and some pastors and teachers . . ." (Ephesians 4:11).

THE CALL summons many ministers with unmistakable clarity. Others struggle—some in knowing, others in yielding. God calls some people in their youth. He calls others at various stages of life. Some people surrender to God's call with eagerness, others after years of doubt and questioning.

How do you know whether God has called you? I've lost count of the number of inquirers who have asked that question over the years of local church service, denominational service, and seminary classes. My first response is what most pastors say: "If you can do something else and be happy, do it." Note that I did not say, "If you can't do something else, do this." Some people think ministry is a place for people who cannot be successful in secular employment. Perhaps a few ministers fit such a description, but people who would fail in business will generally fail in ministry too.

Ministry demands a vigorous combination of skills like few other vocations. It requires the kind of long hours doctors and lawyers experience but without the corresponding compensation. Conflict is sure; tenure can be short; pay is paltry; and every person in the congregation is your employer. Sounds like a dream job to me. Ministry is one job in which you will be absolutely miserable if you do not have THE CALL.

THE CALL will keep you where God wants you when nothing else will.

You will want to quit nearly every Monday morning, but you won't because of THE CALL. (I heard one minister say he never took Mondays as a day off because he didn't want to feel that bad on his own time.)

You will wonder why you didn't go to work at the factory or get that medical degree or learn more about insurance sales. You will be tempted to send that job application to your college buddy. But you won't because of THE CALL.

Your wife may wonder why she didn't marry Tom, Dick, or Harry. Your children may ask why Daddy has to be away so many nights taking care of other family's problems. You may want to scream into the night air, "Why!" But you won't because of THE CALL.

- THE CALL is a tug on your heart that does not allow a "time out."
- THE CALL is an emptiness that cannot be filled by anything except God's Will.
- THE CALL is a freedom to turn away from the kind of success all your friends want so you can surrender to the only achievement worthwhile—hearing God say, "Well done, good and faithful servant."
- THE CALL comes sometimes through quiet contemplation and sometimes in the heat of service.
- THE CALL may have a specific scriptural accompaniment, and it may come from the general knowledge of God's Word.
- THE CALL is God's option on your life.
  - His purpose worked out in your life
  - His will expressed through your life
  - His strength enabling your life
  - His life flowing through your life[1]

Ultimately, THE CALL must be confirmed not merely by family and congregations but by God. In my case, the confirmation came in the joy I felt anytime I was able to serve Him—whether in my youth group at church or the Youth For Christ meetings after school, whether preaching in a cell at the county jail, being the actor in the youth musical, *Good News*, or finally pastoring a church. Over the years, God has continued to test, and to confirm, THE CALL. When times were really desperate in ministry and a friend offered me a good-paying secular job, THE CALL brought me back to reality.

Life offers many less-traveled roads for the average person. Those persons whom God calls can wander down many of them, but they will only find peace on the one with this road sign: "THE CALL."

Tom was minding his own business, and maybe yours, as a law enforcement officer for over twenty years. He had been a deacon and was active in his church. God began touching his heart about the pastorate. He resisted at first. Having never been to college, he wasn't sure about starting over in school. After praying for two years, he finally became convinced that God wanted him to preach and to prepare. He began pastoring a small bivocational church and simultaneously started seminary classes. He regularly testified how God has blessed both decisions and has provided for his family throughout the experience.

Consider the Qualifications

Some people confuse God's calling with personal desires. One way to determine if you are on the right track is to consider the biblical qualifications for a minister. Some people might argue that Paul's letters to Timothy and Titus spoke only of senior pastors and deacons. I doubt Paul knew what a senior pastor was. His lists of spiritual and practical qualities apply equally to ministers who preach in the pulpit, lead a youth ministry, serve on the mission field, or pastor in some other way.

Read what Paul wrote under the inspiration of the Holy Spirit:

> This is a true saying, If a man desire the office of a bishop (pastor), he desires a good work. A bishop (pastor) then must be blameless, the husband of one wife, vigilant, sober, of good behavior, given to hospitality, apt to teach; Not given to wine, no striker, not greedy of filthy lucre; but patient, not a brawler, not covetous; One that rules well his own house, having his children in subjection with all gravity; (For if a man know not how to rule his own house, how shall he take care of the church of God?) Not a novice, lest being lifted up with pride he fall into the condemnation of the devil. Moreover he must have a good report of them which are without; lest he fall into reproach and the snare of the devil (1 Timothy 3:1–7).

> If any be blameless, the husband of one wife, having faithful children not accused of riot or unruly. For a bishop (pastor) must be blameless, as the steward of God; not self-willed, not soon angry, not given to wine, no striker, not given to filthy lucre; But a lover of hospitality, a lover of good men, sober, just, holy, temperate; Holding fast the faithful word as he has been taught, that he may be able by sound doctrine both to exhort and to convince the gainsayers (Titus 1:6–9).

While these passages use the term *bishop* rather than *elder*, both words clearly refer to the pastor. Vocational ministry is a good work. It deserves good ministers. That's why a pastor should not be a "novice," a new believer. The devil offers enough problems to the mature pastor. In addition, the minister should possess certain qualities to serve God's people effectively:

1. **Blameless.** People will blame you for enough when you don't deserve it. Don't give them reason for accuse you of wrongdoing.

2. **A husband of one wife.** Does Paul's statement mean a single man cannot be a pastor? Most scholars agree that Paul did not exclude single

men but was emphasizing the need for men not to have more than one wife. However, many churches in Eastern Europe and other parts of the world take this admonition to mean that a pastor must be married.

Does this admonition mean a minister cannot be divorced and remarried? A textual reading of "one woman man" gives more liberal interpreters flexibility of allowing for pastors who have been divorced and remarried. They argue that polygamy was common in biblical days, and a pastor should not be polygamous.

That argument is disingenuous at best. While polygamy was common among nonbelievers, all Christians were expected to be monogamous. Why, then, would Paul have a special note about the marital status of pastors if he did not mean to exclude serial polygamy (divorce and remarriage) as well? The best interpretation excludes men from the pastorate who have been divorced and remarried. This statement does not mean they cannot serve God and His church in some ways, but not as a pastor.

Another consideration may help here: Do you want the spiritual leader of your church to meet some stripped down, bare bones qualification with plenty of asterisks and exceptions? Or do you want your spiritual leader to meet the highest of qualifications and be the best example possible for the believers?

Also, does Paul's consistent reference to the male gender preclude women from serving as pastors? It does. While women may serve honorably in many ways, even as missionaries or in many church ministries, Scripture specifically limits the pastorate to men.

3. **Ruling his own house well, having his children in subjection with all gravity.** Ministers' children don't have to be angels, but they should not behave in a way that brings rebuke on the ministry. The emphasis is on the minister's ability to "rule well his household" rather than the expectation that Preacher's Kids be perfect. Kids will be kids and churches should not place unfair burdens on preachers' children. At the same time, a man might need to reconsider his calling if his children are so disobedient that the police have to come to the parsonage. Paul's argument is that a man cannot rule well the house of God if he can't take care of his own house.

4. **Vigilant.** The Greek word means "temperate, self-controlled." If a man cannot control his own desires, how can he lead others to holy living?

5. **Sober.** Now it's really important that a man not be a drunkard (as seen in later verses), but that is not the meaning of this word. Like *vigilant*, the word *sober* means to be serious minded and self-controlled. Being sober does not require that the minister never laugh or enjoy himself. Believe me; you'll need a good sense of humor in this work.

6. **Of good behavior.** Paul used a word that suggests modesty and a quiet spirit that produces a respectable lifestyle.

7. **Given to hospitality.** Ministry is a people business. You cannot spend all your time in the cloister of your office preparing sermons and organizing programs. You must love people. As a counselor of ministerial students for several years, I've used a number of tests to help them understand themselves and find the kind of ministry to which they are best suited. I was surprised to discover that several had difficulty with people. Some lacked the ability to relate to groups; others had problems opening up to people on an individual basis. If, like Charlie Brown, you love humanity but can't stand people, join the community club or do relief work somewhere, just stay out of the pastorate!

8. **Able to teach.** The minister must be able to take what he has been taught and relay the Word of God faithfully to others (1 Timothy 3:2; Titus 1:9). He uses sound doctrine to exhort and convince.

9. **Not given to wine.** Like the issue of divorce and remarriage, these four words (actually two in the Greek) cause heated discussions between ministers who believe in total abstinence from alcoholic beverages and people who do not. The latter group argues that the text only calls for the minister not to be a drunkard or brawler.

Some younger ministers accept the use of beverage alcohol. They argue that the Bible does not have a clear prohibition against drinking. They tend to overlook the larger body of Scripture that obviously warns against the dangers of alcohol as a beverage. Can someone who uses beverage alcohol legitimately claim to do so for the glory of God? (1 Corinthians 10:31).

I agree with the former group—a minister should avoid all use of alcoholic beverages. After all, do you really feel like the man in the pulpit is filled with the Spirit of God when you've seen him on Saturday night imbibing the spirits? If you keep the highest standards, you will never be embarrassed by the teenager who asks what kind of beer you were having at the restaurant. Remember, we are called to a HOLY calling.

10. **Temperance.** This quality lets us know that it is just as bad being intemperate in our eating habits as in our drinking. The average pastors' conference offers plenty of evidence that some men may be doing all right when it comes to avoiding liquor but are failing terribly when it comes to gluttony. Medical problems notwithstanding, a grossly overweight minister is a poor example to a congregation struggling with their own temptations.

11. **No striker or brawler, but patient.** Some ministers may feel like demonstrating their pugilistic prowess after a lively business meeting, but the representative of the Prince of Peace cannot be quarrelsome or eager to get into a fight, physically or verbally. Allow the fruit of the Spirit to come through your life so people will see love, joy, peace, longsuffering, gentleness, goodness, faith, meekness, and temperance (Galatians 5:22–23).

12. **Not greedy of filthy lucre.** Frankly, I smile at this a little bit, knowing how much more most ministers could make if they took their skills into the business world. Still, some men will compromise just to keep their paychecks coming rather than take unpopular stands in the pulpit or at committee meetings. The bottom line is you can't be in this business for the money. Otherwise, you will fail that other ministerial test: not being covetous.

13. **Holy.** Saving the best and all-encompassing point for last, Paul echoes the admonition, "Be ye holy, for I am holy" (1 Peter 1:16). Consider how many times Scripture reminds Christians in general, and ministers especially, of the importance that we live holy lives: (Leviticus 11:44–45, 19:2, 20:26; 1 Peter 1:15–16.) We represent the Holy One. The Holy Spirit lives within us. God's Holy Name is at stake in the way we live.

I do not presume to add to Paul's list, but another qualification should also be considered by one praying about the call to vocational Christian service. Rather than add to Paul, it summarizes Paul—**a minister must love the Lord first and foremost and above all other things in life.**

Your motivation for ministry must not come from a desire to meet family expectations, or a personal need simply to help people. If YOUR CALL emerges from a heart in love with Jesus, it will be like that pure spring water gushing from the earth—it cannot be stopped.

What about spiritual gifts? Scripture does not require a specific gift for being a pastor. Some writers claim Ephesians 4:11–13 lists prophets, apostles, evangelists, pastors, and teachers as spiritual gifts. Actually, Paul does not mention spiritual gifts in this passage. He says God has given persons with these ministries to the Church for the equipping of believers. The role of pastor or pastor/teacher is not a specific gifting for the minister but a type of minister given to the church.

Other scholars refer to Romans 12 and 1 Corinthians 12 when enumerating spiritual gifts. Neither passage was intended as an exhaustive listing of spiritual gifts. Rather, Paul emphasized the use of whatever gifts one has for the unity and edification of the Church.

Corinthians, especially, has been misunderstood as some believers focus on supernatural manifestations, such as speaking in tongues. The true example of speaking in tongues was first observed at Pentecost. In this case, the disciples spoke not in unknown languages but in known languages they had not learned (Acts 2:7–12). Proper hermeneutics does not support the claim that 1 Corinthians 13:1 endorses the idea of an angelic, or heavenly, language. Paul was using a rhetorical argument. He did not speak with an angelic language any more than he gave his body to be burned (1 Corinthians 13:3).

> *Spiritual gifts do not determine what one does in Kingdom work but influences how one serves.*

The Corinthians had many heresies and problems. Paul used their own arguments to show their error. Here, he argued that whatever kind of spiritual manifestation they claimed was worthless without love. Similarly, in 1 Corinthians 15:29, Paul was not giving credence to the act of baptism for the dead. Rather he used their heretical practice to argue against their false teaching that there was no resurrection from the dead.

In any case, spiritual gifts do not determine what one does in Kingdom work but influences how one serves. A pastor may benefit from having the spiritual gift of exhortation, but a pastor with the spiritual gift of helps can also be successful. Each one simply serves the congregation differently. The first may be a gifted speaker, while the second is known for compassion and service. However, both can be effective servants of the church.

The Call to a Place

You've responded to God's call to vocational ministry. What now? How do you end up where God wants you to be? God's call to a specific place should be as clear as the overall call to ministry.

Each church or mission field will be special. None is more important or better than the other regardless of convenience, prominence, or pay scale. As London and Wiseman observed: "Every assignment is holy ground because Jesus gave Himself for the people who live there. Every place is important because God wants you to accomplish something supernatural there. Every situation is special because ministry is needed there."[2]

Many Next-Gen ministers respond to the strong pull of missions among the vast unreached people groups of the world. Others prefer to engage in church planting rather than struggle with established structures of a traditional church. One survey of seminary students indicated fewer than a third planned to serve as pastors of existing churches. Practically none envisioned themselves in bivocational churches, even though bivocational pastors serve 42 percent or more of churches in many states. No God-called minister has the right to limit the Lord regarding the place or type of position in which he will serve. Whenever you're tempted to do so, reread the little book of *Jonah*. It describes the results of trying to ignore God's direction as to one's place of service.

How do you know which place is the right one for you? Does God pull your heart toward a place? Does He drop your name into the mailbox of a Pulpit Committee or a Youth Minister's Search Committee or a mission agency? How does it happen, and how will you know it is right when it does happen? The next chapter will help you prepare for and respond to God's calling to specific places of service.

Chapter 5

GOD'S CALL TO A PLACE

"Now when they had gone throughout Phrygia and the region of Galatia, and were forbidden of the Holy Ghost to preach the word in Asia, After they were come to Mysia, they assayed to go into Bithynia: but the Spirit suffered them not. And they passing by Mysia came down to Troas. And a vision appeared to Paul in the night; There stood a man of Macedonia, and prayed him, saying, Come over into Macedonia, and help us" (Acts 16:6–9).

Like Paul, you may have in mind the kind of place you want to serve. Perhaps you want to be close to family, so you say, "God, I'll serve you as long as it's not too far away from mom and dad." Maybe you see larger churches with vast resources as your destination, but you want to start at the top (who has time to work your way up?). Responsiveness may determine your vocational GPS. After all, who wants to spend years among people who resist the Gospel?

Paul's motivation was more spiritual than these examples, but his direction still missed God's plan. Asia certainly needed the Gospel, as did Bithynia. Philippi was not on Paul's radar. God had other plans. God knew a seller of purple cloth (Lydia) and a hardened jailer who needed Jesus. How could they believe in Him Whom they had not heard? (Romans 10:14). God knew a church would spring up in the wake of Paul's ministry that would minister to him as he sat in a Roman prison ten years later. That experience produced one of the most poignant letters of the New Testament (Philippians).

Your first goal is not to find God's will but to yield to God's will, whatever it may be. He is Sovereign, not us. He knows exactly where we need to be. Determining God's call to a place begins with getting in touch with Him. As you commune with Him, have a submissive spirit and delight in God Himself. Don't try to figure it out on a human level, but "trust in the LORD with all your heart; and lean not unto your own understanding. In all your ways acknowledge him, and he shall direct your paths" (Proverbs 3:5–6).

God does not play hide-and-seek with His will. He greatly desires that we know and do His plans. If we surrender our will to His and find great joy in His presence, He will show clearly whatever step He wants us to take.

Preparation and Education

If you surrender to God's call to vocational ministry, prepare yourself now for whatever He may call you to do later. Most pastors will advise their would-be preacher boys, "If God calls you to preach, He calls you to prepare." Part of preparation involves education. Some people are so eager to get started in ministry they want to skip this foundational part of preparation. A small church (or perhaps a larger one) may be willing to call you just as you are and you may do well at that point. What about the future?

As a young minister, I had the opportunity to serve a very large congregation, but to do so meant bypassing seminary. I sought the advice of a seasoned minister who had taken that road years earlier. He asked me, "What has God called you to do and be when you reach age fifty? What education, training, experience, and skill will you need to fulfill His call?" I knew I could get by for a while without formal education but could not accomplish what God wanted me to do down the road unless I paid the price in advance.

You may not be able to predict a specific place of service that far in advance, but you should know the kind of preparation you will need for the future. Lay a strong foundation. You will have a lifetime of ministry building on the groundwork. If you take shortcuts now, you will struggle through a lifetime of catching up or making excuses as you try to fake it. Avoid the diploma mills that give you a certificate without giving you an education. You won't fool anyone, and you can seriously handicap yourself.

First, if you are a preaching pastor, skipping formal education means you will have to develop about 150 sermons a year without the biblical and theological knowledge to dig deep week after week. Many pastors go from one church to another and simply turn over their sermon barrel every two years, repeating the same poor sermons they used before. Some pastors use other people's sermons from the Internet or in books of sermons or at pastors' conferences. However, if you will dig your foundation deep with knowledge and skill to "rightly divide the word of truth" you will never run out of material for sermons, lessons, or counsel.

Second, many pastors fail because of lack of leadership skills. They end up leaving churches involuntarily as much as from conflict over theology. Make sure your preparation includes courses in working with people, administrating committees and ministries, counseling, and the basic skills of pastoral ministry.

Third, a few pastors have tried to enhance their résumés with certificates from unaccredited institutions, taking shortcuts to credentials. Other pastors have faced termination because they falsified their résumés. Don't do that. You will hurt, not help, yourself and the church. Take the high road of preparation. You are not simply adding an alphabet soup of degrees to your résumé; you are developing skills, knowledge, and character to last you a lifetime.

To Résumé or Not to Résumé, That Is the Question

As in most areas of employment, experience is highly valued as a qualification for ministry. How to get that experience in the first place can present not only a practical, but also an ethical dilemma. Once ready to serve, perhaps even while in college or seminary, how do you connect with a potential place of service?

In many denominations, the ecclesiastical organization and polity make it easy for a young minister to find his first place of service or to change fields of work. Ministers are simply placed by an ecclesiastical hierarchy. One hopes the will of God and the desire of the local congregation are sought.

In congregational denominations, each church is a local, autonomous body. The people decide who will be their pastor. They often resent and resist any efforts by a denominational officer or a friendly pastor to suggest someone for their ministry needs. Others welcome recommendations and openly advertise for résumés. In either case, how does the name of a potential minister and the church in need of a minister get together? One way is through résumé sharing and résumé services.

Some ministers do not believe in sharing résumés. They trust God knows where they are and believe He will move them when He is ready. A similar mindset argues that because the Holy Spirit must inspire a sermon, it is therefore unspiritual to prepare a sermon. Both attitudes forget that the Holy Spirit often works through the tools we yield to Him. Having a résumé does not circumvent the work of the Holy Spirit. It is merely a tool in His hands.

Think of a résumé as a letter of introduction rather than as a way to induce a church to call you. If you are in school and have not found that initial place of service, or if you face the end of a ministry without a place to go, having a résumé provides an introduction to churches searching for a minister. The Holy Spirit remains the Prime Mover between ministers and churches.

On the other hand, many ministers are too quick to spread their résumés, trying to leave a bad situation, trying to get a better situation, or just fishing to see what might be out there. They are constant candidates, never settling into a place of ministry but always on the move to the next pasture.

Some ministers enlist friends to recommend them to churches. They send out résumés with glowing testimonials to qualifications and experience. In the arena of public elections, seeking supporters, making campaign speeches, and putting out promotional literature are common practices, but are these activities proper in a divinely called ministry?

Some denominations employ résumé services to aid churches and ministers looking for one another. Placement offices of theological schools are inundated with graduates who have the necessary academic credentials, but who have not received an invitation to exercise their newly acquired skills. Real estate and insurance offices, hardware stores, and supermarkets are not what these eager and idealistic young people had in mind when they entered seminary.

An unwritten rule prohibits most ministers from approaching a prospective church directly. The suggested alternative is to use a third party to send a letter of recommendation, along with a résumé of the candidate. We are not being too mystical when we affirm the leadership of the Holy Spirit in bringing pastor and people together. He Who knows both and the gifts of each is in the best position to make these introductions. Certainly, human intermediaries may be instrumental, but the best marriages are not initiated by the candidates themselves.

A deacon was helping a former pastor move to his new place of service. While visiting with the Minister of Music at the pastor's new charge, he asked if the musician knew of a prospective minister for his church. The Minister of Music recommended an associate minister in another city who had been praying about entering the pastorate. The introduction bore fruit and the church called the young associate to his first full-time pastorate.

A sense of divine leadership by the church and the minister is indispensable to extended tenure. In discussing elements of longer pastorates, R. Dwayne Conner noted that biblical churches believe in "a God-called, a God-placed, and a God-tenured ministry." He declared, "In the mystery of that inner call and the call of the church, 'deep called unto deep,' and there was the conviction that God was in the process of establishing a covenant relationship between that pastor and that congregation. It was that conviction which often sustained and encouraged both the pastor and the congregation through the years and enabled them to discover God's purpose."[1]

At the same time, ministers should feel no shame in sharing with associates and friends a desire to serve. Still, if you are already in a ministry, the best course would be to allow the Holy Spirit to work in His own way and time. The minister can experience a quiet confidence that God will move him when He is ready. Until then, he can go about his ministry without the constant restlessness that marks the search for greener pastures.

If you have no church, discover people in need of ministry, and meet that need. Like Paul and Timothy, if there is no church, start one. More Search Committees are impressed by someone busy about the work than someone waiting for the phone to ring.

For ministers needing help, most Baptist state conventions, national denominations, and seminaries offer services known as church–minister relations. More than résumé services, these offices provide help for ministers who are completing their seminary education, have been forced to leave a church without a call to another, or feel strongly the need to be available to interested churches. The services help churches who need assistance in finding potential ministers for consideration. Many churches, especially smaller ones, may not understand the basic process of how to call a minister. They also need help in getting information on qualified candidates. Too, mission agencies have personnel offices that receive résumés from ministers who sense a call to the mission field.

Ministers and churches in need of these services may contact these agencies directly or through their websites. Southern Baptist ministers can go to www.sbc.net to access the denomination's minister search process. Ministers can also contact state conventions and local associations. At each state convention website, a link to the state church–minister relations office will prompt the seeker to contact persons by phone or e-mail. Many state convention and seminary websites offer automated résumé services in which the minister can insert his résumé information, which is then shared with churches that contact the church–minister relations offices. Churches also can access these sites and submit their requests for certain types of ministers.

Preparing Your Résumé

If you feel comfortable with offering a résumé, what should it look like? As with any letter of introduction, a résumé should have several overall qualities:

1. **Honest**—A résumé should only contain truth. Don't pad your résumé. Search Committees are not impressed that you won the spelling bee in the sixth grade. Increasingly, Search Committees do not accept at face value your claims of education or experience. Be sure your claims will bear up under investigation.

2. **Clear**—A résumé should help churches get to know the minister and his wife. The arrangement of information should be easy to read.

3. **Complete**—Educational achievements should include the name and address of the institutions, the degrees earned and the dates of completion, and any areas of specialization. Lists of previous places of employment should include the years of service, titles of the positions, names of the church or ministry agency, complete addresses of the institutions, phone numbers, and e-mails of key contact persons.

4. **Personal**—Committees want to know your family. Share the names of your spouse and children (along with dates of birth— of your children, not your spouse, she would not appreciate that!). Note special hobbies and interests, but don't go overboard lest the committee think you plan to spend five days a week fishing or golfing.

5. **Brief**—Committees do not want to read a dissertation. For example, if you want to note your doctrinal beliefs, you don't have to explain your position on the top fifty doctrines. If you agree with your denomination's statement of faith, such as the Baptist Faith and Message, simply say that. Churches are well able to look up those documents and ask appropriate questions.

What to Include

At the top of the page, put your name (include a title only if you have a doctorate; avoid "Rev.") address, home and cell phone numbers, and e-mail address. A nice family photo (in color if possible) should adorn the top right- or left-hand corners. Avoid settings that are too formal (such as the wedding portrait of one minister and his Bride complete with wedding gown) or too casual (like the minister who used a picture of his family on the beach in bathing suits).

Include a brief statement about your calling (pastoral ministry, youth ministry, etc.) and why you are open to a new place of service.

Describe your educational background by listing degrees earned, beginning with your most recent and working back. Include the degree, any specialties (such as BS, business major), date earned, and the name, address, and phone number of the institution. If you have specialized seminar training, list them in order after listing your degrees. (Example: Advanced Pastoral Education—University Community Hospital, Tampa, Florida, 1996).

Describe your ministerial employment beginning with your current (or most recent) position. Include the dates of service, the title of the position, the name of the church or agency, and its address and phone number. Give a summary of the location in one sentence. (Example: "Mount Zion Baptist Church is a congregation of five hundred members in a county seat town.") Give a one-sentence summary of your work. ("As Youth Minister, I was responsible for Sunday School, the Wednesday night youth service, visitation, summer camp, and all events and activities for the senior high and middle-school students.") Don't exaggerate or brag about accomplishments. Keep each entry short. List your supervisor if you were not the pastor. If you do not want the committee to contact your current employer, note that request.

Describe any secular employment beginning with your most recent position. Unless the work relates directly to the ministry position you are seeking, just list the dates of service and the names and addresses of the employers. Do not feel compelled to state that your job at the supermarket was to sweep the floors and take out the garbage. However, if you supervised other employees, were responsible for organization and management of an organization, led marketing campaigns, or other pertinent tasks, a prospective church might find that information helpful in assessing your leadership skills.

List any published writings, honors, and other items that are truly noteworthy and offer insight into your skills and experience.

Finally, list four to six references. Be sure to obtain permission before using their names in your résumé. Use a variety of people, including previous pastors, professors, deacons and other laity, and friends. Include names, church (if a minister), position held, address, phone number, and e-mail address.

Print your résumé on good stock, not copy paper. A light color or white is preferred since many committees will photocopy extra copies for members.

Truth-in-Packaging

Truth-in-packaging laws were instituted in the marketplace because some merchants and manufacturers refused to give consumers all the information about a product. In some cases, blatantly inaccurate information has been placed on packages to make a sale. Is it time for ecclesiastical "truth in packaging?" Is it ever ethical for a candidate to tell less than the truth, the whole truth, and nothing but the truth in his communications with Search Committees and churches?

Résumé writing services in secular industries suggest ways for prospective employees to highlight their successes while bypassing embarrassing failures. Unfortunately, some of those ideas have been absorbed into the Christian world. Some ministers simply eliminate from their résumés those churches where they have had problems. They find various ways of disguising lost years, succeeding with committees that do not do their homework. Unearned academic degrees, untraceable specialized training, even fictitious places of service have been found on résumés of the more dishonest candidates.

A résumé should be a complete and honest accounting of one's training, ministry, and references. It should not gloss over the difficult parts, nor should it embellish one's successes. The résumé is to be a polite and proper introduction, not a sales tool.

Working with Search Committees

The average Search Committee will work through all of the résumés they have collected, praying until they settle on one person to study further. At that point, the committee may contact you for more information.

Unfortunately, a few uninformed churches will interview several people at the same time. If you find yourself in such a situation, you may want to decline an interview until the committee decides to focus on you. Similarly, you should not actively negotiate with more than one church at a time.

Pray to see if the Holy Spirit is leading you to leave your current ministry. Do not merely test the waters or shop around for a new church. God will lead you somewhere if He is not finished with you where you are.

Don't feel like you have to move quickly. God rarely makes you feel like you are five minutes late for the plane. Even if you are having difficulties in your church, do not allow panic to call you to the first church that dials your number.

Try to determine whether the committee is focused on you or if it merely is getting additional information. If you are still one of several pastors under consideration, you may not want to give out sensitive personal information, such as a credit check. At that point, let the committee know you would be happy to have them conduct credit and background checks if you are the one person they are considering.

When the time is right, cooperate. A church is prudent in wanting to know if the prospective minister has been a good steward with his finances and whether he has had legal difficulties. However, insist that the committee not make copies of your financial information. Ask them to return the originals to you after being reviewed. You may request that only one or two members of the committee handle the documents and give a report to the committee rather than having your personal data float around unsecured.

If the committee asks for audio or video recordings of your sermons, send two or three, not just your sugar stick favorite. You may also want to send copies of written outlines for each of the recorded sermons. Make sure the recordings are well-done, not full of crackling static.

When you talk to people, be nice. You may or may not feel called to this church, but these people will remember the impression they get. A Christian gentleman will honor the Lord in relationships. "Let your speech be always with grace, seasoned with salt, that you may know how you ought to answer every man" (Colossians 4:6).

Preparing for an Interview

Investigate the Church and the Community

An Internet search can provide some information. A church's data is often available in the denomination's annual publication of proceedings. See how the church has progressed over the past ten years, not just how it is now.

Contact the chamber of commerce for community information. The United States Census Bureau also has valuable information about the demographics. Go to www.census.gov. Demographical information specific to the church field also may be obtained from denominational or seminary sources.

If you want to see the church and community in person, you may drive through the community and go past the church, but do not show up at the church uninvited.

Prepare Your Family

Pray together as husband and wife and as a family. Discuss the possibilities of going to this church with your spouse and older children. Make sure they are open to a move. While you are the spiritual leader of your family, this a family decision. Many teenagers will be more open to a move if they are part of the decision. Family involvement does not limit the spiritual leadership of the minister; instead, consideration of your family enhances your influence.

Prepare yourself and your spouse for questions the committee will ask.[2] Generally, they will ask about your salvation testimony and call to ministry, your educational background, and your experience at other churches. If you have had difficulties in previous pastorates, be open and truthful in answering. Be prepared to answer doctrinal questions honestly and succinctly. The committee may also ask about your vision for their church. Admit to them that while you have some ideas, you would be foolish to outline a vision without knowing more about them, the church's history, and the community. Acknowledge that you have certain ministry tools you probably will bring with you and explain how these tools/ministries could help their church.

Your wife should expect to be asked about her role in the church, especially as to how she supports you in your ministry. She may also receive inquiries about your children.

Prepare Lists of Questions You Want to Ask the Committee

Honestly answer questions and honestly ask questions. You are having a discussion with these people about your mutual futures. Do not be afraid to ask difficult questions, but don't be difficult in the asking. You will help yourself by thinking through lists of questions you want answered prior to the interview. You want to know about the church's history, but frankly you should have studied the church in some depth prior to the interview. Here is an opportunity to see the church's past from the viewpoint of people the church has entrusted with its future. Politely inquire about previous pastors and staff ministers with regard to their successes, relationships, and present ministries. Ask about what they consider to be the church's high and low points, its successes and failures. How did they celebrate victories and how did they handle problems?

Also request information about how the church is doing currently. Are they experiencing additions or subtractions from the membership? Is the congregation at peace or in conflict? How would they describe their worship services, ministries, and general atmosphere? Where is the church going? Does it have a plan to which it is committed? Does the congregation have the financial resources to meet its needs and pursue its future?

Generally, the first interview is not the appropriate occasion to ask about compensation. However, if the committee does not bring up the issue, be sure to have a solid discussion about how the church will provide support for your family before committing to going to the church in view of a call.

Your spouse may also have questions. Discuss these in advance. You might verbalize her questions in advance or she may prefer to ask them herself.

During Subsequent Interviews

Promises

If the committee makes any commitments or promises, ask if the church has voted to approve these or if the church will do so prior to a call. One Search Committee agreed to provide a signing bonus to help a prospective pastor pay a debt made to his previous church. Because the committee did not seek church approval in advance, the minister accepted the call to the new church only to find out, once there, that the church Finance Committee was not willing to recommend approval of the financial arrangements.

On the other hand, another church had a similar situation, but voted on the financial package, including a loan to the pastor for housing, in advance of the call. You can imagine which situation resulted in a happy ministerial marriage.

Process

Be sure you understand and are comfortable with the process the church will use for the weekend when you go in view of a call. Neither the church nor the minister benefit from a rushed courtship. Take time to get to know people. A good schedule includes having the minister and his family enjoy dinner with the deacons and Search Committee (and their spouses) on Friday night. Saturday could include a morning activity with the youth followed by a church-wide get-acquainted lunch. Saturday night should be free so the minister and the people can prepare spiritually for Sunday. At the most, a quiet dinner with the Search Committee might cap off Saturday night. On Sunday morning, the minister would do well to make a courtesy call on the Sunday School classes before they begin their lessons. Leave at least half an hour for prayer and preparation prior to the morning service.

Some churches will vote after the morning service after the minister speaks. Others will wait until the Sunday night. Still others will delay a week before voting. The last option provides a problem for the minister and his current church, since he likely will face questions from his church without being able to inform them of his response to a call to the new church. In addition, people voting the following week may have been absent when the prospective pastor visited.

Most churches have a specified percentage of positive votes before a minister can be called. A divided church may find it hard to meet a high percentage. One church went without a pastor for nearly two years because no candidate could generate the required 75 percent vote. However, few pastors would dare accept a call to a church without a strong vote. You don't want to start out with a significant number of people opposed to your ministry. You should consider the situation and your inner sense of God's call before arbitrarily setting a percentage of the vote you will require before accepting the call.

Pressure

Once you go before a church in view of a call, you will feel pressure to accept the call regardless of the vote. You may worry that your current church will not allow you to stay if you decline the call to the new congregation.

Do not go in view of a call unless you are prepared to accept the call, but don't be afraid to decline if you and your family determine that this move is definitely not God's will. It is as sinful to go when God says to stay as it is to stay when God says to go.

Informing Your Present Church

Some pastors try to keep the visit to a prospective church as secret as possible, fearful of backlash if people know he may be seeking to leave. An interesting phenomenon is the anger people feel when you contemplate leaving them. They love you and may feel rejected or even betrayed by the suggestion that you would prefer some other people to them. Anger is a natural part of the grief they experience.

On the other hand, if you are not open with some people, and fail to get the call, you may lose your ministry anyway. You probably should not discuss a possible move while negotiations and interviews are underway. A good middle road is to let your current leadership know when you go in view of a call. Let people know you are simply seeking God's will just as you did when you came to their church. Invite them be your prayer partners through this final stage of the process.

Points of Contact

Stay in close contact with the Search Committee chair throughout the process. Make sure you have good, accurate information about the attitude of the church and any concerns that may be floating around the congregation.

After the church votes to call you, the Search Committee may feel it has done its job. The committee or some other group should responsible for helping you move—not just moving your household and office furnishings, but getting settled in with your new staff, committees, financial processes, and other aspects of beginning a new work.

The people who were a part of calling you to this church have reason to expect to be especially close to you and your family as you begin the new ministry. Be careful. One pastor and his wife were delighted that the Search Committee chair and his wife wanted to spend time with them socially after the call and move were executed. However, as he tried to build relationships with other couples, the committee chair and his wife became inordinately possessive and the relationship was seriously damaged.

Handling Financial and Personnel Issues

You are not guilty of seeking "filthy lucre" (1 Timothy 3:3) if you want to know how the church plans to support you and your family. Remember, these people are putting their families into your care, and you are putting your family into their care. It doesn't hurt to remind them of that relationship.

Financial Packages

The Internal Revenue Service tax code changes from time to time. The following information is not intended to replace sound advice from a qualified tax accountant; it is for educational purposes only. Consult with an appropriate financial advisor before making decisions. Another good resource is the website of Guidestone Financial Resources of the Southern Baptist Convention (www.guidestone.org). This site has several good, and usually current, guides for churches and ministers regarding compensation. A minister and a church should consider several important issues:

Salary

The salary is not the total compensation package. Salary is what a minister uses to provide meat and potatoes, clothes and cars, and the other needs of his family. Generally, a pastor's salary will be comparable to the average family in his congregation. In smaller and bivocational churches, the minister may have to supplement his salary with a second job, or his wife may have an additional income.

The church should provide as well as possible for its minister and his family, heeding the apostle Paul who wrote, "For the scripture says, 'Thou shalt not muzzle the ox that treads out the corn.' And, 'The laborer is worthy of his reward'" (1 Timothy 5:18).

Housing Allowance

A minister's housing allowance includes whatever is involved in providing lodging, furnishings, and utilities, but has several limitations established by law. The amount of the housing income tax deduction is the lesser of the amount the church establishes, the actual amount spent, or the fair rental value of the home plus furnishings and utilities. The housing allowance is not exempt from Social Security and Medicare taxes. The legality of the minister's housing allowance is under review by federal courts. Ministers and churches should always seek qualified legal and accounting advice from attorneys and certified public accountants.

Parsonages: A parsonage is part of housing allowance. In addition, the church can set aside an additional amount of money for the minister and label it "housing allowance" to cover utilities, furnishings, maintenance, and other expenses that the minister must pay to keep up the home.

During negotiations with a Search Committee, a minister should ask for a written agreement with the church outlining what aspects of parsonage maintenance and repairs are the responsibility of the minister or the church. A pastor would be wise to pay his own utility bill and make that part of the housing allowance, thus minimizing complaints by church members of bills being too high in the summer or winter. If the minister uses a cable service or incurs other expenses related to utilities, these costs may be included in a housing allowance.

Benefits

One problem ministers have with compensation packages is the perception that their incomes are too high. This misperception usually comes from having the entire package listed as income to the minister. The average factory worker or insurance salesman compares his paycheck to the minister's total compensation. The worker does not stop to consider that his pension plan, his insurance, and any business expenses are not included in the paycheck. To keep church members from comparing apples and oranges, a church should list benefits and expenses separately from salary and housing.

A loving church will provide for retirement benefits in an amount at least equal to 10 percent of the minister's salary and housing allowances. In some cases, denominational entities match contributions to qualified funds. A minister could ask the church to set aside an additional part of his salary for retirement payments.

Other benefits could include insurance for health, life, dental, and disability coverage. A minister may also use a salary reduction agreement to set aside funds for a health savings account or a health cafeteria plan to reimburse him for out-of-pocket and deductible expenses not covered by insurance.

Business Expenses

Separate from the salary and housing and the benefits listings, a church should budget whatever business expense allowances it plans to provide. How these expenses are handled is important not only for taxation purposes but also for maintaining trust and integrity between the church and the minister.

A business expense should not be considered income to the minister; it is simply the church's provision for expense the minister incurs in doing his job. Wise ministers are frugal with expenses. Wise churches use an accountable reimbursement plan to handle expenses. An accountable reimbursement system is one in which the minister reports expenses, along with receipts and documentation, to the church, which reimburses the minister dollar for dollar. Miles driven in the minister's personal vehicle should be reported along with documentation and reimbursed at the IRS standard approved rate.

Some ministers ask the church to set aside part of their salary through a salary reduction agreement for books and education. In the case of books, a written agreement should specify whether the books belong to the minister or to the church. Having such details outlined in advance and kept in written form can help both parties avoid unpleasant disagreements when the minister moves to another church.

Other Personnel Matters

Finances are not the only matters that require negotiation. Vacation time, the number of revivals allowed, responsibility for paying supply preachers, and many other aspects of the ministry relationship should be negotiated in good faith.

Ask about the expectations regarding office hours versus being out on the church field. One pastor of a large congregation was dismissed because of conflict over office hours. A seemingly minor consideration became reason for ministerial divorce because of unrelenting positions of two parties. The problem could have been avoided by a thorough discussion of job descriptions and work habits.

If the church does not have a role description, the negotiation period is an excellent opportunity to create one that incorporates the desires and expectations of all parties. Again, honesty and sensitivity are keys to agreements, which produce long-term cooperation and success.

Moving Expenses

Usually the church or missions agency that calls a minister will pay for moving his family to the new field. However, churches have a wide range of interpretation as to what these expenses include. One church paid for the rental van and gas, but the pastor had to pack, load, and drive the truck. The church people were kind enough to help unload the truck once it arrived at the parsonage.

On the other extreme, a suburban church allowed the pastor to employ a moving company that packed, loaded, moved, and unpacked both household furnishings and office materials, including a large library of books and a dozen file cabinets.

Some churches believe home ownership helps the minister's family develop a commitment to stay for a longer time. They may offer financial incentives to help first-time homeowners with down payments and/or closing costs. The minister should be careful not to take advantage of a willing congregation and to consult a tax professional about potential tax liability.

When love, respect, and the desire to honor the Lord motivate the parties, the art of negotiation can be a positive process for creating a covenant relationship between pastor and people.

Bivocational Ministry

Nearly half of the churches are served by a bivocational minister. These servants of God are not part-time pastors but usually devote as much time to the church as if they were fully funded by the congregation. However, since the average church has just over sixty persons present on a given Sunday, money is rarely available for smaller congregations to provide adequate support for the pastor. Pastors called to these churches take on secular work to supplement their family income.

Bivocational ministry is honorable. The apostle Paul worked as a tent maker on occasion to support his ministry as a church-planting missionary. Like Paul, bivocational pastors sometimes struggle to balance all of the demands on their time. In addition to their secular workload, they prepare sermons, visit the sick and sinful, conduct weddings and funerals, meet with committees, teach lessons, train leaders, and lead all the other ministries of the church. At the same time, they wrestle with having enough time to meet the needs of their families.

If a church or church-planting opportunity arises and you feel God's call, but the congregation cannot provide full financial support, talk with them about serving bivocationally. Some churches think that having a bivocational pastor is like getting half a minister. Help them to understand that the nature of the pastor's job allows him to care for the people and, at the same time, provide for the family.

If a church is not able to fund the pastor's family needs and is unwilling to allow him to take on additional work, perhaps God is not leading you to that particular place of service. Certainly, the pastor must live by faith, but the church also bears a responsibility for caring for the minister's family just as he cares for their families.

Accepting a bivocational ministry position means committing yourself to good time management so you can handle triple obligations of family, church, and secular job. Multiply yourself by developing lay leaders, especially deacons, in the church who can help visit hospitals, members who are confined by physical limitations, and others.

Remind your members that they do not really need for you to be in the office as much as simply to be available. With the advent of cell phones and other technology, most ministers can reach out to persons in need within a reasonable amount of time after the member calls them.

Fellowship with other ministers and theological education are low on the average bivocational pastor's list of priorities because of time restraints. Both activities will actually help the bivocational minister handle his work more effectively and efficiently. While difficult to schedule in the short run, over the long haul a pastor will find ideas and encouragement from ministerial fellowships and seminary training helpful. Sermons will come more quickly and easily. By making time for these two activities, busy pastors will find help for church programming, ministry concepts, advice on dealing with difficult situations and people, and other issues.

The limits of this book will not permit extensive advice focused specifically on the bivocational pastor (although every chapter has application for the pastor in bivocational and fully funded settings). One of the best resources for bivocational ministers is the book *Uniquely Bivocational—Understanding the Life of a Pastor Who Has a Second Job: For Bivocational Pastors and Their Churches* by Ray Gilder. Gilder is nationally recognized as one of the most prominent leaders in bivocational ministry.

Ordination

Being set aside for the Gospel Ministry will always be a sacred moment in your life. Having responded to God's call to vocational Christian service and being called to your first church can be overwhelming in itself. The service in which a church invests you with its affirmation as God's minister humbles you as godly men lay hands on you and pray for you. Such a trust must be honored with noble and faithful service.

Ordination involves more than being licensed to preach. Often a church will issue a "License to Preach" when a young man exhibits a response to the call to ministry. The license merely affirms him and commends him in his pursuit of preaching the Gospel. Ordination involves being set aside in a larger way. Both churches and the government identify ordained ministers differently than laypersons who minister.

Usually, you will seek ordination when you are called to your first church as pastor, although staff ministers are often ordained as well. Generally, the church that has called you will send a request for ordination to the pastor of your home church (or other church of your choice). Sometimes, the candidate can make the request personally. Being ordained by the calling church is not wise. If you were to be fired from the church, it could revoke your ordination as well. Only the church that ordains you can defrock you.

Your home pastor will probably interview you and set a date for two events. First, an ordination council of ordained ministers will be called together by the pastor. This committee will talk with you about your calls to salvation and to ministry. They will ask you doctrinal questions to make sure you have a sound theology. They may inquire about your family, your personal life, your devotional and prayer habits, and other matters. Once the committee feels you have met biblical qualifications, they will recommend to the church that you be ordained.

After the church votes to proceed, the ordination ceremony will take place. Ordination is a church function, and the entire church (and the congregation you will be serving), along with ministers from the area, will be invited to participate. The pastor likely will consult with you about who participates in the service. Someone will bring a charge to the candidate, someone else will deliver a charge to the church, and a third person will preach the ordination sermon. Interspersed will be prayers and songs. At the end of the service, you will be asked to kneel while the ordained ministers present (and perhaps others) will come by one by one. They will lay hands on your head or shoulders and pray for you individually.

After the service, the members of the ordination council will sign your ordination certificate. Keep this certificate in a safe place and make back-up copies. In some places, like West Virginia, you will have to produce your credentials (i.e. the certificate) in order to get a license to perform marriages. In any case, this certificate will be a constant reminder of the confidence each person expressed in you by the laying on of hands and signing that document. In addition, it will be a daily motivation to live and serve in such a manner as to honor the Lord and fulfill your ministry.

Chapter 6

THE MINISTER'S FAMILY

"For if a man know not how to rule his own house, how shall he take care of the church of God?" (1 Timothy 3:5).

Before a man can lead a flock of families, he must learn to guide his own. Every Scripture that applies to the husband and wife, parents and children, applies to the minister and his family. In addition, the Bible addresses several specific principles related to ministerial households.

The Priority of Family

Scripture places a high priority on the pastor's ministry to his wife and children. Too many ministers succeed in the pulpit but fall short at home. A pastor can lose a church and start again, but if he loses his family he has lost his ministry altogether.

Some ministers think putting the church before the family is a quality of spiritual leadership. Actually, Scripture declares, ". . . if any provide not for his own, and especially for those of his own house, he has denied the faith, and is worse than an infidel" (1 Timothy 5:8). Granted, this particular text addresses the specific issue of caring for widows. Still, the larger principle, I believe, is valid for our consideration.

The minister is, first and foremost, the pastor of his own family. Can he evangelize strangers on the street and not lead his children to faith in Christ? Will he be successful in discipling a congregation if he has no time to teach his family how to walk with Jesus? Will his wife or children not feel neglected if the pastor spends evening after evening offering pastoral care to others and not have time for his family?

Certainly, the role of pastor demands many hours invested at inconvenient times, but his normal regimen should provide his family with convincing proof that he loves them. Most ministers can distinguish between legitimate emergencies that take him away from the family dinner table and those calls that could easily be rescheduled for another time.

Expressing Love for Family

We cannot take it for granted that our wives and children know we love them. **They need to hear, see, and experience our love.** If a minister never tells his children that he loves them, he should not be surprised when they rebel not only against his leadership but against the God he serves. They may reason that if their earthly father is representative of the heavenly Father, they do not want either one.

Our wives also need to hear those sweet, irreplaceable words: "I love you." I never go to sleep without telling my wife that I love her. If I'm traveling, I make it a point to call home and talk about the day. Before saying goodbye, I always tell her, "I love you." When I talk to my children and grandchildren, I want to end the conversation or phone call with, "I love you." Throughout the day, we need to express love verbally and in many other ways.

Making time for individual family members, as well as for the family as a whole, shows them you love them as persons, not just as a group. Your wife needs some undivided attention from her husband. Your children also need that multitasking dad to turn off the TV, close the computer, hang up the phone, set down the book, and focus on them. Eye contact and listening express love more than gifts, cards, or other material things.

Remembering special events shows your loving care. At the beginning of each year, I enter all the birthdays into my calendar. My wedding anniversary goes into the May 30 slot. If your children have special school activities, put them down in your schedule as soon as you know about them. If they play sports, jot down the game schedules and make that appointment as important as a meeting with the deacon chairman.

Having these events already on the calendar will help you respond when someone calls you about having a meeting or wants you to do something at that time. You can simply respond, "I'm sorry. I have an appointment. Can we schedule that meeting for later (or earlier) in the day?" Most people are reasonable and willing to accommodate your schedule. Surely, some emergencies arise, but if you limit interruptions to your family schedule to true emergencies, your family will generally understand.

Ministering to Your Wife

Your wife has many demands on her life. She raises the children, prepares meals, washes and irons the clothes, and generally manages the household. All the while, she has expectations by church members to attend meetings and social events, serve in the church, and be available for last-minute calls by well-meaning church ladies. In the meantime, she wants to care for her husband and help him in his ministry.

A loving husband recognizes his wife has many needs. She has spiritual needs, so pray and worship with her. She has emotional needs, so love and listen to her. She has intellectual needs, so encourage her as she reads and expands her mental horizons. She has physical needs, so help with the house and the children so she can get some rest!

Wives need romance in their lives. This need is not merely physical, but emotional and spiritual. For women, the intimate aspect of marriage is more emotional than physical, though both are important. Take your wife on date nights regularly. Without expectation of sex at the end of an evening, spend time with her in a socially enjoyable setting. Recall your early days of courtship and relive some of those silly, fun, spontaneous times you shared.

Like the rest of your congregation, **your wife needs to grow spiritually.** Her development as a disciple of Christ should prompt you to spend time with her in spiritual growth activities—prayer, Bible reading, worship, ministry, etc. The two of you will grow together in Christ as you encourage one another in communion with Him. At the same time, give her time for quietly reading Scripture and other Christian literature. Encourage her to attend special women's events, such as Bible conferences. She will discover biblical insights for her life and have the opportunity to meet other like-minded women.

Help her to fulfill God's calling on her life. Many ministers' wives had felt God's call to special service long before they married their pastor husbands. However, once in a church setting, the wife is often relegated to a support role. Some ministers even expect their wives to be somewhat of a personal secretary, handling tasks the church administrative assistant should do. Resist that urge! Do not demean your wife by having her make your phone appointments, type your papers, or perform other such work. Respect her enough to allow her freedom to find her own place of ministry.

Protect your wife from unrealistic expectations by church members or others who try to impose their agenda onto her. When interviewing with churches, I am inevitably asked, "What will your wife do in the church?" I smile and answer, "Whatever she wants to do." From the beginning, I want the people to know they are not hiring two people for the price of one. My wife has always supported my ministry and been active in the church, usually teaching children's Sunday School classes. Still, the kind of ministry she chooses has resulted from her response to God's call.

Also, **protect your wife from carping criticism** by carnal people. Unfortunately, some churches have gossips whose function is to misuse their tongues. Scripture warns about this problem. "The words of a talebearer are as wounds, and they go down into the innermost parts of the belly" (Proverbs 26:22). If your wife (or children) suffer the wounds of a gossip, be man enough to confront the source. If the gossip is a female, meet with her and her husband together, explain the harm that has been caused, and express the need for repentance and an apology. Follow Matthew 18 all the way when this happens the first time and you likely will not have to handle it again.

Provide a Home: Some smaller churches will provide a church-owned home, called a parsonage. The advantage is you don't have to come up with a down payment to purchase a home. In addition, you'll find it easier to relocate if you don't have to sell a house. Among several disadvantages, you are not building equity, you aren't getting a tax deduction, and you're living in a house the congregation feels is theirs. Your wife may feel inhibited about painting walls or putting up pictures on the walls. People in the church may drop by unexpectedly to borrow something for the church. Firmly but kindly help church members understand this is your family's home. You may have to assert yourself to secure your wife's ability to keep her home as she wants, but most church members will understand and support your need for privacy.

If possible, you may find it better to rent an apartment or buy a house. Again, this choice has its advantages and disadvantages. In some small towns and rural areas, good housing may be difficult to find. Let your wife lead in finding the kind and location of the place she wants to call "home." Whether you rent, buy, or live in a parsonage, help your wife and children make it their own.

Provide Financial Security: Financial security, or the lack of it, is one of the primary sources of stress in marriage. The vast majority of pastors do not make as much money in the ministry as they would in secular business. Often, the minister's wife has to manage household expenses with a narrow margin of income over outgo. Wise husbands do not place on their wives the burden of having to decide what bills to pay if money is insufficient. As the leader of the home, take the initiative to manage the money in partnership with your wife so she senses you are committed to finding a way to provide financial stability and security for the family. You may have to find a way to produce extra income or reduce obligations, but the stress of living within a budget is not nearly as great as the problems that come when you do not.

Above all, **love your wife as Christ loved the Church**. Christ loved the Church sacrificially "and gave Himself for it" (Ephesians 5:25). Paul used that example to demonstrate the self-giving love a husband has for his wife. All Scriptures related to how a husband should treat his wife apply to the pastor as well. Sometimes we preach truths for our congregations and forget to hear those principles for our lives. If we will live out the biblical principles of marriage, we will not only improve our own families, we will set clear examples for couples in the congregation.

Nurturing Your Children

We would need another book to address all of the issues related to a minister's children, particularly since their needs change as they grow through different developmental stages. Still, some basic tips can help you serve your children and, in doing so, fulfill your ministry.

Set the Example—Children follow what they see, not just what they hear. The minister's children (they really don't like to be called PKs) and teenagers know whether Dad's sermon is lived out at home. Paul's admonition for Timothy to be an example to the believers (1 Timothy 4:12) starts in the family.

Spend Time—Don't believe that quality time substitutes for quantity of time. Our children need both. They need to be with us. Granted, the older they get, the less time they want. Still, at whatever age, your children and teens need time with us. As mentioned before, they need individual time, one on one, with us. While they appreciate family experiences, they love having Dad focus in on them personally.

Sit and Listen—Our kids do not need us to solve their problems so much as they want us to hear what they are saying. Really listening to them shows we value and respect them. Listen to what is not being said as much as to what is verbalized. Sometimes the nonverbal communication really speaks what the heart is trying to say. Have an open body language that invites them to open up. Often it is not just the major issues of life but the small talk that becomes most valuable over time.

Show Interest—What do our children and teens find interesting? Don't demand they take up fishing or golf simply because that is what you enjoy. Observe how they spend their time when free to pick an activity. Join in or just watch. Being genuinely interested in whatever they feel is important to them lets them know you really care.

Show Up—Whenever your child or teen has a special day at school, a ballgame, or even the piano recital, show up! Not much will substitute for being there. My daughters especially remember two events growing up. My youngest daughter's birthday came while away at church camp. I bought a huge cake for the entire group, drove several hundred miles, and surprised her with a big happy birthday.

Our oldest daughter graduated some years later with her master's degree while I was serving as executive director for the West Virginia Convention of Southern Baptists. Her graduation coincided with a national missionary commissioning service that I had worked over a year to secure for our state. In explaining to the people why I was turning over the service to my associate, I said, "Ten years from now you will not remember whether I was at this meeting, but my daughter will remember whether I was at her graduation." At least one minister's wife thanked me for the example that it was okay to put family needs up front.

Shut Up—Preachers tend to talk through problems. We communicate so often through preaching and teaching that we think the natural response to any difficulty is to talk about it. Sometimes our children, and especially our teenagers, do not need or want a sermon.

> *Often, the most poignant words are those we refrain from speaking.*

They need us just to love them, to hug them in heartaches, and sit with them in sorrows. Often, the most poignant words are those we refrain from speaking.

Seize the Opportunity—Deuteronomy tells parents to share God's Word with their children: ". . . when you sit in your house, and when you walk by the way, when you lie down, and when you rise up" (Deuteronomy 11:19). Teachable moments come through the normal course of daily life. Use those opportunities to draw close to your family and help them draw close to God.

Secure Them—Protect your children. Their environment overflows with enemies of God who would like nothing better than to strike down the shepherd by attacking his children. Protect them from getting caught up with the wrong peer group. Sometimes you have to protect them from themselves. Your job is to love them and nurture them, even when doing so is not a lot of fun—for them or for you.

Part of security is **discipline**. Learn what kinds of discipline motivate each of your kids. What works with one will not work with another. Be careful not to lower yourself to a shouting match or debate with your children. Explain why they should make certain choices based on God's Word rather than simply saying, "Because I said so." Also, avoid provoking your children "to wrath" (Ephesians 6:4). That word means "exasperation." Overdiscipline, or disciplining your children in anger, will only provoke them to anger in response. Learn the appropriate and effective ways to handle each situation redemptively. After all, isn't that how your heavenly Father disciplines you?

Another aspect of security involves **having time in one place** to make friends, do well in school and church, and otherwise build a life. If you come home from deacons' meetings moaning and groaning about how unfair they are, you produce insecurity for your children and unknowingly poison their attitudes toward church. Also, be careful how you handle relocation to new ministries. As you pray about God's will regarding an opportunity at a different church, consider the effect moving might have on your children and, especially, on your teens. The final determination must be God's promptings, but He may use your family to help you discover His direction.

POIMEN—SHEPHERD

The Shepherding Pastor

"And he gave some, apostles; and some, prophets; and some, evangelists; **and some, pastors (poimen/shepherds)** *and teachers; for the perfecting of the saints, for the work of the ministry, for the edifying of the body of Christ: till we all come in the unity of the faith, and of the knowledge of the Son of God, unto a perfect man, unto the measure of the stature of the fullness of Christ"* (Ephesians 4:11–13).

Chapter 7

BEING A GOOD SHEPHERD

"I am the good shepherd, and know my sheep, and am known of mine. As the Father knows me, even so know I the Father: and I lay down my life for the sheep" (John 10:14–15).

The primary paradigm for ministry is that of the Good Shepherd Himself. Jesus' most familiar portrayal of His relationship with His people was that of one who knows, feeds, leads, and protects his sheep. The tenth chapter of John's Gospel is replete with figures of speech that describe that relationship. Christ's model of shepherding is not only appropriate for pastors but for all varieties of service. The evangelist should have the same care for the flock as the local minister. A student minister must know and care for his young charges as a shepherd would the youngest sheep or risk inevitable rejection by intelligent teens who respond only to genuine love.

Jesus' model offers several key aspects of faithful pastoral ministry:

Know the Flock (John 10:14, 27)

Once a minister has been called to a place of service, what is his most immediate concern? A good beginning sets the standard for a good tenure. For the new undershepherd to get off to a good start and maintain an effective ministry, he will to follow the example of the Good Shepherd Who knew His sheep and called them by name. They also knew Him and followed Him (John 10:14, 27).

One of the misconceptions of contemporary ministry is the popular idea that a pastor can be a communicator or pulpiteer without being a shepherd. If the pastor is a good shepherd, he will not begrudge the amount of time required for home and hospital visitation. He will not yield to the urge to play hide-and-seek in his study but will recognize his duty and privilege to be among the flock, getting to know them and ministering to them the balm of relationship.

People come to church looking for closeness, touch, and fellowship. They expect it from the congregation; they demand it from their ministers. Yet, among the hectic programs of modern churches, some ecclesiologists would argue that a heavy visitation schedule would be out of date, unwelcomed, and drain the pastor's time. Many younger ministers feel that they should only invest precious hours visiting the lost and handling crises situations. Their attitude is "If they need me, they can call me." One new pastor boldly announced on his first Sunday that he simply would not be visiting church members' homes unless they specifically requested him to. The inevitable conflict that ensued was not surprising.

Addressing the modern crisis of poor leadership in churches, James Means observed that "shepherding has been deemphasized in favor of administrative efforts, slick performances, program management, recruitment of personnel, building budgets, and the like. Deep within the church, but often unverbalized, is a fundamental hunger for leaders who obviously know God and know how to pray, preach, teach, disciple, equip and shepherd!"[1]

To overcome such a leadership deficit, ministers must pay the price of investing time with all sorts of people. Not all people are easy to know. Others may avoid the minister because of sin in their lives. Like a dark place that resists intrusion of the light, these families do not want their secrets exposed to the local parson who stands before them Sunday by Sunday. Still, the minister must try by whatever means possible to bridge those barriers.

Feed the Flock (1 Peter 5:1–2), Preach/Teach

"If you love me," Jesus told His disciple, "feed my sheep" (John 21:17, paraphrased). A good shepherd is not content with merely gathering the lambs into the sheepfold. He accepts the continuing responsibility of caring for them. Basic to this care is the feeding of the flock of God. Balanced with the visitation ministry of the pastor is his preparation and delivery of the Word of God through preaching and teaching by means of public proclamation and personal discipleship.

> *A good shepherd is not content with merely gathering the lambs into the sheepfold. He accepts the continuing responsibility of caring for them.*

The bleating of the sheep heard in many churches is caused by hunger. Hearts still cry out to their shepherds, "Is there a word from the Lord?" To tell preachers that they ought to preach is like encouraging lions to roar or roosters to crow—it ought to be the most natural of activities. The plea of this paradigm is not merely to offer up a homily, pet peeve, or philosophy, but to feed the sheep, to nourish them through the means of preaching, teaching, and discipling.

A later chapter will further address the subjects related to preaching, but here suffice it to encourage a balanced diet. The whole counsel of God's Word is needed to produce healthy Christians. Doctrine, inspiration, counsel, instruction, edification, and evangelism combine to nurture the congregation.

Many believers need more personal feeding tactics than just the public forum. While the place of the pulpit is neither outdated nor replaceable, it can be supplemented with personal instruction. One-on-one discipleship and small Bible study/fellowship groups (Sunday School) are important ways to help parishioners who require individual attention. These believers are not necessarily babes who must be spoon-fed the Word. Sometimes, they are mature workers whom the pastor develops into leaders. Such work cannot be accomplished wholesale; it must be retailed on a personal basis.

Another way of feeding the flock of God is through worship. Spiritual worship involves individual and group participation in the adoration of the Most High. When believers humble themselves and open their hearts to God's presence, they find meat for their souls that cannot be found elsewhere. The minister's role is to educate people in the ways of worship, to provide an atmosphere that enhances worship, and to lead the congregation in its corporate expression of worship.

Lead the Flock (John 10:3–4, 27)

The Youth Pastor waxed passionately eloquent as he pled for people to win souls. "Why is it that for the past six months our baptistery has been full of dust rather than souls?" he asked. Sitting in the pew, I wanted to return the question to the pulpit. A herculean restraint was required not to rise and ask the speaker, "I'm guilty as charged, but what have you been doing the last six months?" Pointing out others' faults is easier than leading in correction. Perhaps that is why many preachers take the low road of beating the sheep rather than leading them.

Servant leaders walk in the steps of the Master Who garbed Himself in the towel of a slave and washed the feet of His disciples.

Pastors who refuse to lead the flock disregard the biblical example of the successful shepherd found in John 10:3–4. Churches desperately want a pastor who is a leader, someone who knows them, who knows their Lord, and who can meld all together to impact their society for God. Yes, some family chapel types of churches are dominated by patriarchs or matriarchs who want someone to preach three times a week but not interfere in the leadership of the church life. Still, congregations look for a shepherd who can lead them in knowing and doing God's will.

Ethical issues of leadership include using manipulation rather than motivation, exercising status rather than earned leadership, using a position for ego appeasement or financial gain, and misusing people. Servant leaders walk in the steps of the Master Who garbed Himself in the towel of a slave and washed the feet of His disciples. Such a model seeks out the needs of others and aligns them with the accomplishment of the ultimate will of God. When men see their own good integrated in the general purposes of God, they are highly motivated. On the other hand, a manipulator will maneuver people who genuinely want to serve God, using their noble motives for self-serving interests.

Basic to Christian motivation is a spiritual value system. When the leader helps a congregation to define and clarify its goals, he unveils a pure source of continual energy. The Christian Church has unique values that are in contrast to the world, neutralizing typical carrot-stick, guilt-shame, or other secular motivations. In fact, some nonreligious industries are discovering this fact and considering their own values. Tom Peters claims most excellent companies are "value-driven."[2]

Christian values center on God's holiness and love. His holiness requires a reciprocal righteousness in living by His followers. "Be ye holy, for I am holy" (1 Peter 1:16). Our inability to match His rightness of life requires the understanding of atoning mercy and love. Scripture reminds us that "We love Him, because He first loved us" (1 John 4:19), and "If God loved us, we ought also to love one another" (1 John 4:11).

When applied to the Christian minister, he is motivated to live in such a way that honors his heavenly, holy Father and that ministers to the needs of his fellow human beings. The ministerial leader who accepts his role as servant, determines to avoid manipulative techniques, and embraces value-driven motivation will find a grateful flock who will respond to such love by following.

Protect the Flock (John 10:11–13)

The Good Shepherd laid down His life for His sheep. The good undershepherd does the same. Enemies of the flock of God are found everywhere. God's people live in a hostile environment—a world that hated the Son and that will despise all who follow Him. Within the church itself, Christ warned of "wolves in sheep's clothing" (Matthew 7:15). Sometimes, the sheep themselves are their own worst enemies. In each case, the guardian of the flock is charged with protecting the sheep's well-being. Laying down one's own life physically is rarely demanded in Western societies. However, the pastor must often take actions that require constant death to self.

The world system is a natural enemy of the flock of God. Jesus told His disciples, "If the world hates you, you know that it hated Me before it hated you. You are not of the world, but I chose you out of the world, therefore the world hates you" (John 15:18–19). The New Age movement, mass-media ethics, and peer or community pressures are just a few aspects of the worldly assault on the Church.

False religionists are also enemies of the sheep. Jesus described these predators who would try to enter the sheepfold through some means other than the door. Cult groups usually fit this description. They are well dressed and articulate as they knock on the unsuspecting church member's door. Many Christians are not grounded well enough in their faith to counter the indoctrination of a missionary of false doctrine.

The shepherd must protect the flock from this kind of intrusive attack. One way he can guard the people is through education. By preaching and teaching the deeper matters of biblical truth, the pastor can prepare people for inevitable challenges from cultic representatives. Interfaith witness classes take them one step further and enable them to respond with a positive Gospel presentation. *A way - Example*

A Louisiana pastor encountered two Jehovah's Witnesses at his home. After they made their presentation, he insisted on sharing his Gospel. When they left, he refused to give them free reign among his flock. House by house, he visited alongside them, making sure the people knew who these strangers were and, when allowed into the home, refuted their arguments step-by-step until, exasperated, they left the community. Rude? Perhaps, but it is better to be impolite to a representative of the enemy than to allow one small sheep to stray. *Protect the Flock*

Other potential enemies include persons within the sheepfold who would do harm to the sheep. Some church members have never been saved but have positions of prominence and influence. Others are saved but have given themselves to carnality, seeking to rule over the flock. In each case, when their authority is contested, they viciously attack the challengers, whether pastor or fellow sheep. If the pastor is involved, these wolves in sheep's clothing will pounce on any of the sheep who support him.

In one church, a pastor who won a vote of confidence in spite of strong opposition from long-standing power brokers saw his supporters singled out and, one by one, surrounded by the opposition. They fled the church. In a short time, the pastor was forced to leave, not just because of the dwindling support but because people he loved were being hurt in the process. Sometimes, the shepherd lays down his ecclesiastical life to keep the sheep from being injured on his account.

Chapter 8

BEGINNING WELL

"And we desire that every one of you do show the same diligence to the full assurance of hope unto the end: That you be not slothful, but followers of them who through faith and patience inherit the promises" (Hebrews 6:11–12).

The best way to end well is to start well. Dorothy would never have found the Wizard of Oz if she had not begun on the Yellow Brick Road. Beginning well in any new enterprise significantly affects the prospect for success.

Some ministers approach new beginnings with excitement and anticipation; others confess to an element of fear for the unknown lying ahead. Make sure you are starting well on the issues that matter for eternity. Wanting to please the new congregation tempts the incoming minister to waste time on the inconsequentials, to be drawn into activities that drain your energy and consume your efforts. Decisions about what you do and don't do at the start of your ministry will set a pattern for years to come.

Get Your Family Settled In

Starting up a new ministry generates excitement and anticipation. Eager to get moving with progress at the church, pastors often forget that their families are also starting fresh. The first people needing your ministry is your own family. A wise minister understands that his family provides a foundation from which he can serve others.

No small amount of stress surrounds a move to a new place. The house has yet to become home. Potential friends are still strangers. Having left familiar surroundings, your family may experience discomfort with the prospect of settling in to foreign territory. Take time to help your family get adjusted to their new home. You will have plenty of time later to set up your office files.

Help Your Wife Feather the Nest

A woman's home is an extension of herself. However nice the house might be, it will not become home simply by unpacking boxes and hanging pictures. Take time to discuss how your family would like their house to look. Do walls need repainting? Should the carpet be cleaned? What plants need repotting? Letting your wife and children personalize their house and their individual rooms helps transform the house into a home.

Prioritize Time with Your Spouse and Children

Make a point to eat together as often as possible. Family time around the table provides opportunities for sharing, laughing, discussion, and bonding. Having some type of routine lends stability to the family structure and eases the transition. The world may be a bit chaotic around them, but at home the family should feel safe and relaxed.

Have some fun time each week. When our children were younger, our family established the beginning of each weekend as "Friday Family Fun Time." Your family needs to enjoy your new home. Discover together your new environment. See the sights. Find new places to eat out. Go for a picnic at the park. Attend local concerts, fairs, festivals, and other activities that make your new community special. You will not only have a good time, but you can meet many of your new church members, neighbors, and potential church prospects.

Take your wife for a date every week. Spend some time each day talking about the house, community, schools, problems, dreams, and fears. As with the children, don't try to analyze every comment or solve every problem. Listening to her and sharing with her builds solid communication and strengthens relationships. She needs the affirmation of love, security, stability, and companionship.

Confide in your wife, but avoid pouring out all your frustrations on her at the dinner table. She wants to be part of your life and ministry, but she needs your spiritual leadership to face problems with faith, not fear. Build a partnership in the ministry. She will find her own place at the church if given the freedom to accept or decline responsibilities.

Interact Every Day with Each Child (or Teen)

Listen to them. Don't simply ask, "How was school today?" Share something about your day and encourage them to talk about their experiences. Have they met new friends? What are their teachers like? What kind of homework do they have? Is the cafeteria food good? How are the sports teams? Watch for symptoms of anxiety and offer a listening ear that doesn't respond immediately with a father's fix-it attitude. Don't explain away or minimize difficulties. Let your children know that they are important and that you understand their fears of being in a new place.

Get Acquainted

Know Your Church Family

Jesus said, "My sheep hear my voice, and I know them, and they follow me . . ." (John 10:27). If a good shepherd wants the flock to follow him, he must get to know them.

Your church family usually will help you get settled into your home. The people often are eager to get to know their new minister and his family. Accept invitations to eat with them. Attend group functions. Ask Sunday School classes, youth groups, deacons and their wives, and other organizations if they have social events at which you and your family can meet several people without being overwhelmed by the whole church at once.

Make learning names a priority. People love to be called by name. When people introduce themselves to you, say their name aloud and associate their name with something about their physical features to aid your memory. If the church has a pictorial directory, get a copy for each of your family members. Ask the church secretary to make notations about relationships. Who is related to whom? Are some pictured individuals no longer living or have they moved away? Time spent learning names and relationships is one of the best investments you will make.

Get Out of the House and Meet the Neighbors

Fear of new people and places can cause family members to hide out at home. Instead of integrating into the new community, they launch out only when they have to venture forth to school, church, or the grocery store.

Depending on the local culture, some neighbors will offer a friendly welcome. They may offer to help you move in or bring food so you don't have to worry about preparing meals while unloading the moving van. In other places, you may have to take the initiative to meet people who live near you. Look for ways to get acquainted and develop friends.

Remember, you are not just beginning a new ministry; you are beginning a new life. Help your family find ways to get acquainted with their surroundings and the people who make up your church and community.

Help Your Wife and Children Make New Friends

Encourage them to invite new acquaintances to your house for a cookout or other activity. Establishing your home as a welcoming place helps your children build friends on their turf rather than having to break into cliques in foreign territory.

Become involved in local organizations like PTA and Little League. Community involvement cannot take the place of ministry, but it can become part of ministry as well as help your family integrate into the local society. Your wife and children will meet people who can become friends. Getting involved also shows you are interested in the overall well-being of the community. Many of the people you meet will be unchurched, providing great opportunities to develop witnessing relationships.

Become Familiar with the Territory

D. L. Lowrie suggests you ask the minister's Search Committee or the church secretary to prepare a packet of information about the community prior to arriving on your new location. He observes that most Chambers of Commerce have packets with maps, schedules of community activities, and locations of schools, parks, hospitals, businesses, malls, and other important places. Ask for a list of emergency numbers. Knowing how to dial 911 is not enough when your child spikes a fever your first night in a new town.[1]

Buy a good map. In large cities, map books are available commercially. In rural areas, go to a well-equipped truck stop and ask for a topographical map book of the county. Such books will show county roads, as well as mountains and rivers, which are often omitted on regular maps.

Drive around with your family. Observe the kinds of neighborhoods. Notice how people live. Each community has a routine. By learning how your neighbors interact, observing their schedules, and seeing their interactions, you and your family will become more comfortable with your new home.

Learn the Community's Seasons of Life

Most towns have a life cycle. Agricultural communities revolve around planting and harvest seasons. Small towns may focus on school athletics, county fairs and festivals, community events, and local businesses. Larger cities often have major sports teams that provide camaraderie and conversation. Also, large cities are really composites of smaller neighborhoods, each with distinctive atmospheres.

Get Organized

Gather Information

Even before arriving on the church field, ask the Search Committee or the church secretary to assemble sets of information vital to your ministry. Either in a notebook or electronic format, these lists will aid your understanding of the church organizationally and personally. As you constantly contact different individuals or groups, having this information at your fingertips makes your ministry more efficient. Included in the basic data should be the following:

1. **Church directory.** As mentioned, a pictorial directory is preferred so you can match names, faces, and relationships. If the church does not have a professionally published directory, you can enlist an amateur photographer to take pictures of members over the course of several weeks. Using a database, the secretary can insert photos into family data cards available to you electronically or in a printed copy.

2. **Organizational lists.** Ask for lists of deacons, church officers, committees, Sunday School or small-group Bible study leaders, discipleship workers, youth and children's ministry leaders, etc. Each list should contain all contact information for each person (name, address, phone, cell phone, e-mail, and any other information available). Having the data for an individual repeated on several lists may seem redundant, but if you are calling several deacons or other leaders, you do not want to have to flip back and forth into the church directory each time.

3. **Shut-ins and hospital patients.** Scripture emphasizes the value God places on the widows and orphans—persons least empowered in a society. Discover early those members who cannot attend church because of physical limitations, whether they live at home or in assisted-care facilities. Also ask for regular updates of hospital patients and be faithful to visit them. Ministering to these saints of God will bless you as much as you might be a blessing to them.

4. **Prospects.** Smaller churches may not have a formal file of prospects, but church leaders will have some knowledge of people who have visited the church but have not made decisions about membership. Other churches may have sophisticated databases of prospects for evangelistic and church-growth visitation. Develop a workable system for discovering, maintaining, contacting, and following prospects.

5. **Constitution and bylaws.** Some Next-Gen leaders view constitutions and bylaws as encumbrances. They want to move quickly without limitations of rules and regulations. However, effective organizations need basic structures and agreement about how to proceed in various matters. The church has built its structures over time and generally trusts them. Learn the bylaws and work within them. If adjustments are needed, take time to build trust relationships and learn why things are the way they are before trying to institute significant changes.

6. **Budget and financial reports**. Some smaller churches do not have a detailed budget. They tend to operate like a large family, with everyone being a part of deciding on expenditures as they come up. Larger churches find having a budget to be more effective in guiding the financial planning of their ministries. You not only need to know the details of the church budget, but you want to understand how it was developed and why items are included.

Gather several months of financial reports. Knowing how money has been spent will give you an idea of the values and habits of the congregation and individual ministries. Also, developing graphs showing monthly income and expenses over the course of a year or two provides insight into the church's financial life cycle. Some months reflect larger income. December often has the largest revenue due to end-of-the-year gifts. Other months will have more expenses than income. Summer is notorious because of Vacation Bible School, youth camps, higher utility bills, quarterly literature purchases, and other expenses while income is reduced due to people traveling on vacations.

7. **Minutes of business meetings.** Lowrie urges new pastors to study the minutes of business meetings over the past two or three years.[2] Knowing the history of the church's decisions will guide you in directing the congregation through new decisions. In addition, if you know the church has experienced significant conflict over certain issues in the past, you can avoid stepping on those minefields as you lead the people into the future.

8. **Church calendar.** When you arrive, the church will already have made plans for several months in advance. Often churches repeat past events simply because they've always done it that way. Do not immediately write off traditional activities. Sometimes those occasions have lasting value for the congregation. Use what is already calendared and develop new approaches to help organizational leaders improve what they've been doing. At the same time, avoid giving the impression that you know more than them about how activities should be conducted. People generally resist anyone who seems condescending or arrogant. As you build trust, lead the organizations to envision new opportunities that, consequently, impact the calendar.

Get Started

Meet with Your Leaders

Ministerial staff, deacons, committee chairmen, and other leaders will be eager to meet with you. They want to know you and your vision, but they also need you to know them and understand their ideas and concerns. Take time to understand leaders as individuals, not mere cogs in the ecclesiological machine. Tom is not just the chairman of the deacons; he has a wife, children, and a job that are important to him. Understanding people, their dreams, and their heartaches will help you forge strong bonds with this larger team of following leaders.

> *Take time to understand leaders as individuals, not mere cogs in the ecclesiological machine.*

Learn the tasks of each group as they see them. Gather job descriptions (if they exist) for each ministry team. If adjustments are needed, build a base of trust before trying to transform the organizations. You may discover that these people have solid reasons for operating in certain ways.

Ask about how the church has worked in the past. Discover what issues presented opportunities and obstacles. Learn how they handled decision making and conflict resolution. What has worked? What didn't work? Why? What are the traditions of the church and how has the Kingdom benefited by them?

Ask about their view of your work and the church's future. Conflict often begins with unmet expectations. During the search process, you discussed the role of the new pastor. Individual leaders may have different concerns and desires for their minister. Encourage them to share their thoughts, but at the same time gently lead them to make adjustments if their expectations are unrealistic.

Inquire about present plans and upcoming important events. Each organization and ministry leader will already have developed strategies, plans, and events. Talk to them about their vision. Why do they want to do whatever it is they are doing? What do they hope to accomplish? What are their goals? How do their plans fit into the overall vision and mission of the church? Learn as much as you can about what and why they are doing certain activities before you try to introduce a vastly different agenda.

Establish Good Work Habits

Establish habits for study and sermon development, counseling, hospital calls, home visitation, and administrative tasks. Many clergy exist in the extremes of being slothful or supermen.

For unmotivated preachers, an average week's work might consist of a few hospital visits, a knock or two on a prospect's door, hours spent sitting in an office in case a deacon might stop by, and a Saturday night perusal of borrowed sermons. The majority of ministers, however, are found at the other extreme—trying by superhuman effort and seventy-hour weeks to accomplish something great for God, inevitably encountering exhaustion, frustration, and failure.

Paul reminded the leaders at Corinth: "We are laborers together with God" (1 Corinthians 3:9). This work is indeed that—work. The average layperson may have some vague idea of the minister being called for emergencies at odd hours of the night, but few outside the vocation fully appreciate the constant demand on the minister's time.

In a church survey concerning the laity's concept of how the pastor spent his time, people expressed ignorance at the total hours expected of the minister. They believed the pastor should spend at least thirty hours preparing his sermons, ten hours counseling the hurting, and twenty hours visiting the lost, the sick, and others. The church had no idea how many hours were designated for various administrative tasks, including committee meetings, staff meetings, financial planning, calendar planning, program planning, and other nonoptional matters.

On the other hand, pastors should not use their lack of daily accountability to become lethargic in fulfilling their ministry. Ezekiel warned that pastors are held accountable for their stewardship: "And the word of the Lord came unto me saying, Son of man, prophesy against the shepherds of Israel, prophecy and say unto them, thus says the Lord God unto the shepherds: Woe be to the shepherds of Israel that do feed themselves! Should not the shepherds feed the flocks? You eat the fat and you clothe you with the wool, you kill them that are fed but you feed not the flock. The diseased have you not strengthened, neither have you healed that which was sick, neither have you bound up that which was broken, neither have you brought again that which was driven away, neither have you sought that which was lost, but with force and with cruelty have you ruled them. And they were scattered because there is no shepherd and they became meat to all the beasts of the field, when they were scattered. . . . Therefore, O you shepherds hear the word of the Lord; thus says the Lord God, Behold I am against the shepherds and I will require my flock at their hand, and cause them to cease from feeding the flock; neither shall the shepherds feed themselves anymore; for I will deliver my flock from their mouth, that they may not be meat for them" (Ezekiel 34:1–10).

Throughout Scripture, people are commanded to work industriously. The fourth commandment certainly indicates the importance of the Sabbath day but only after making the equally emphatic statement that one should work the other six days! The writers of Proverbs agreed that the diligent laborer would be blessed, but the lazy person would remain in poverty (Proverbs 6:6–11). The faithful pastor heeds the wisdom writer's advice: "Be diligent to know the state of your flocks, and look well to your herds" (Proverbs 27:23).

Jesus said the laborer is worthy of his hire (Luke 10:7). He expected His followers would be vigilant in their work. Christ warned the disciples that they should be found "doing" upon His unannounced return (Luke 12:43).

For a minister to accept money from the tithes and offerings of God's people and not carry out the tasks of ministry is to rob the people, the church, and God Himself! Time theft cost American employers billions of dollars each year. Faked illness, extra-long lunch hours, habitually arriving for work late and leaving early, using company time for personal business, and other dishonest tactics have contributed to this enormous cost. For ministers entrusted with the souls of men and the Church of Christ, such thievery bears most severe consequences.

Certainly, no one benefits if the minister ruins his health and family by trying to do all the work himself. Still, in every successful ministry there is a minister who gives himself diligently to the work.

Many ministers "burn out" rather than "rust out." Someone aptly pointed out that the compulsion to be in perpetual motion eighteen hours a day, seven days a week, is as wrong as the perpetual inertia of slothful ministers. Sin like this can be avoided if the minister accepts that he does not labor alone but in cooperation with others called to share in the task of ministry.

Connect with the People

Some Next-Gen pastors believe personal visitation does not work in a sophisticated society. They prefer to make contact electronically, believing e-mail, text, or social media is more efficient, as well as culturally acceptable. However, people still like to see their ministers in person.

Not all visits have to occur in the home. Younger pastors tend to make pastoral contacts in many ways, often over breakfast or lunch at a local restaurant or coffee house.

Granted, people may not be open to cold calls. Making appointments for visitation insures the pastor does not waste time traveling to a home when no one is present. Appointments also insure people are expecting a visit. You don't want to arrive when people are eating a meal, entertaining guests, or embarrassed by unkempt households.

Visit leaders and shut-ins first. You need to build relationships with leaders and their families because they influence so many others. At the same time, you want to visit shut-ins (whether at home or in assisted-care facilities) because they do not have influence. They need to know that they are important to the new pastor. They have not been able to participate in the call of the pastor, so they are naturally curious about you. They can be some of your strongest prayer partners if you will reach out to them early and regularly.

Visit people in the hospitals. Hospital visitation provides the minister a prime opportunity to grow closer to his people. In these hours of physical and emotional need, the pastor joins the team of physicians and, under the guidance of the Great Physician, offers the ministry of healing. This privilege cannot be delegated to others, although it may be shared. Many pastors of larger churches expect their associates to make the daily trek around the hospital circuit while they themselves tend to more interesting tasks. Soon, they discover that even the largest of congregations will not endure such neglect or presumption.

Visit prospects. Many people will visit a church during an interim period before a new pastor arrives. Most will not join until the church calls the minister because they want to know they can sit under his preaching and follow his leadership. Now that you are on the field, these visitors are the most likely to make decisions about salvation and church membership. If you go and get acquainted, they are more likely to respond during an invitation.

Plan to visit all families in the first year. Unless you have an extremely large church, this task is not as difficult as it seems. A church with six hundred people generally has about two hundred families. If you visit four families a week (a task accomplished in about three hours), you can easily see all two hundred families and have two weeks for vacation! Also, you will see many of these families in the normal course of ministry, at hospitals, funerals, committee meetings, and other opportunities. Making pastoral visitation appointments a priority communicates the value you place on your relationships with the people. You will get to know and love them, and they will love you in return.

Have some Sunday School, small group, or organizational fellowships. You and your spouse will meet many more people quickly through social events built around existing groups. Invite the youth group to your home for a hot dog cookout. Ask the deacons and their wives to host a Sunday night dessert fellowship after church. The more people you can meet informally (as opposed to committee meetings or worship services), the more personal your relationships will become.

Meet the community. Don't just pastor the church; pastor the community. Be sort of a parish priest. Walk the neighborhood and meet your neighbors. Systematically work through communities around the town, meeting people in a natural, friendly way. Stop in local stores and greet workers and owners (without interfering with their jobs). Make appointments with civic and governmental leaders. Building relationships on a personal as well as professional level opens many doors for ministry.

Get acquainted with other ministers. While not your first priority, initiating contact with pastors in other churches (within and outside your denomination) will pay lasting dividends. These ministers know the history of the community and your church. They can share valuable insights helpful to your work. They also may become your best supporters. While most ministers cannot openly share their problems with people in their churches, they find wise confidants in relationship with other ministers.

Most of All . . .

Take time for God. If your spiritual health is not a priority, everything else will fail. Beginning each morning with the prayer will affect everything you do that day. Read Scripture for personal communion and devotion, not just to develop sermons and lessons. Everything you do personally and professionally is predicated on a strong relationship with the Lord.

Take time for family. Ministering to your family first provides the foundation for ministering to other families later. At church or in school, don't expect your family to be perfect and they won't be disappointed when you are not. Give them reason to love where they are and let them feel like they are a part of this new home as well as the new ministry.

Love the people. Human beings are naturally reciprocal creatures. In most cases, if you love them, they will love you in return. Some people may not be very loveable, but Christ in you can love through you. As God loved us while we were still sinners, we ought also to love one another, especially those the Father has placed in our care (1 John 4:7–21).

Chapter 9

PASTORAL CARE: KNOWING AND CARING FOR THE FLOCK

"My sheep hear my voice, and I know them, and they follow me:" (John 10:27).

Next-Gen ministers believe in relationships. Knowing the communal nature of postmoderns, Next-Gen leaders intentionally build interactive structures into their churches. From coffee fellowships to small groups for Bible study and fellowship (a.k.a. Sunday School in more traditional congregations), younger leaders emphasize relationships between believers.

To a degree, most pastors live out a commitment to relationships. They understand that you cannot know the flock if you don't walk among them regularly. While text messaging, social media, instant messaging, FaceTime, and other technological tools help connect ministers to their people, unless you spend time with people, relationships tend to be shallow at best.

In beginning a new ministry, we discussed the importance of getting information about people in the church. However, knowing about people does mean you know people. General data can organize your efforts to relate to people, but it merely provides an entryway to actually connecting with the congregation on a regular basis.

Your ultimate goal is not merely to know people but to care for them. The flock of God needs a pastor who will have a shepherd's heart. They need someone to offer counsel, encouragement, spiritual growth, mentoring, and so much more.

> Your ultimate goal is not merely to know people but to care for them. The flock of God needs a pastor who will have a shepherd's heart.

One of the best ways to get to know the people remains connecting with people personally. Sometimes visitation occurs in people's homes. At other times, it happens over breakfast, lunch, or coffee. It may take place at the gym or coffee house. It can occur in the normal course of daily life. The social aspect of personal interaction combines with a spiritual purpose as the minister uses direct contact to build relationships.

How better to get to know members' families? How else will you discover their interests recreationally, vocationally, and spiritually? How can you have the kind of interpersonal exchanges that allow you to know them and them to know you without face-to-face opportunities?

When we think we are too important to interact with people, people will get the idea we love the church but don't care about them very much. Show your people you love them by investing precious time with them. Here are a few ways to do that:

General Principles

General tips for ministering to your people include the following:

Determine your purpose. While random encounters with people can be profitable in themselves, make the most of your contacts by planning your purpose. Are you making this call (in person or by phone) to build relationships, provide pastoral care, engage in evangelism, or help someone in the process of discipleship? Your purpose will determine the kind of contact you make. You may keep in touch with people with technology, but pastoral care requires a personal touch. You can transmit information by text or e-mail, but evangelism best happens face-to-face.

Having your purpose clearly in mind also allows you to prepare spiritually by praying for yourself, the person, and the visit. You can also prepare physically. Dress appropriately to the encounter. Take a Bible, Gospel tract, or other material helpful for the specific objective. Enlist the right person to go with you, if needed.

Create a contact system to keep up with your interactions with church members, prospects, and others. It should be easy to use and kept confidential. The advent of various applications for smartphones and tablet computers allows ministers to create databases of members easily and efficiently. Microsoft Excel or Access, as well as more sophisticated church information computer systems, offer easy ways to track your ministry.

Without a systematic approach, you likely will miss some families, while spending additional time on a few active members.

You may want to categorize the membership by families, home locations, work places and schools, interests, and church involvement. As you make contact with various people, sit down at the end of the day and add notes to your database. Identify the type of interaction, its results, and special information, such as needs, interests, prayer requests, or steps taken in evangelism or discipleship. At the end of each week, do a quick summary, noting whatever follow-up you need to schedule in future weeks. Also, recognize families or individuals who have not been touched recently. Intentionally schedule some opportunity to interact with all the people over the course of the year, lest some be left out.

Set goals. Build in accountability for your contacts. Unless you deliberately create a reasonable level of expectation, you will find yourself making excuses at the end of the year as to why you failed. One church-planting expert advises that new congregations require at least twenty-five to forty visits a week in order to grow. Established congregations may have smaller expectations but will become healthier and grow more quickly if a strong system of regular interaction is in place.

Don't play favorites. You will be tempted to focus on certain people you enjoy and to avoid persons who are annoying, adversarial, or overly dependent. Remember that you are pastor for all the people. Your system will allow you to keep up with the dispersal of contacts. Be sure to see new members, church visitors, and shut-ins. Do not neglect people in nursing homes or hospitals. Discipline yourself to love all the people, and they are more likely to love you in return.

Virtual Visitation

Next-Gen ministers belong to the digital generation. You grew up with technology. Your phone has more computing power than the first spaceship that circled the earth. You are accustomed to using various forms of technology without thinking about it. You don't read newspapers but get information on your smartphone, iPad, or computer. You don't wear a watch or use a desk calendar because time and appointments are on your phone. You don't talk on your phone as much as you use it to text, have FaceTime, instant message, or otherwise communicate.

Technology allows ministers to multiply themselves and maximize time. Next-Gen pastors prefer to use smartphones to text with people rather than to talk with people. Texting is an asynchronous method of communication that does not require the attention commitment claimed by conversations.

E-mail provides another venue for virtual visitation. While less personal, and sometimes less accessible, e-mail allows for quick dissemination of information to several numbers of people at the same time. Be careful not to hit "reply all" unless you really want everyone in the e-mail stream to see what you're saying. Also, remember that whatever you put in print (even electronically) can easily be forwarded to people you really did not intent to include in the communication.

Social media provides another quick way to keep up with people. You can see what is going on in their lives and share photos, videos, comments, and even encouragement from your life. Be careful to protect access to your account and monitor it regularly to protect yourself from hackers, spam, or other infiltration.

Recognize that **technology has its limitations**. Not everyone has a smartphone or computer. While nearly universal for middle- and upper-economic groups, poorer people and older people likely do not have access to technological devices.

When communicating via technology, remember that emoticons cannot convey nonverbal communication like voice inflection, facial expression, and body posture can. Without accompanying expressions, what you type into a text, e-mail, or social media post may be misunderstood. Avoid counseling matters, handling conflict resolution, or any sensitive and confidential matters when using technological helps.

Another limitation is evangelism. A low level of Gospel interaction may occur through text, tweets, and other technological channels, but few people will come to a decision to receive Christ via the cold, impersonal flow of electrons and radio waves.

Public Meetings

Some contacts can be made in public places, such as the local diner or coffee house. Public meeting places can accommodate one-on-one chats or small group (three or four people) interaction. The social element aids relationship building as long as topics of discussion do not become emotional. Counseling, conflict management, and other emotionally charged encounters should never be handled in public venues.

As with home visits, never meet a person of the opposite gender unless that person's spouse, or yours, is present. Not only can one-on-one meetings with the other sex produce unintended consequences, the encounter will be the topic of conversation throughout the community.

Social Interaction

"A man that hath friends must show himself friendly . . ." (Proverbs 18:24).

Relationships often grow deeper through casual, social interaction. Ministers and their wives have many opportunities to be with people, whether at informal gatherings after church, church socials, Bible study group fellowships, or private dinners in homes. You may be with one couple or several, but social interaction is always personal and individual. People want you to know them not merely as church members but as Bob and Sally and John and Mary. Social encounters are wonderful opportunities for you and your wife to get acquainted and build friendships. You may find this aspect of ministry is important to your wife and could meet a vital need in her life.

A much larger book would be required to cover all the issues of social interaction a pastor and his wife might encounter, but here are a few helpful tips:

Be available and approachable. People will invite you to social events if they believe you enjoy that type of activity. Pastors who isolate themselves from people except for ministry activities give the idea that they love the church but don't like people very much. On the other hand, if you are friendly and approachable, individuals and small groups will want you and your spouse to be with them.

Be genuinely interested in others. Task-oriented people find small talk difficult. Simply develop an authentic care for people. Be interested in their lives and ask questions: where they grew up, what hobbies they enjoy, where they work, how their children are doing. You'll find the other person will enjoy doing most of the talking. They will also be interested in knowing about you and your family.

Observe social etiquette. Be on time. Don't overschedule yourself so you arrive late for events. Ask about appropriate dress code when accepting an invitation to a social gathering. Wear clothing that blends in with the occasion. Give attention to personal grooming and hygiene. Initiate conversations; don't sit in a corner expecting people to seek you out. Don't monopolize any individual's time.

Learn names. People like to be called by name. When being introduced, speak the other person's name aloud while shaking hands firmly. Memorize the name (mnemonic devices like word association might help).

Focus. Don't let your eyes or mind wander. Be present mentally as well as physically. Keep eye contact and don't be constantly looking around for the next person to talk with.

Be polite. Social occasions are not the right time for correcting someone, arguing about church business, or discussing controversial issues. Just be nice. Being offensive serves no spiritual purpose.

Don't dominate conversations. Learning the art of social discussion requires different skills than preaching a sermon or teaching a lesson. Remember, social interaction involves mutual sharing.

Enjoy yourself. Have fun. Laugh (but not too loudly!) Let social occasions be a time of personal refreshment for you and your spouse. Yes, you have a ministry purpose of developing relationships with your people, but you have social needs too!

Home Visitation

"And when Jesus came to the place, he looked up, and saw him, and said unto him, Zacchaeus, make haste, and come down; for today I must abide at your house. And he made haste, and came down, and received him joyfully" (Luke 19:5–6).

Among all professions, ministers alone have the understood right of initiation when it comes to making contact with people in their homes. Depending on the culture (generational as well as geographical), many church members expect their pastors to see them in their homes. Older people especially enjoy having the minister pay them a visit.

While most people feel uncomfortable about having someone stop by their homes without an appointment, nearly all church members welcome an appointment by the pastor (and his wife if possible).

The advantages of home visitation include the following:

- People are more relaxed in their own homes. They feel a bit more in control on their own turf.
- People enjoy being hospitable, especially toward the minister and his wife.
- People are more likely to talk about serious issues at home. Few individuals will discuss situations that might involve strong emotions in public places.
- People are more likely to make major decisions, including receiving Christ as Savior, in their own homes. You will rarely win someone to Christ through instant messaging or at Starbucks.
- People are more likely to have the entire family, even the dog or cat, present in a home visit. If the goal is to nurture the family, their home or your home is a good place. (A love of hospitality is one of the qualities Scripture requires of pastors. Inviting people into your home offers a deeper level of relationship than merely seeing them at church.)

As you engage in personal visitation, these tips can help you maximize your efforts and minimize the liabilities:

Make appointments—People respond well when they know you are coming. They have time to clean the house, prepare some refreshments, and avoid interrupting homework or other obligations. Visiting by appointment keeps you from showing up at an empty house and wasting your time. This plan also allows you to make several visits in nearby neighborhoods in a short time frame.

Watch the clock—Not literally, of course. Don't check your watch or phone to see how long you have been at the home, but beware of overstaying your visit. The length of home visits depends on your purpose, the people's schedule, and the culture. In some communities (usually rural), people expect the pastor to stay longer than in urban settings. Older people want their minister to spend more time (and have a piece of pie and cup of coffee) than younger families.

Take someone with you. Multiply yourself and protect yourself—Jesus' method provides a good example for us. He sent the disciples out two by two. Having someone with you allows you to multiply your ministry as you train other people for pastoral care, evangelism, discipleship, and other ministries. It also protects you from embarrassing or dangerous situations. Never, read that again, never—I'll say it one more time—**never** go into a home where a woman is by herself unless your wife is with you. Even if the lady is 110 years old, do not enter a home if she and you are alone. Regardless of how innocent the visit may be, you do not have to succumb to temptations to set the gossip mill churning.

Hospital Visitation

". . . I was sick, and ye visited me . . ." (Matthew 25:36).

When people experience physical pain, illness, and infirmity, they need to know their church, and especially their ministers, care about them. Jesus emphasized the importance of visiting the sick (Matthew 25:36). Our hospital ministry cannot be selectively applied only to people or families we believe are important. Jesus said, "Verily I say unto you, Inasmuch as ye have done it unto one of the least of these my brethren, ye have done it unto me" (Matthew 25:40).

Ministering to people in the hospital not only touches those lives but also families and friends. You may meet more lost people in an afternoon of hospital ministry than a week of sitting in your study. People will see you as a caring person. As they have personal needs arise, they will reach out to someone who they believes cares—you!

You will develop your own philosophy of hospital ministry, but here are a few ideas to get you started:

Get to know the hospitals. Introduce yourself to administrative staff as well as doctors and nurses. Learn the rules of each hospital, including visitation times. Discover the location of various units, such as the intensive care unit, surgery waiting rooms, and chaplains' offices.

Go. When you receive word about a member in the hospital, be prompt to go as soon as possible. At the same time, realize some people may not inform the church about being in the hospital. A very few will even try to make the minister feel guilty if they are in and out of the hospital before he visits them. Don't play hide-and-seek. Explain that you would have been happy to visit if you had known the patient was hospitalized.

Visit when it is most convenient for the patient. Avoid meal times and shift changes. During shift changes, nurses are rechecking vital signs and handling other duties, making an effective visit difficult. Often, procedures are scheduled early in the morning. If you plan to see the patient before a heart catheterization, surgery, or other early-morning operation, you should arrive an hour early. Insurance, as much as illness, often dictates the schedule and length of hospitalizations.

Watch your appearance. Always be clean and look professional. Even if you do not wear a coat and tie, you will command more respect by the medical staff if you take your ministry seriously in the way you look.

Be pleasant. Smile, but don't try to cheer up the patient with a lot of jokes. One nurse complained that ministers sometimes try to be stand-up comics in hospital rooms. Greet other people in the room, including other families, in the case of a semiprivate room or ward.

Be concerned without being worrisome. Don't remark, "My cousin had something like that and died!" Don't ask too many questions, especially about female patients' problems. Don't try to interpret the heart monitors and other machines.

Be careful about what you say. Don't share others' experiences. What your aunt Sadie had has little to do with this patient. Don't be an amateur diagnostician. Let the doctor take care of determining the patient's condition and care.

Be aware of the time. Don't stay too long or run off too quickly. Culture and common sense dictate how long one should visit. In some rural areas, people expect longer visits than in urban settings. The patient's condition and needs should determine the length of the visit.

Be careful. Don't sit on the bed, even if there are no available seats in the room. Hygiene and propriety prevent such familiarity. Use wisdom about touching the patient. Especially avoid touching female patients except to gently shake hands. When shaking hands with a male or female, be careful of intravenous sites and other issues. Wash hands before and after entering a room. If available, use waterless antibacterial hand cleansers, but don't do either while in the patient's room. Note any precautions. Follow directions if signs warn visitors to wear masks and gowns or offer other guidelines.

Be respectful of medical staff. If the doctor is present, wait outside. If the doctor comes in, offer to wait outside; most physicians will not treat or discuss the patient's condition in the presence of nonfamily individuals. If procedures need to be done, excuse yourself and come again later.

Be a good listener. Listen if person wants to talk, but be careful not to overtire the patient. If the patient has a breathing tube, you should do the speaking and not ask questions or expect a response.

Be aware of spiritual needs. Share Scripture appropriately. Having a pocket New Testament with Psalms handy is always helpful. Share the Gospel appropriately. While hospitals are not the place for "turn or burn" evangelistic approaches, patients need to know the hope found in Christ. I have led several people to Christ who became open to the Gospel through a serious illness. Pray. Pray with and for the patient and the family. If the patient has a catheter drain bag on the side of the bed, do not kneel when praying. It embarrasses the patient and the family.

Relationships with Doctors and Staff

Build relationships with the medical staff. Become a part of the healing team. Remember they have jobs to do, so be diligent to help and not hinder. Do not second-guess the doctor or nurse. If you have a concern, speak to a family member privately. Avoid asking the doctor inappropriate questions about the patient's condition; privacy laws require the doctor provide only the most general answers. Avoid asking the doctors, nurses, or hospital administrators for special favors beyond what is acceptable for ministerial involvement.

Remember that doctors, nurses, maintenance staff, administrators, and others need ministry too. While serving as a volunteer chaplain to a cancer ward of a local hospital, I often took time to greet hospital workers by name. The turnover rate of nurses was eighteen months because of the high stress they experienced due to the mortality rate of the unit. Neonatal wards have the same issues.

Take time to listen and pray for workers without interfering with their work. Your investment in focused care for people will bear major returns as people receive comfort, encouragement, and spiritual nurturing. Many of them will be unbelievers. Your authentic care will open the door for opportunities for sharing the Good News.

Chapter 10

WHAT DO YOU DO WHEN SOMEONE DIES?

"And (Jesus) said, 'Where have ye laid him?' They said unto him, 'Lord, come and see.' Jesus wept. Then said the Jews, 'Behold how he loved him!'" (John 11:34–36).

Death visits every home. While the Holy Spirit is the ultimate Comforter, people also need and expect their pastor to minister comfort and encouragement. Unfortunately, some ministers are uncomfortable around the strong emotions accompanying grief. Others see the whole issue of funerals as an interruption to busy schedules. Good shepherds follow the example of their Lord in demonstrating love and compassion for people experiencing the pain of loss.

When Jesus showed up at a funeral, He raised the dead. Pastors today may not be able to raise the dead, but they should develop skill in raising the living. Three biblical accounts of Jesus' ministry demonstrate practical principles for serving people when someone dies.

Go and Minister to the Family

When His friend Lazarus died (John 11), Jesus returned to Bethany and found his family and friends grieving. Jesus had delayed several days before going to Bethany because he planned to raise Lazarus from the dead and wanted enough time to pass so no one would have any doubt that Lazarus was dead before being brought back to life. When the time came, he went to join the family at Bethany.

A pastor should go to see the family upon hearing about a death of a church member or one of their close relatives. Hurting people need their shepherd's ministry. His presence during their pain affirms not only his concern, but represents God's care as well.

On arrival at the house of grief, don't discuss the funeral arrangements or assume that you will be asked to do the funeral. Simply be there with them. Your ministry of presence and prayers will go far in comforting the grieving.

Understand Their Range of Emotions

When Jesus arrived at Lazarus' funeral, people were openly mourning. In her grief, Martha, Lazarus' outgoing sister, seemed to confront Jesus and appeared to blame Lazarus' death on Jesus' absence. "Lord, if you had only been her, my brother would not have died" (John 11:21). Her sister, Mary, also mentioned Jesus' absence, but in a quieter expression.

People exhibit different kinds of emotions following the death of a relative or friend. The initial stages of grief include shock, disbelief, and anger. Sometimes grieving people express intense emotions. In some instances, their feelings may be misdirected toward one another, the deceased (especially in the case of suicide), or anyone who happens to be in the line of fire, including the minister. Understand their state of mind and help them to identify their emotions and express them appropriately.

Comfort the Grieving

Jesus ministered to Martha with comfort, to Mary with empathy, and to the crowd of unbelieving mourners with demonstration of power that led to faith. He comforted Martha with the promise that her brother would rise again. If the deceased was a believer, we can comfort the family with the knowledge that their loved one is alive and well in Jesus' presence and will one day rise again at Jesus' Second Coming. If the deceased was not saved, the minister focuses on the believing family and offers the comfort of the Holy Spirit. Assure them that the Holy Comforter will be present alongside them throughout their grief. In such cases, focus on the living, not the dead. After all, they are the ones who need God's grace now.

Express Empathy

Jesus' empathy was evident in the verse that ranks as the shortest, yet most poignant, of all Scripture: "Jesus wept" (John 11:35). Some readers think Jesus wept because He was about to bring Lazarus back from heaven, yet Jesus did not weep when He raised the son of the widow at Nain or Jairus' daughter. Other commentators believe Jesus cried because of the unbelievers, but He did not do so when confronted by other doubters.

No, Jesus wept as a natural response of grief before the tomb of His friend. The people who witnessed His tears understood His emotion. "How much He (Jesus) must have loved him (Lazarus)." Sometimes we forget that Jesus was all human as well as all divine. He felt the same emotions you and I would feel at the tomb of a beloved friend or relative. He was not afraid to reveal His feelings.

Ministers empathize with their flock. Weep with those who weep and rejoice with those who rejoice (Romans 12:15). Pastors may shed tears if sincerely moved to do so. Not every situation produces such a strong emotional response as does the loss of a friend. Still, loving shepherds find ways to express their empathetic compassion to grieving family and friends.

Offer the Ministry of Presence and Prayer

At the home of a man whose daughter died, Jesus focused on the immediate family—Jairus and his wife (Mark 5:22–43). When you visit a grieving family, be courteous towards other people, but focus on the family. Be careful not to offer vain platitudes like "I know how you feel." Some well-intentioned comments cause more harm than good. When my father died, I actually received a sympathy card with a handwritten note: "I guess God needed your father more than his family." Such nonsense not only is untrue theologically, it causes spiritual and emotional pain in the bereaved.

Listen as much as talk. Draw the family out to the extent that they feel like talking. Encourage them to experience good memories of the past. Share an appropriate Scripture as the occasion lends itself. Prayer is always helpful when done so sincerely and not as something people simply do because they do not know what else to do.

Encourage Trust in Christ

Jesus encouraged Jairus' family to moderate their grief with trust in Him. A funeral is a powerful venue to demonstrate the efficacy of faith in Christ. Nearly every appropriate sermonic text contains a bridge to share the Gospel. You will preach to more lost people in a typical funeral than at any other time. Without turning the funeral into an evangelistic revival service, the preacher can powerfully portray the hope that lies only in Jesus.

Demonstrate Compassion

At the funeral of a widow's son, Jesus ministered with compassion (Luke 7:13). Entering the town of Nain with His disciples, Jesus encountered the funeral procession of a young man who was the only son of a widow. In that culture, without family to care for her and no safety net such as Social Security, this woman faced not only the grief of losing her son but a life of poverty. Luke records, "And when the Lord saw her, he had compassion on her." Although the people were moved at this miracle, Jesus did not ask for faith as at the raising of Lazarus or Jairus' daughter. He acted strictly out of compassion.

One ministerial student confessed that he disliked funerals because he did not feel genuine compassion for people experiencing grief. Part of the reason was he had never experienced the death of a close friend or relative. He would learn quickly that a pastor without compassion is a pastor without a ministry. Throughout Scripture, Jesus is described as being moved with compassion. If we are to follow His example, we must find His heart and embrace His loving compassion for people.

> *A pastor without compassion is a pastor without a ministry.*

Practical Suggestions

- **If the family asks you to conduct the funeral, make an appointment to come back and discuss details.** At that time, encourage them to share fond memories of their loved ones. Such information, as well as favorite Scripture verses, poems, and song lyrics, can help personalize the funeral message. When discussing the funeral, demonstrate tenderness while working through necessary details of the service. If new to the community, you will benefit by talking with the funeral home director about customs and procedures.

- **Gently ask someone about the deceased's faith.** If the person was a believer, get the family to discuss church involvement and other elements of the person's faith life. Such testimony can be a powerful encouragement for lost family members to trust Christ. If the deceased was not a believer, the family will already be experiencing more intense grief than otherwise. Such a funeral does better to focus on the living more than on the dead. Comfort the surviving believers and share a tender witness with the lost.

- **If you did not know the deceased well, ask family members to share remembrances.** Getting them to talk about their loved one not only gives you information you might use in the eulogy, but it is therapeutic for people in grief.

- **Talk with the family about details of the funeral.** Where will the service be held? At the funeral home or at the church? If the latter, make sure no other activities are going on in the vicinity of the funeral. Having a youth recreation program going on while people are mourning is unhelpful at best.

Ask about plans for music. Make sure the songs are appropriate. The adult daughter of one family actually suggested "Stairway to Heaven" as a song for a Christian funeral! Discuss whether the family will arrange for musicians or if they need your help. The family should not assume the church musicians or sound technicians are always available. Work with them to help with such details.

- **Work out an order of worship.** Contemporary families often want to participate in funerals for their loved ones. As you plan the service, involve relatives and others who had been close to the deceased. They recognize the pastor's unique role in conducting the worship service and expect him to provide comfort and counsel from a scriptural basis. Still they want to be part of saying goodbye to their kin.

Often, family members or close friends will share testimonies during the eulogy. Others may sing, share poems, create videos, tell stories, or say prayers. Next-Gen pastors encourage and assist in a variety of expressions of love by relatives and friends. Still, some people do not know what is appropriate for a Christian funeral and need the minister to guide them.

Gently lead families to share with you in advance whatever they intend to say or do in the funeral. By having them submit their poems, testimonies, and songs, you not only can help them avoid uncomfortable moments, but they also benefit by having thought out in advance what they will say.

A typical funeral service might include the following:

Prelude—Usually the funeral home director will have a local pianist or organist play softly in the background or he will use appropriate recorded music to develop a quiet atmosphere prior to the formal service. The funeral home or the family may put together a video of family pictures with a musical background. The video may be played during the visitation or as a prelude to the service.

Song—The first song should bring the people into a frame of mind conducive to worship. It should be appropriate to the Scripture and prayer, which follow.

Scripture and Prayer—If more than one minister participates in the service, one might lead in Scripture reading, prayer, and the eulogy, while the other delivers the message.

Eulogy—Share remembrances of the deceased. Acknowledge the family. You might have family members enlisted in advance to share testimonies, stories, poems, and other remembrances.

Song—The second song helps prepare listeners for the minister's message. It likely will be a favorite of the family or the deceased.

Message—The funeral message balances comfort for the family and sharing the Gospel for lost persons attending the service. You can, and should, take advantage of helping people to know Christ's Good News. Still, remember the difference between a revival service and a funeral.

Many texts from both Testaments provide the opportunity to personalize each funeral message. The minister who merely reads a standard service from a standardized Minister's Manual, giving the same sermon for every funeral, will soon lose the respect of his people. They quickly recognize the lack of effort and see it as an absence of concern and love.

Watch your time. The average funeral service is thirty to forty-five minutes long, depending on the number of speakers. Work with participants in planning the service. One of the main challenges involves multiple ministers who share messages or family members whose testimonies are not well prepared in advance. Talk with everyone in advance to insure a well-flowing funeral service.

Final Respects and Recessional—Every place has its own culture for funerals. In some cases, the funeral directors will have the congregation file by the casket as they exit the room (particularly if the casket remains open during the service). The family is the last to view the deceased. In other places, the people merely exit in a recessional.

At the Funeral Home

Most families will schedule a visitation time, either the day or evening before the funeral or during the hours prior to the service. Attend the visitation. Spend time with the family, but don't take up all their time. They have many friends to acknowledge and distant relatives who have traveled for the service.

When time for the funeral service arrives, have prayer with the family just prior to moving into the chapel. As the funeral directors prepare to move the casket into the chapel, walk at the head of the casket. You will lead the casket each time it moves, including at the cemetery.

At the end of the service, stand by the head of the casket if the family desires a final viewing during recessional. When everyone has left the chapel, lead the casket procession to the hearse and stand nearby while the pallbearers load the casket into the vehicle.

Going to the cemetery, you may wish to take your personal vehicle. However, make sure it is clean and in good condition. If your car is not appropriate for the funeral procession, you may ride in the hearse with the funeral director.

At the Gravesite

Lead the casket procession to the grave. Be careful not to step too closely to the open grave, especially if the area has experienced rain recently. Grave walls can give way and you may find yourself falling in!

Stand at the head of the casket. When everyone is ready, share a few final words. Read appropriate Scripture passages. Psalm 23, Psalm 100, and 1 Thessalonians 4:13–18 are excellent verses. Watch your time. Gravesite services generally last no more than fifteen minutes.

Focus on helping people say good-bye. Don't be maudlin. Never say, "Dust thou art and to dust thou shalt return." The concept of interment is difficult enough for grieving families without morbid visions of the grave. Pray to close the service. Shake hands with family, and then stand to the side while everyone leaves the gravesite.

Do not wait around for an honorarium. The family or the funeral home may give you a gift, but you should never expect payment for serving God's people during their time of grief. If asked what your fees are for the funeral, simply say you are happy to help the family since the church provides your salary.

After the Funeral

If the church provides a meal for the family, they generally will expect you to participate, but you do not have to remain for an extended time. Later, visit the family later to see how they are doing. Remember, grief doesn't end with the funeral. Keep in touch with family. Be aware of anniversaries and key dates for grief ministry. Birthdays, wedding anniversaries, holidays, and special days (such as Mother's Day or Father's Day) can be especially difficult during the first year after a death.

> Remember, grief doesn't end with the funeral.

Help with transitions as appropriate. Some widows may not have family to help with issues that the deceased handled before. Skilled church members may offer help in financial planning, legal issues, or even ordinary tasks such as winterizing vehicles.

Special Situations

Stillborn and Miscarriage

How do families deal with death before life? Certainly, life begins at conception and a baby is a child before birth. However, when the child dies in the womb or is born dead, pain tears through a family's hearts. Depending on the situation regarding a miscarriage, a family may not hold a funeral. Stillborn children or miscarriages that occur later in term often result in formal services. In either case, the worship of God in a funeral or memorial service will help the family through some level of closure.

The minister can extend Christ's comfort and compassion and lead the congregation to surround the family with loving support. Rather than a theological treatise about what happens when an unborn child dies, the family needs the assurance of God's grace for them as well as their child. Affirm their hurting hearts and help them toward healing.

After the service, stay in touch with the family for several months at least. Emotions, especially for the mother, will remain deep and raw. The couple may try to have another child too soon in order to replace the one who died. Help them see future children not as replacements of the lost child, but as gifts from God in their own right. If the couple is not able to have children again, try leading them to find acceptance in God's present work in their lives. Adoption may be an option, but adopted children should not be consolation prizes, as they are special children on their own.

Death of a Child or Teenager

Few funerals are more difficult than that of a child or teenager. No death seems timely to people who have lost loved ones, but a life lost in childhood or youth seems especially painful. Understand the level of grief the family is experiencing and adapt your approach appropriately.

You may sense deep emotions welling up in your own heart. As Jesus wept at the grave of His friend Lazarus, you should not feel ashamed if you find your eyes filled with tears and voice choked with emotion.

A pastor and I stood by a family in a doctor's office shortly after a child died suddenly. The child's mother was still holding the deceased four-year-old, rocking back and forth, and weeping uncontrollably. The pastor not only wept along with the family at this sight, he could not hold back tears when he preached the funeral several days later.

Circumstances surrounding the death of a young person often affect the level of emotions experienced by family and friends. Sudden loss due to an accident or violence may produce more intense feelings than death after a long illness; however, both situations are extremely painful.

Be prepared for family members who question God's love and goodness. I stood with the father of a sixteen-year-old youth who drowned earlier that day. He wanted to know why a loving God would allow a child to suffer and die. I affirmed God's love and tried to help the grieving dad realize that even if he knew the "whys" of his son's death, he would still feel the hurt. Also, our heavenly Father understood what it meant to have a Son die. God loved this father even with his doubt and pain.

Realize pain, not intellectual doubt, causes questioning. Remind the family that God understands their pain and wants to comfort and strengthen them. Do not try to explain questions, but don't casually dismiss them either. Rather, love the questioners and help them sense God's love and presence in the midst of their pain.

After the funeral, as with other tragic deaths, stay close to the family. People who do not work through grief often turn their anger toward whoever is closest. Husbands and wives sometimes express their pain in such a way as to hurt one another, however unintentionally. At the other extreme, some hurting people turn inward and withdraw from others. Husbands and wives may feel shut out by their spouse and sense rejection when they need one another the most. Such situations compound the tragedy of loss when divorce ensues.

You may have to intervene with loving counsel and force such couples to confront their lack of healing and misplaced emotions. Lead them to discover healing at the hands of the Great Physician. Help them turn outward and begin meeting each other's needs as a path toward restoration.

Suicide

Tom's father ended his life suddenly and unexpectedly. Facing bankruptcy, he believed his insurance policies were his only option to provide for his family. He did not consider the heartbreak his wife and children would experience. No one knows what he was thinking in those final moments, but sadness and grief remained after joy and hope were abandoned.

Funerals for suicides should not dwell on reasons for the tragedy, for not even a suicide note explains the deceased's motives. Knowing why the person chose such extreme action does not ease the family's pain.

The primary focus for the funeral is lifting up the living to the throne of God from Whom they can obtain mercy and find grace in their time of need (Hebrews 4:16). Assure the survivors they can anticipate hope for the future. Demonstrate God's love with Scripture and experience. Help them think of fond memories of the past, not the immediate horror of the present.

The family will still be in shock as they walk through the motions of the funeral. Help them begin the turn toward acceptance of their new reality. Teach them to trust God in the midst of their pain and anger. Most importantly, keep walking with them long after the funeral.

Watch out for symptoms of danger among surviving family and friends, especially if the death is of a teenager. Many schools bring in trained counselors after the suicide of a student because of the high incidence of other teens who may take their lives either in response to their grief or as they see their friend's suicide as an option for dealing with their own problems.

Death Due to Violence

Funerals for victims of crimes may be delayed longer than normal. Usually, coroners perform autopsies to determine cause of death and any circumstances that may help solve the crime. Families whose loved ones undergo medical procedures not only struggle with the delay, but with the idea of the autopsy itself. Interaction with law enforcement officers can further complicate their emotions, especially if family members were witnesses.

Use the delay to help the family process their pain and work with their grief. Help the church and friends of the family provide practical as well as emotional and spiritual support. The survivors may need simple acts, such as food preparation, lawn mowing, or other assistance as they focus on the ongoing trauma.

Absence of a Body

In some cases, the deceased's body is not available for a funeral. Such instances are commonly due to war, disaster, fire, flood, drowning, or unexplained disappearance (as in the case of an abduction that results in death). Unless witnesses give firm evidence that the person actually died, the family may resist accepting death's reality. Without a physical body, survivors may cling to the belief that somehow their loved one escaped and may still be alive. Without forcing them to surrender hope, walk with family and friends as they process the situation and their grief.

At some point, the family may have a memorial service. In rare occasions, they might insist on burying an empty casket or urn to commemorate the deceased. Remember such is their decision, not yours. Help them to use whatever type of service they choose as a means to express love and remembrance. Such a service can be a major turning point in bringing closure.

Military Funerals

If the deceased had been a member of the armed forces, the family may request a military funeral. A local chaplain from the deceased's branch of service usually will work with you to implement appropriate honors. Generally, the service at the funeral home does not involve the military other than having the casket draped with an American flag.

At the gravesite, the minister will offer whatever Scriptures, prayers, and comments he desires and then turn the service over to the chaplain. The chaplain has a standard format to follow but may offer personal words, especially if he knew the family. Following the benediction, an honor guard may offer a salute involving multiple rifle shots (blanks, naturally). Finally, two officers will formally fold the flag, insert the casings from the rifle cartridges, and present the flag to the closest family member on behalf of a grateful nation.

Fraternal Orders

Some fraternal orders have certain rituals, which families may insist on being part of the funeral, usually at the gravesite service. Each minister should investigate the nature and meanings of such rites and determine if they fit the purpose of Christian worship. One such order uses symbols and language that specifically assigns salvation to the good works of the deceased. It teaches Jesus was not God but was an emanation from God. More like occult Gnosticism than Christianity, its members occupy the pews of average churches. Although such rituals may involve Scriptures and invoke the name of God, their theology conflicts with the Bible.

Should the minister feel he cannot participate with such a funeral rite, he should discuss the situation with the family in advance. He may assure them of his love for them, and gently, but firmly, explain why he cannot be present for the ritual. In some cases, be prepared for a strong, negative reaction, especially if the deceased or family members were strongly involved in the order.

Grief Ministry

Grief does not only afflict people who have lost loved ones in death. Any major loss, including divorce, a house fire, firing from a job, or even moving away from friends and family, can trigger grief responses. The church has a responsibility to minister to grieving members long after the immediate period of loss has passed. Grief does not punch a time clock. It hangs on long after the loss has occurred.

The pastor is not the sole caregiver. Deacons and other trained members can assist in ministry to people in grief. In the aftermath of grief due to the death of his wife, Dr. Kenny Bruce developed a grief ministry training program for deacons. His plan provides an excellent model for church grief ministry. The following section is provided with his permission. This outline does not include everything in Dr. Bruce's work, but offers

> *Grief does not punch a time clock. It hangs on long after the loss has occurred.*

understanding and help in grief ministry.[1] [The basic outline below (in bold) comes from "Training Deacons to Minister to the Bereaved," a Doctor of Ministry Project Report by Dr. Kenny Bruce. Comments are offered by Jere Phillips.]

Everyone grieves. Everyone grieves in different ways and to different degrees, but each of us experiences the pain of loss. David, king of Israel, grieved deeply over the deaths of two sons: one was the child of his adulterous relationship with Bathsheba, the other was an adult son who had rebelled against his father. The first died in infancy; the second died violently. David experienced anticipatory grief over the sickness and impending death of the infant. He expressed posttraumatic grief over Absalom's demise (2 Samuel 12:13–23, 18:24–19:8).

Anticipatory grief: Family members of persons with terminal illnesses or other life-threatening conditions may go through aspects of the grieving process prior to the actual death. Knowing the loss looms ahead, they experience shock, disbelief, anger, bargaining, and many other stages of grief although their loved one is still alive. If cognizant, terminal patients often grieve their own loss in the time leading up to actual death.

Actual grief: Any loss prompts a series of emotions and responses. A family whose house burned down often expresses similar sentiments to those of a couple that divorces or a family of someone who dies. The levels and intensity of grief and its manner of expression may vary due to a number of factors.

Variable Influences on Grief

- **Family attitudes**—Some families express emotions openly and vigorously. Others internalize feelings and frown on displays such as weeping. The latter often have more difficulty working through grief than the former.
- **Patterns of stress management**—People handle stress differently based on personality type, learned behavior, culture, situational environment, or other factors. Grief is one of the most intense sources of stress, with the loss of a spouse or a child producing more stress than nearly any other experience.
- **Intensity of attachment to lost one**—Obviously, the greater the love, the larger the loss. Even the death of a parent or spouse does not invoke as much grief if relationships were not close during life. At the same time, some people experience more intense grief in the form of deep-seated guilt if they perceive they were at fault in having a poor relationship with the deceased.
- **Social acceptance of emotional expression**—Various cultures and subcultures differ as to what is proper regarding emotional expression. Some ethnic groups may maintain a "stiff upper lip" while others freely vent deeply held feelings.

Stages of Grief

Elizabeth Kubler-Ross was one of the best-known advocates for recognizing the various stages of grief people experience. Her book, *On Death and Dying*, has been a primary source for many studies. However, her book does not recognize crucial elements of human experience as they relate to God in the process of grief. Dr. Bruce's study offers a broader, more appropriate approach to understanding grief.

In reviewing these stages, one must understand that not everyone goes through each stage and not every stage is experienced in order. Grief is a messy business. How one reacts to the grace God offers during loss greatly affects the length, nature, intensity, and outcome of the grief process. Pastors should be aware of these stages and engage sufferers with compassionate ministry appropriate to each.

1. **Shock**—When I heard my mother had died suddenly of a heart attack, I was stunned. It couldn't be true. I was away at school when she died and repeatedly declared that she must just be sick, not dead. Even when her death was confirmed by a family member, I sat in unbelief, unwilling to accept my new reality. Denial may be especially difficult if the survivor is not able to see the deceased due to distance or other circumstances.

2. **Express Emotions**—Weeping is normal for people who experience loss. We cry because the one we loved is gone. We cry because we are left with an empty place in our lives. We cry over the good things of the past that we will miss in the future. We cry because of the pain strangling our hearts in agony.

Some people feel very angry at this point. They may express anger toward others they feel are responsible for their loss. They may sense anger toward themselves, especially if they had past conflicts with the deceased.

Guilt and blame also emerge during grief. Survivors may feel guilty over real or imagined offenses involving the person who has died. Often, a close family member might say something like, "I should have done more . . ." On the other hand, they may point fingers at other relatives saying or thinking, "You should have done more . . ."

Emotional expression will differ based on the variables. Some bereaved will react to loss very strongly and may be resentful if others do not express the same level of emotion. Emotions are natural as long as they do not overwhelm the person or harm others. Mourners who internalize their feelings often take longer to heal and may remain in unresolved grief for several months or longer.

3. **Depression and Loneliness**—The funeral may not be over before loneliness and depression set in. One pastor friend expressed his emptiness in the weeks after his wife's death: "Every day I experience the absence of a presence and the presence of an absence." People who have suffered loss have their lives turned upside down. The person who was so much a part of their lives is gone. Even when

they go to church, they feel out of place because their Bible study class has couples and they are now single. The pew where they sat feels odd without that person by their side.

Family and friends of grieving people may be confused by bereaved persons' changing moods as they ride the roller coaster of pain, broken only by brief escapes to normality. Grief-stricken individuals may suffer varying degrees of weariness as they tire emotionally as well as physically.

During this stage, the survivor may be in real danger of seeking a rebound relationship just to escape the loneliness. After months of extreme grief, one widower became involved with another woman and soon married. He needed relief from his pain and found hope in a new relationship. Sometimes new relationships are beneficial. In many cases, such marriages turn out tragically as the couple realizes that what brought them together was pain of the past rather than anticipation of a future together.

Depressed individuals may seek medical help. If the physician does not spend enough time with the patient to recognize the grief-induced depression, the resulting treatment may rely more on pharmaceutical aids rather than spiritual solutions.

4. **Physical Distress**—Prolonged stress of any type can produce physical symptoms. The agony of loss, especially lasting over a lengthy period of time, can cause hypertension, ulcers, immune system disorders, high blood pressure, weight gain or loss, difficulty sleeping, anxiety, and other problems. Medical consultation should be sought quickly if these or other problems emerge.

5. **Panic**—Depending on the intensity of the grief and the intrapersonal resourcefulness of the grieving person, panic attacks may ensue. A widow may have a strong sense of insecurity, particularly related to finances. If the deceased took care of money and business matters, the survivor suddenly faces immediate financial challenges without the requisite knowledge to handle them.

Widows and widowers may experience fear of a future without their spouses. Even simple issues like social interaction present unsettling possibilities. Previously, they were accustomed to socializing with other couples, now they feel out of place. Younger persons might sense that former friends feel threatened by the presence of a newly single person.

Some grieving people cling to the past, keeping everything exactly as it was before; others flee the pain associated with the departed. Constant reminders of the deceased appear in every room—the table where they ate, the TV room where they spent evenings, the bed they shared. A desire to escape may prompt the sale of a family home, moving to someplace new to get away from memories of the past.

6. **Guilt**—Even the most faithful, giving, and helpful people may experience guilt as part of grief. False guilt involves an irrational belief that they should have done something more for the deceased. On the other hand, some bereaved may sense true guilt because of unresolved conflict, harmful words and deeds, or other actions that hurt the person who has died.

Symptoms of guilt manifest in many ways. Some family members assume responsibilities related to the deceased, including financial obligations for the funeral, debts to be paid, and caregiving for other family members. They may make decisions related to the deceased. Carrying emotional baggage can burden the survivor emotionally, spiritually, and financially.

7. **Anger**—In addition to the initial emotions expressed after a loss, bereaved individuals who do not reconcile their grief in a reasonable length of time may grow increasingly irritable. Their anger may be directed toward God for letting their loved one die, or they might resent others for actions related to the deceased or themselves. Some grief-stricken people may be angry against the deceased for real or imagined offenses. Children may feel anger toward a parent who died, as if the parent chose to leave them.

Unresolved problems related to disposition of money and possessions may produce conflict with relatives. Inward strife may motivate striking out at others in frustration. Ongoing stress can build up and overflow with lava heat, hurting everyone in its path.

8. **Resist Turning**—Many mourners resist leaving the grief state. They may have an unspoken sense that returning to normal activities represents a betrayal of the deceased. Instead of recognizing their loved one would want them to get on with life, they hold on to an image of the past. They might keep the deceased's room as it was when he/she was alive. They often refuse to dispose of possessions, clothing, and anything else that reminds them of the loved one.

9. **Hope**—Eventually, as grieving people respond to God's grace, they can begin to accept their new reality. Although they may not have resolved all issues, they can move forward, anticipating God's

working in their lives. Ultimately, they will begin seeking to return to life. It will not be the life they knew in the past but life as God can make it for their future.

10. **Affirm Reality**—When survivors begin to affirm their new reality, they gain a sense of peace and freedom. Unfortunately, not all people achieve this state of resolution. Some remain in the harmful stages for the remainder of their lives. However, people who allow the Holy Comforter to work in their hearts can find a peace that passes all understanding through Christ (Philippians 4:7). Whereas along the way they may have struggled with their belief in the goodness of God, they finally emerge with a renewed faith and restored joy in the Lord.

Ministering in the Stages

Ministers, deacons, and other caregivers are better prepared to help when they understand the specific stage of grief each person is experiencing. Using descriptions of the stages, try to identify where the survivors are in their grieving process. The variable influences differ from one person to the next, requiring a variety of approaches with various members of the family. A general plan of ministry will develop as you consider the following practical suggestions:

Shock—During the initial reaction, grieving people need the minister simply to be there. He is not only a friend, he also represents the Lord. In a very real way, the minister's reputation as a man of God should produce a sense of God's presence. God's love, grace, mercy, and strength can flow through the conduit of the pastor's ministry. Prayers should be genuine, not merely an escape valve during conversations when you don't know what else to say.

Shock often paralyzes entire families. They are so consumed with their loss, they do not think of simple, ordinary tasks to care for themselves. Pastors and deacons can enlist a caring congregation to help with ordinary tasks such as food preparation, cleaning the home, mowing the yard, and other mundane but necessary activities.

During this stage, observe the family closely. Watch for signs that the grief may become overwhelming. In rare situations, distraught survivors may take extreme actions harmful to themselves and others. Intervene with firm compassion, helping the sufferer work past the immediate pain.

Express Emotions—Some ministers sense discomfort when other people express strong emotions. Others react with strong empathy and shoulder the emotional level of the sufferer. Instead of shutting down their feelings, encourage appropriate emotional expression.

Sit alongside as they weep. However, male ministers should resist the natural inclination to place an arm around female grievers. Sometimes the pastor can achieve much by sitting quietly while the mourner works through the pain either verbally or emotionally.

When appropriate, offer to pray with the family. If possible, get them to pray silently or aloud for themselves and each other. Help them express their feelings to God, much as David did in his Psalms.

Scripture should not be used as an artificial substitute for genuine empathy or to stifle emotions, but it can be a powerful part of grief ministry. Think about what passages may be helpful prior to going on the pastoral visit. Have a small New Testament with Psalms on hand. Reading from God's Word allows God to speak directly to the people.

Depression and Loneliness—Some ministers react to grieving persons with empathy up to a point. However, they may lose patience with people who express the constant sadness and hopelessness of depression. Insensitive pastors may dismiss negativity with encouragement to "get over it."

Caring spiritual physicians recognize the symptoms of loneliness and offer affirmation and love. People in this stage need encouragement to reengage in activities, especially with other people. Enlist church members to invite the griever to church, Bible studies, group activities, and social events. The bereaved likely will resist at first but may respond with gentle, but persistent, entreaties by friends.

Exercise can provide a very positive activity on many levels. Often, even simple walks can get the person out of the house. Engaging in physical activity aids the sufferer emotionally as well as helping keep the body healthy. Simple encouragement will not likely motivate the grieving person to start exercising. Have church friends to invite the sufferer to join them in various activities, accomplishing several positive goals.

Watch the grieving person closely for signs that depressive behavior and attitudes are becoming overwhelming. One widower went to the cemetery nightly, lay down beside his deceased wife's grave, and begged God to let him die. He recognized his danger and took the wise step of removing several guns from his house so he would be less likely to act on his depressive thoughts. Unfortunately, neither his pastor nor his family knew his sadness had reached such a state. His recovery took much longer, as he suffered his loss alone.

Physical Distress—Pastors should not become amateur diagnosticians. However, they should be close enough to grieving parishioners to recognize physical symptoms of prolonged grief. Ministers and family members can encourage the bereaved to seek medical help and make lifestyle adjustments to overcome physical problems associated with extended grief and its accompanying stress. A relationship with local physicians may help ministers be part of the healing team committed to the person's welfare physically as well as spiritually.

Some grievers may disregard physical problems. A few actually embrace suffering as misguided penance for false guilt related to their loss. Pastors can help these people rethink what is worth striving for. As they regain a desire for recovery, they will more likely cooperate in their physical rehabilitation.

Panic—If you recognize symptoms of the panic stage or if mourners talk about having feelings of fear or anxiety, be careful not to dismiss their concern. Affirm them and try to understand the source of panic emotions. Work with family members to provide a higher level of care to protect the sufferer during vulnerable moments.

If panic attacks relate to specific issues (such as financial concerns), enlist church members with appropriate skills to help address those concerns. Often, when they see the source of their fear coming under control, grievers feel more confident and begin to gain a sense of peace.

Encourage family members to watch the griever's nutrition. People at this stage may either avoid eating altogether or use comfort food to satisfy their anxiety. Either choice can be harmful physically and emotionally.

Guilt—If the bereaved express feelings of guilt toward the deceased, try to determine if it is genuine guilt or false guilt. In false guilt, survivors wish they could have done something differently, as if their actions could have forestalled death. Encourage them to recognize their limitations. Help them recall the many good things they did prior to the person's death. Affirm recognition of their love for the deceased.

In the case of real guilt, bereaved people constantly revisit previous conflicts, arguments, lack of care, or, in some cases, actual harm done to the person prior to death. They wrestle with how to reconcile with someone who has died. Help them express their contrition and lead them to find forgiveness, not from the deceased who is no longer present, but from their God Who is there and will be with them forever.

Share Scripture related to being reconciled with people and with God. Sample passages include 1 John 1:9. Affirm God's desire to forgive and His provision of Christ's atonement to make restoration possible. Remind grievers that Christ's blood is powerful enough to overcome any sin. Encourage them to repent of genuine sin and accept God's forgiveness.

Anger—When grieving persons persist with anger (regardless of the object of the anger), ministers must balance the need for empathetically encouraging the expression of emotions and the responsibility to confront them with the need to forgive. Prolonged anger often falls into bitterness. Lead them to forgive whoever is the object of their anger. Share Scriptures such as Colossians 3:13: "Forbearing one another, and forgiving one another, if any man has a quarrel against any: even as Christ forgave you, so also do yourself." Another good passage is Ephesians 4:32: "And be kind one to another, tenderhearted, forgiving one another, even as God for Christ's sake hath forgiven you."

Resist Turning—Survivors who resist moving forward with their lives may need assistance dealing with unresolved issues. Gently but firmly get them to talk about the loved one. Reviewing memories (both good and bad) can bring the relationship into the present. When you discover problems that hold the grievers back, help them work through each in turn.

Encourage participation in relationships through ministry to others and group activities. The church may offer grief support groups, which allow sufferers to compare experiences and encourage one another to become more open and move forward. However, churches must be careful not to segregate grief survivors. Bereaved people need to normalize activities and reintegrate into socialization, work, and ministry.

If the bereaved has resisted disposing of the deceased's clothing or other personal articles, enlist church members to offer help in gathering, cleaning, and removing the items. If they see the clothing going to a good cause—a benevolent ministry or someone in need of clothing—they feel better about letting go of their belongings.

Encourage participation in group activities. Sometimes asking grieving persons to help you minister to others can help them shift their attention from themselves. Helping other people puts their own problems in perspective and gives them a sense of well-being.

Hope—As the bereaved move into hope, help them toward positive resolution. Affirm decisions they make about their future. At some point, they may desire to build new relationships, yet fear others' opinions as if moving on were somehow a betrayal of the deceased. Children, especially older teens or adult children, may need to give a parent permission to begin dating after an appropriate time. The widow or widower needs acceptance by family, friends, and church members in order to begin a new chapter of life.

Affirm Reality—Persons who experience loss never forget the past, but they begin to accept their new reality. Affirm their strengths and offer support for their choices for the future. Help them see God and life as good. As they normalize their situation, accept their new lifestyle as it fits into God's pattern and plan.

Grief is real. It hurts. While no one enjoys it, everyone must walk grief's paths many times, for death and loss are parts of life. If you understand grief's elements and are intentional in ministering to people experiencing loss, you will give evidence of being a loving, competent minister, and the congregation will become known as a caring church whose ministry is a channel of God's grace.

Chapter 11

PASTORAL COUNSELING MINISTRY

". . . and his name shall be called Wonderful, Counselor . . ." (Isaiah 9:6).

"Unqualified and unprepared." Many ministers describe themselves with these words when asked about their counseling ministry. Seminaries rarely require more than one or two courses in ministerial counseling for the average master's degree. Graduates are left to self-education through reading, seminars, and discussions with peers. Theological education trains us how to parse Greek or Hebrew verb forms. We are able to list the kings of the northern and southern kingdoms of Israel and Judah. We can debate important topics on the tongues of the average people, like supralapsarianism. (NOT!) However, when our people come to us with the deepest pain of human experience, we are unprepared.

Next-Gen pastors not only encounter the typical kinds of cases their forefathers experienced—counseling related to premarital and marriage issues, parenting, career determination, conflict resolution, drugs, and others—they also confront issues their granddads never imagined. How would you counsel a transgender person who had a sex change and later became a Christian? If you enter the military chaplaincy, how do you handle a same-sex couple wanting to be married? Should an AIDS patient be allowed to participate in communion? What should a teenage girl do about other students who engage in cyber-bullying, leaving her in tears and contemplating suicide?

This short chapter will not equip you to open a clinical counseling practice. Still, you should find some help in handling the kinds of situations typical to the average pastor. It is not exhaustive in examples but offers principles, direction, and resources that will help you as you help your people.

Who Is a Pastoral Counselor?

Take a look in the mirror. What do people see when they enter your office looking for help during the most challenging episodes in their lives? Hopefully, they will observe the kind of person described here.

An Authentic Christ Follower

People expect their counselor to know Jesus Christ and to follow Him in everyday life. His walk must match his talk. People will not follow someone who says, "Do as I say, not as I do." No true change can happen in a counselee's life unless God works such transformation. Without Christ, no counselor has anything to offer of lasting help, for only in Christ can the counselee become right with God. The counselor only serves as one of God's instruments of change if he lives out an authentic relationship with Jesus Christ.

A Biblical Scholar

The only authority by which a counselor may speak into another person's life is the Word of God. Counseling cannot be biblical unless the counselor studies Scripture and becomes proficient in understanding and applying biblical principles to life. One does not necessarily have to achieve a doctorate in theology to counsel, but the more rooted a person is in the Bible the better he is able to help others.

An Accountability Partner

Biblical counselors love people enough to confront them with their sin and to hold them accountable for walking in accordance with God's Word. True love does not let someone continue in lifestyles contrary to God. Sin is destructive. Pastoral counselors are strong enough to lovingly challenge counselees regarding sin and righteousness.

A Compassionate Friend

He wasn't a professional. No elaborate diplomas lined his office walls. As far as I knew, he had never attended a counseling class. He was just a Christian friend who was willing to listen with compassion and empathy. As I poured out my heart, he did not interrupt. There was not a hint of boredom or "I know the answer; hurry up so I can give it to you." His genuine concern did not restrain the sharp insight into Scripture that he offered. When our talk ended, I not only felt the correct biblical answer had been reached but I exhilarated in the warmth of an authentic friendship.

A Competent Counselor

At the same time, simply being a friend is not sufficient without developing competencies for counseling. The pastor should learn as much as possible in order to offer the best counsel to his people.

Secular mental health experts often see ministers as unqualified poachers, intruding into a specialized field for which they are considered to be unprepared and unwanted. Unfortunately, many Christians feel the same way. They think of pastors as being useful in spiritual areas, but not of much use when it comes to "the real world." Believing mental and emotional problems stem solely from a medical model, counselors and counselees alike may discount the benefit of ministerial counseling.

Decades ago, Jay Adams enlightened pastors to their rights and responsibilities as counselors. He and other biblical counselors pointed out the importance of seeing problems related to spiritual issues, whose solution comes not from secular sources but from the Word of God.

Ministers have a responsibility to become highly proficient in skills related to listening, understanding the root problems based on Scripture, identifying spiritual principles involved in people's lives, and leading them into discovering and applying biblical solutions. Too many people are injured by often well-meaning ministers who take their abilities for granted simply because they hold the position of pastor without developing their capabilities as counselors. We owe both our congregants and our Master the highest level of competence possible.

> *Ministers have a responsibility to become highly proficient in skills related to listening, understanding the root problems based on Scripture, identifying spiritual principles involved in people's lives, and leading them into discovering and applying biblical solutions.*

A Healthy Healer

People who struggle with severe difficulties often desire to help other people with problems like theirs. However, "wounded healers" (Henri Nouwen) or "fellow strugglers" (John Claypool) do not make the best counselors; they often have yet to find the answers for their problems. Healing counselors live biblically healthy lives. They manifest a right relationship with Christ. They understand how to solve life's problems from a scriptural basis. They have a positive outlook on life, a strong emotional constitution, and an empathetic spirit. Their source for counseling lies not in personal struggle, but in clear application of biblical principles.

A Confidential Confessional

Malpractice! That was the charge in the lawsuit against the priest. The plaintiff argued her right to confidentiality was breached when her pastor exposed her confession. In another case, the alleged failure of a pastoral counselor to maintain a confidence resulted in a lawsuit for $5,000,000!

In recent years, taking the preacher to court has been an increasingly common problem. Malpractice insurance for clergy, a relatively new concept, has become increasingly important in the wake of rising vulnerability of clerical counselors. Legal action has become the response of choice to many parishioners who feel (justly or not) their counselor has betrayed their confidence. Misconduct and lack of competence have also been charged in suits against clergy who counsel.

People come to their ministers for personal counseling for several reasons. They assume the preacher is a maintainer of confidential issues shared in private counseling. Scripture urges Christians to confess their faults to one another and to pray for one another that they might be healed (James 5:26). In order for this ministry to be effective, it must be confidential. When a preacher shares a privately shared matter with someone else, he not only breaks trust with the counselee but with the entire congregation. How can a flock trust a shepherd who uses their personal problems as sermon illustrations?

A Releasing Relationship

People come to a pastor for counsel during their most vulnerable moments. The intensity of need, which precipitates a counseling visit, can present a problem to the counselee and to the minister. Unless the pastor understands his role properly, he may be manipulated into playing God for every parishioner with a problem. The pastor might enjoy being the provider of every solution, the answer to every question—for a while. Ultimately, the dependency of his people will become an albatross around the neck of the counselor and a stumbling block to their growth and health.

The goal of counseling must be the release of the individual, not continued dependence. Just as Jesus developed His followers so they might make proper decisions before He left them, even so the undershepherd must guide counselees into personal responsibility under the guidance of Scriptures and the Holy Spirit. Personal growth is never gained when another assumes one's responsibility in life.

A Forgiving Fellowship

The compassionate friendship of the pastoral counselor must find wider expression in the *koinonia* of the congregation if a genuinely healing environment is to be created. The unwed, expectant mother-to-be may find empathy from the minister, only to be received with reservation by the Christian community. A recovering alcoholic might find understanding in the heart of a counselor, but never be invited to the women's auxiliary tea party.

As the spiritual leader of the church, the pastor cannot avoid his responsibility to do everything possible to create a loving, healing environment among the church family. Naturally, it is unfair to hold him responsible for every immature response by a few parishioners. However, whether the overall tone will be one of acceptance and forgiveness or one of judgment and estrangement will be influenced by the pastor.

Forgiveness does not mean excusing behavior without repentance or change in life. A truly healing fellowship helps members by holding up scriptural standards for life. When people sin, we do not help them by overlooking wickedness. However, when people repent, confess, and ask forgiveness of God and others, they should be received with love and support (2 Corinthians 2:5–11).

Why Should You Offer Pastoral Counseling?

Given the availability of clinical counselors, mental health resources, and professional psychologists and psychologists, why should you offer pastoral counseling at all? Why should you risk taking on the problems of other people? After all, you have enough to handle just being a pastor! Precisely. You are a pastor. Shepherds love their flock and cannot ignore injured sheep. Healing is part of their nature, or should be.

Perhaps you would find it helpful to take a few minutes and develop your own **philosophy of counseling**. Try following this outline:

- **What do you believe about human beings?** Are people made of two parts (material and nonmaterial; physical and spiritual) or of three (body, soul, and spirit—1 Thessalonians 5:23)? In reality, it does not matter because people are integrated wholes involving body, spirit, mind, will, and emotions. They are complex beings whose various parts interact with each other to relate to God above them and the world around them.

Think about the people you encounter each week. They were born with a sinful nature, dead in sin and trespasses. If they have accepted Christ, they are reborn and are being refashioned by the Holy Spirit into Christ's image (Romans 8:29; 2 Corinthians 3:18). Nevertheless, they grapple with sin and circumstances. The nature of the Body of Christ involves the interdependency of each person on the rest of the Body to help with those struggles.

- **What do you believe about the nature of human problems?** Certainly some people have difficulties of organic origin that require medical assistance, such as in the case of tumors, thyroid problems, and other physical diseases. However, most of the problems for which people seek counseling involve sin, either their sin or the sin of other people. Yes, some people will seek counseling for simple decision making, career determination, problem solving, and other issues that are not sin related, but most of your counseling will involve someone who is wrestling with the results of sin.

- **What do you believe about your role in helping people?** When you accepted God's call into His service, you opted out of the privilege of having a private agenda. In becoming a pastor, you put yourself into a unique relationship of responsibility. While you should not feel the weight of other people's poor choices and difficult situations, you ought to love them enough to help them bear such burdens that were never designed for any individual.

Galatians 6:2 urges us to "Bear one another's burdens, and so fulfil the law of Christ." Yet, three verses later, Paul advised, "For every man shall bear his own burden." Conflicting verses? No. Paul used two different words for *burden*. The second involves the normal responsibilities of life, which each person must manage. The burden demanding assistance is that overpowering load that requires the help of fellow believers. Our roles as ministers should not lead us to assume the normal responsibilities of others' lives, lest we encourage irresponsibility. When our people struggle with the issues of life beyond their abilities, God's call places us alongside them—not alone, but with the divine Paraclete (the Holy Comforter).

- **What do you believe about healing?** Does God still heal people? If we believe that an omnipotent Creator has the ability to heal injured people physically, mentally, emotionally, and spiritually, do we have a role in such healing? If so, what?

James instructed, "Is any sick among you? Let him call for the elders (pastors) of the church; and let them pray over him, anointing him with oil in the name of the Lord" (James 5:14). Verses 14 and 15 address the importance of prayer for the sick. The use of oil was not a supernatural anointing but represented the partnership of medicine and the prayer of faith. People need knowledgeable, competent shepherds who can bring needy people into contact with the spiritual resources of the Great Physician.

- **What resources do you have to offer?** Fortunately, we never approach people or their problems alone or empty-handed. David Benner reminds us of the powerful resources Christian ministers bring with them to the counseling ministry, including the Spirit of God, the wisdom and Word of God, the congregation of God, and prayer—conversation with God.[1]

Jesus promised the **Holy Spirit** would be with us, guiding us into all truth (John 16:13). As we need wisdom and insight into a particular issue, we need only ask and God will give it liberally through insight into God's Word (James 1:5). God's Spirit not only guides both minister and congregant into spiritual understanding of problems and solutions, but He convicts the sinner regarding his need to repent and return to God. Since most of the counseling problems you will encounter relate to someone's sin, you are absolutely dependent on the Spirit to bring the individuals to repentance and renewal.

We never counsel merely from personal experience but from the **Word of God**. Otherwise, a young pastor could not help an older believer. Someone who had never struggled with alcohol or drugs would be unqualified to aid an addict. Help for hurting people does not depend on human experience, wisdom, or advice. Rather, God's Word, given under His inspiration, is profitable for doctrine, for reproof, for correction, for instruction in righteousness: . . ." (2 Timothy 3:16).

Scripture must be the primary resource in our healing ministry, for it alone "is quick, and powerful, and sharper than any two-edged sword, piercing even to the dividing asunder of soul and spirit, and of the joints and marrow, and is a discerner of the thoughts and intents of the heart" (Hebrews 4:12).

> *Scripture must be the primary resource in our healing ministry, for it alone "is quick, and powerful, and sharper than any two-edged sword, piercing even to the dividing asunder of soul and spirit, and of the joints and marrow, and is a discerner of the thoughts and intents of the heart" (Hebrews 4:12).*

In addition, we have the benefit of God's people, **the congregation**. Within each church, God has placed numerous people with skills, experience, expertise, and willingness to help you minister to wounded believers. If you will equip them to apply their gifts correctly, such members can be able co-laborers in helping others.

Prayer and faith are dual priorities in counseling. We believe that communicating with God is effective. We not only pray for counselees, but we pray with them and lead them to pray for themselves and one another. They need to believe God cares for them and wants to work in their lives, so we pray believing. "Without faith *it is* impossible to please *him*: for he that comes to God must believe that He is, and *that* He is a rewarder of them that diligently seek him" (Hebrews 11:6).

- **What are the goals of your counseling ministry?** What are you trying to accomplish? Various Christian counseling theorists offer a variety of goal statements. My personal goal for Christian pastoral counseling is "an abundant experience of life found in Jesus Christ through the power of the Holy Spirit in accordance with Scripture." You would be wise to study biblical counselors like Charles Solomon,

Jay Adams, and others, and then develop your personal philosophy and goal of counseling.

However you state your goal, I pray that it includes the desire that "When the counseling sessions are ended, the primary goal is not a problem solved or mere personal insight or even happiness, but a person who is at peace with God and himself/herself" (Source Unknown).

Prepare Yourself to Counsel

Physician, heal thyself. The Genesis Principle says like produces like. Each species reproduced "after his own kind" (Genesis 1:21–25). If the goal of counseling involves people becoming spiritually mature, capable, responsible followers of Christ, the counselor must be such as well. Pastors begin preparing themselves for counseling by considering their own lives first. Developing healthy qualities, learning to live in a God-honoring manner, and gaining practical life skills enables ministers to help others achieve those goals in their lives.

Be a Lifelong Student

Study the Bible. The only authority pastors, or anyone else for that matter, have in helping others is the Word of God. Scripture relates to every aspect of life. The principles found in the Bible are relevant to every generation and every need. It is sufficient and authoritative. Consider the practical life applications found in the Sermon on the Mount, the Proverbs, Paul's teachings, the narratives of both testaments, the guidance of the law, and the hope found in grace.

Study Human Nature. Observe people—how they act and interact, how they communicate and miscommunicate, how they grow and mature. Watch their behavior, listen to their conversation, feel their emotions. As you learn about people as individuals, as well as within relationships, you will gain insight into what makes a healthy person. You also will grieve over their tendencies toward sin. Seeing sin's destructive consequences, you will be more motivated to help them escape sin through Christ.

Study counseling. Read the best books by solid biblical counselors. Take courses and seminars from reputable teachers. Learn various methodologies and understand which approach works best in different situations. Consider their ideas within the context of Scripture and make sure they line up with the Bible. Investigate case studies to understand how to approach various problems. Gain skill in application of biblical principles in helping people.

Pray Constantly

Pray to experience communion with Christ. Being a person of prayer keeps you in intimacy with Christ. You cannot help people by yourself. Only as you abide in the Vine can you bear fruit, especially fruit that spiritually nourishes your counselees.

Pray for yourself. Pray that you might know Christ more fully each day. Pray to resist temptation (Mark 14:38). Pray to grow as a disciple of Christ.

Pray for your people, even before you know what problems they might bring you that day. Be the intercessor for your congregation. As their spiritual leader, you have a special role in protecting the flock through prayer (Colossians 1:9; 1 Timothy 2:1).

Many problems may be avoided if the pastor leads the people to develop a commitment to intercessory prayer for one another. Spiritual warfare is real. Satan desires to attack God's people. Like a roaring lion, he roams about seeking whom he may devour (1 Peter 5:8). Like a murderous thief, he seeks to steal, to kill, and to destroy (John 10:10). Build a hedge of intercessory prayer around your people. Bring them before God's throne with love and compassion. Seek God's intervention for their lives and families.

Master a Process

The practical processes for counseling might follow several legitimately biblical Christian methods. Depending on your philosophy, you may find one particular method that you believe follows Scripture most faithfully. On the other hand, you likely will find help from several different methodologies to use in varying situations. Provided the epistemology has its foundation in biblical truth, you will probably benefit from working through various writers to your own approach.

Your process should include (as a minimum) the following:

1. Setting the Place for Counseling

Generally, counseling should take place in your church office. Never bring the counseling into your home; otherwise, you will find people calling and coming by at all hours. Also, you may put your family into risky situations with more volatile counselees. At the same time, be hesitant to counsel people in their homes. You cannot control the environment, including children and pets, which may lead to awkward encounters.

Set your office up in a way that is conducive to counseling. Having several chairs is preferable to using a couch, especially when counseling females. You may prefer not counseling from behind your desk, but have a means for writing notes as you listen.

Make sure your office door has a window built into it. You can provide privacy by placing your counselees with their backs to the door. However, counseling in a closed room, especially if it involves children or women, can be hazardous to the minister's reputation.

Never counsel women without the presence of their husbands or, alternatively, your wife. Cross-gender counseling can be problematic, not only in emotional confusion but in recognizing real problems. Women are much more capable of reading between the lines with other women, just as men understand their own gender more easily.

If you find it necessary to counsel after normal business office hours, make sure you do not counsel women alone. One minister was totally innocent in his counseling ministry to a woman whose work prevented her from coming to the office until evening. Still, the presence of the minister's car and the woman's car outside the church offices at night caused such gossip that his ministry was irreparably damaged.

2. Scheduling Appointments

While some people will stop by your office or talk with you in the hallways informally, serious counseling is best done by appointment.

Appointments:

- allow you and the counselees to set aside quality time without interruptions
- help you prepare for the sessions spiritually, mentally, emotionally, and physically
- provide opportunity for more controlled environments, including having someone present when counseling persons of the opposite gender
- prevent multiple counseling sessions from happening too close to one another. You need time to debrief the previous from one session and prepare for the next
- keep counseling sessions from continuing beyond the point of positive results. When counseling extends past an hour, you and the counselee may become too weary emotionally and spiritually for productive benefits

3. Establishing the Counseling Relationship

Discover the issue that prompted the counselee(s) to seek your help. Listen carefully. Don't jump to conclusions about what the real issues might be. Resist the temptation to try solving the problem before you understand what the underlying problem might be. Many people seeking pastoral counseling mistakenly expect to receive a spiritual inoculation in one visit. Help the counselee(s) know the problems did not occur overnight and likely will require more than one counseling session to resolve them. Communicate clearly as to how you are willing to proceed, including time and location of counseling as well as what is and is not appropriate regarding contacting you.

4. Making an Evaluation

Gather as much information as possible. Adams has a good Personal Data Inventory that can help provide basic data regarding contacts (address, phone, e-mail, etc.), family history, medical history, and other important information.[2]

Listen. Use active listening to discover the real problem. "He that answers a matter before he hears it, it is folly and shame unto him" (Proverbs 18:13). The Bible is sufficient in counseling, but what part of the Bible is needed for which problem? If you misdiagnose the underlying issues, you will administer the wrong remedy.

Probe. Ask good questions that generally cannot be answered with a simple yes or no. Listen for what is not being said as well as what is being said. Observe body language, including facial expressions.

5. Establishing a Plan of Counseling

Based on your evaluation, determine the nature of the surface problem, but go deeper to discover the underlying cause. (For example, is the problem related to anger and arguing? What makes them angry? Over what do they argue?) Look for spiritual issues and begin to match biblical principles to the problems. Make notes as you go along, assuring the counselee(s) that your notes are confidential and you keep them in a secure location. Where you observe sinful actions and patterns, lead the counselee(s) to recognize the need for repentance and correction. Encourage follow-through.

Based on the nature of the problem, you and the counselee(s) should agree on a course of action, including a schedule of future counseling sessions. Adams and other counselors recommend homework, activities to be accomplished by the counselees between sessions. Homework advances the progress of counseling and places responsibility squarely on the counselee(s).

Keep your goal in mind. To help counselees become healthy, responsible, Spirit-filled followers of Christ, several objectives must be achieved. Counselees must accept responsibility for their actions. Most counseling you encounter will involve sin. Adams rightly notes their need to repent, having acknowledged wrongdoing and demonstrating godly sorrow for their sin.[3] Go further, however, to help counselees stop destructive actions and develop biblical lifestyles.[4]

Many secular counseling methods focus on emotions, helping people feel better. Biblical counseling recognizes feelings are the product of behavior. Use Scripture to confront unbiblical behavior with a view toward repentance and change. Other methods focus on changing the belief system that produces behavior. Biblical approaches also emphasize repentance from sin and developing right lifestyles based on scriptural principles.

Recognize that people are incapable of changing themselves without God's help. God's Holy Spirit empowers His people to live in a way that glorifies Him. Paul acknowledges that God in us enables us to will and to do His good pleasure (Philippians 2:13). Charles Solomon teaches counselors to guide counselees ultimately into the Spirit-filled life in which Christ guides and controls the individual as He becomes the center of one's life.[5]

Follow through with various approaches until problems begin to be resolved. Space does not allow for extensive investigation of counseling techniques here. As you study biblical counseling books, make sure the author has solid bases in Scripture for his methods.

6. Bringing the Situation to a Satisfactory Conclusion

Once major problems are resolved, take deliberate steps to return the relationship to precounseling status. Before starting the counseling process, you were the counselee's pastor. Then, you became the counselor. Now you must go back to being the pastor.

In some cases, you may find it necessary to refer the counselee to another counselor or medical professional. If the person has medical problems, experiences hallucinations, or expresses issues beyond your ability to help, you should help bring the counselee into contact with a physician or a more advanced biblical counselor who can offer assistance.

In the case of referral, be sure the person you engage is committed to biblical counseling, is professionally competent, and is willing to work with you as the counselee's pastor. Help the counselees understand you are not abandoning them and that you will continue to minister to them as pastor.

> As you recognize the Great Physician has chosen to use you in helping His people, you can embrace this role and have the extreme privilege of seeing hurting people experience healing, sinful people find forgiveness, and wandering sheep return to God's green pastures.

Assure counselees that you remain available to them, but avoid setting up a situation in which they are tempted to manufacture problems to maintain dependence and contact with you.

Counseling involves some of the most difficult and painful aspects of people's lives. You may be uncomfortable with many of the issues brought to your office. You may wish to hand them off to someone else and avoid getting your hands dirty. Yet, God has placed these people into your care. As their shepherd, you do not have the option of ignoring them, especially when they need you the most. As you recognize the Great Physician has chosen to use you in helping His people, you can embrace this role and have the extreme privilege of seeing hurting people experience healing, sinful people find forgiveness, and wandering sheep return to God's green pastures.

Chapter 12

MARRIAGE IN A NEW MILLENNIUM

"Therefore shall a man leave his father and his mother,
and shall cleave unto his wife: and they shall be one flesh" (Genesis 2:24).

Marriage in the new millennium poses the possibility of joy and the difficulty of hard challenges for Next-Gen ministers. In contemporary culture, marriage happens later in life. Part of the reason is the mind-set of young adults. According to a study by the Barna Group, 82 percent of adults in their 20s anticipate being married, meaning 18 percent intend never to marry. Thirty percent are not sure about the validity of traditional marriage. Among young adults who intend to marry, 60 percent want to live with a potential spouse before marrying, eliminating one of the reasons for marrying at a younger age. Also, 69 percent want to be financially secure before marriage.[1]

Increasingly, couples will include interracial, interethnic, and interreligious pairings. Many will have met through an online dating service.[2] Their attitudes about morality and religious commitment (or lack of it) will have affected their sexual involvement prior to marriage.

Next-Gen ministers will encounter couples who are living together, some with children, who have no awareness that they have been doing anything wrong. Many will have had multiple sexual partners over the years. Pastors will be approached by same-sex couples wanting a Christian wedding (not to mention transgender issues). Even so-called normal couples will approach weddings with various sets of complications, included blended families. Many of the couples' parents will have been divorced. Blended families present interesting logistical questions, including deciding who will walk the Bride down the aisle.

Still, anticipating their wedding day, young Brides (and their mothers) imagine an event filled with happiness. They envision the beauty of a ceremony with a flowing white dress, bright flowers and burning candles, surrounded by stirring music, family, and friends. A wedding equates fulfillment of hopes and dreams.

Mothers of the Brides spend countless hours planning intricate details, while Fathers of the Brides spend countless dollars making it all possible. With the average wedding costing over $20,000, each new idea translates into added lines on Dad's credit card bill. While many weddings are much simpler (and less costly), the investment remains considerable.

Stress builds up as Mom and Daughter (and perhaps Aunt Sadie) have different ideas about wedding plans. Add the financial concerns, the logistics of managing relatives and friends coming to town (housing, food, time to visit in an already pressing schedule), and the inevitable unforeseen complications (with dresses, caterers, florists, photographers, and scores of other elements), and the ingredients are in place for tragic conflict.

Into this emotion-filled setting walks the pastor. He wants the ceremony to be done well, not only to fulfill the Bride's expectations but to honor the Lord. He wants the family's relationships to be strengthened rather than strained through the process. He wants the Father and Mother of the Bride to emerge from the wedding with fond memories, not financial disaster. He wants the Bride and Groom to establish a strong basis for a sustainable home, not just a service to tie the knot.

Some ministers dislike conducting weddings and spend little time preparing. They try to avoid the drama that often accompanies the family interactions while planning the ceremony. They generally use the same, short wedding service each time, often read verbatim from a published Minister's Manual. Such an approach does a disservice to the family, to the many people who will gather, and to the Lord.

Jesus demonstrated His sanction of marriage as He performed His first public miracle at the wedding in Cana of Galilee (John 2:1–2). Marriage has been part of God's plan for building the good and propagation of the human race since He gave Eve to be Adam's wife. God knew that it was not good for the man to be alone, so he created the woman and "it was good" (Genesis 2:18–25). Eve was not merely Adam's mate; she was his wife. "Therefore shall a man leave his father and his mother, and shall cleave unto his wife: and they shall be one flesh" (Genesis 2:24).

> Good shepherds invest in the couple through solid premarital counseling, serious preparation of a wedding sermon specific to the Bride and Groom, and intentional follow-up to encourage strong homes after the honeymoon ends.

The phrase translated "God made a help meet for man" (KJV) does not mean "help mate." The Hebrew word rendered *meet* actually means "suitable or corresponding to." Adam and Eve were what each other needed. Since God performed that first wedding in the Garden of Eden, marriage has recognized His hand in creating the foundational building block of the family.

Serious pastors recognize they have a responsibility to minister to a large number of people through wedding ceremonies. We have an obligation to insure the couple prepares themselves mentally, spiritually, and emotionally for their new lives following the wedding. We have an opportunity to proclaim God's idea of love and grace to the family and a multitude of friends who hear the wedding sermon.

Good shepherds invest in the couple through solid premarital counseling, serious preparation of a wedding sermon specific to the Bride and Groom, and intentional follow-up to encourage strong homes after the honeymoon ends.

Before the Wedding

1. Ask Yourself Some Basic Questions:

Am I Legally Empowered to Perform a Wedding in This Specific County and State? Some states require that a minister register with the county or parish court clerk prior to performing a wedding. A few states require pastors to obtain a certificate empowering them to conduct weddings. Regulations in some places allow ministers to perform weddings if they are merely licensed or ordained. The laws of the state where the wedding will take place, not the minister's residence, determine legal guidelines.

Weddings may not take place without a proper marriage license. Ministers should require the couple to present their license at the beginning of the rehearsal for the ceremony. Take note of the dates for which the license is valid. Some states have waiting periods between the time the license is issued and the wedding.

For Whom Will I Conduct a Wedding? Some ministers conduct weddings for anyone upon request. Such conduct demeans the ceremony and the ministry itself. A Christian wedding should reflect the Lord Who created marriage as a blessing for His children. It should not be cheapened by societal pressures to conform to contemporary culture.

Important questions to resolve include the following:

Are the Bride and Groom Followers of Jesus Christ? Decide in advance whether you will perform marriages based on the Christian faith of the participants. Scripture advises Christians not to marry unbelievers. "Be not unequally yoked together with unbelievers: for what fellowship has righteousness with unrighteousness? and what communion does light have with darkness?" (2 Corinthians 6:14). Based on this biblical principle, Christian young people would do well not even to date nonbelievers since dating leads to love and marriage. During counseling, the minister may be able to lead unbelievers to Christ but should be careful not to have someone make a false confession merely to be married.

This principle should not give believers an excuse to divorce non-Christian spouses. In fact, Scripture clearly advises them to maintain the marriage in hope that the husband or wife might be saved (1 Corinthians 7:13–15). Still, this situation applies to persons who are already married and does not provide grounds for believers entering a marriage with unbelievers. Paul was referring to persons who became Christians and whose spouse had not yet been converted.

Has Either Party Been Divorced? Another issue involves prior marriages. Obviously, if an individual's previous spouse has died, that person is free to remarry (Romans 7:3; 1 Corinthians 7:29). Scripture is clear, however, regarding divorce. God's plan is for a man and woman to remain married for life. To divorce and remarry results in adultery (Matthew 5:32). The sole provision Jesus made for divorce is sexual infidelity. Paul allows freedom for Christians whose nonbelieving spouses abandon them (1 Corinthians 7:15).

Some contemporary pastors make exceptions for divorce that takes place prior to salvation, but they have no biblical basis for such a position. Divorce is not the unpardonable sin. God's grace can certainly deal with all sin, including divorce. However, the Bible seems clear about God's standard for marriage.

Some pastors perform weddings for anyone, regardless of divorce. Others perform no wedding when one of the parties has been divorced. A biblical pattern seems to allow for marriage between Christians even if one has been divorced based on one of the two biblical exceptions. You will have to search God's Word and base your practice not on what is easy or popular but on the solid ground of Scripture.

Increasingly, Next-Gen pastors wrestle with this issue as they encounter more blended families. Also, as unchurched people compose a larger part of the population, more people grow up as non-Christians, divorce, become believers, and then want to marry. Ministers must come to a biblical position in relating to various situations they will encounter.

Is the Bride Pregnant or Has the Couple Been Living Together? In a sexually permissive society, ministers will commonly encounter people involved in unwed cohabitation, casual sexual liaisons, and other sinful activity. The Bride-to-Be may be pregnant or already have children. When asked to perform a wedding in such cases, pastors need to make decisions based on biblical foundations. Such a position honors God and is in the best interest of everyone involved.

Some ministers do not conduct any weddings if the Bride is pregnant or if the couple has been living together. This approach does not take into consideration Moses' statement: "And if a man entice a maid that is not betrothed, and lie with her, he shall surely endow her to be his wife" (Exodus 22:16).

Other pastors make no demands on the couple and simply perform the ceremony, thinking they are expressing grace. The latter position dangerously mistakes license for grace and does the couple and the congregation more harm than good.

A more biblical approach allows a wedding after the man and woman deal with their sin through confession and repentance. In one church, I encouraged the couple to make a public confession and repentance. They agreed and the church responded overwhelmingly with grace, love, and forgiveness. As a result, the couple was able to feel at home in the congregation and the church accepted them. Another byproduct of this approach was the example it set for other young people. Teenagers knew that sexual immorality was sin and should be taken seriously. At the same time, their congregation expressed biblical compassion, godly grace, and Christian love.

Are the Bride and Groom Active Members of Your Church? Often, people in the general community will ask a pastor to marry them. They want a church wedding but are not members of any church. Why should a church hold a wedding for nonbelievers? If the man and woman are Christians, they should be married in their own church under the authority of their pastor.

Some exceptions appear reasonable. One of the parties may have formerly been part of this church but moved away to go to college. It is natural for them to want to be married in their home church among their family and friends.

In a different scenario, a couple may be members of a very small church and anticipate a large wedding. Churches often accommodate one another. However, you should have sound policies concerning with what type of churches you will cooperate. For example, if the couple belongs to a church of a different faith and order from your congregation, hosting their wedding (much less performing the ceremony) could create an appearance of approving false doctrine.

Special Issues in Contemporary Culture

Participation: Couples are no longer content to experience the ceremony passively; they want to participate actively, from writing their vows to singing or playing instruments, to sharing their Christian testimonies. Wise ministers will guide the couple into prayerful planning of each element to insure the results honor the Lord and benefit everyone present.

Same-Sex Weddings: God's design for marriage is between a man and a woman. Increasingly, however, states and federal laws have created a conundrum for churches, individuals, and businesses regarding gay marriage. Christian businesses (such as photographers, florists, wedding consultants, caterers, lodging providers, and others) are experiencing lawsuits if they do not give equal service to all persons seeking a state-legalized marriage, regardless of the religious beliefs of the service providers. Churches also must decide how to address potential challenges to their positions on biblical marriage.

Pastors not only have to substantiate their practices as to conducting weddings, but churches may encounter legal challenges unless their policies clearly delineate who may hold weddings in their facilities. For example, if a church allows nonmembers to rent its facilities for weddings, homosexual couples conceivably could sue the church if denied equal access as heterosexuals. In addition, even if the church restricted its policies to include only members or family of members to use the facilities, a member could claim the right to use the church for a same-sex wedding. Some churches are using Alliance Defense Fund's definition of marriage, writing it into their church's bylaws for added support. Courts generally give churches wide latitude to determine its policies as long as the policies are clearly stated and consistently followed.

Covenant Marriage: Covenant marriage is a growing opportunity for biblically based marriages to find strong state support. Several states, such as Louisiana, formally endorse covenant marriage with legislation codifying the covenant relationship of a husband and wife. Covenant marriages begin on a more solid basis and tend to be more secure because of the deliberate nature of the marriage. Covenant marriage adds a legal contract between the wedded couple based on several provisions:

1. The couple must specifically sign an agreement that they are entering a covenant marriage.
2. The couple must participate in substantial premarital counseling prior to the wedding.
3. If the couple later contemplates divorce, they agree to engage in counseling to seek reconciliation before filing for divorce.

2. Set and Follow Wedding Policies

Instead of having to decide about every variable in each wedding, pastors benefit from having preestablished, biblical, practical policies. Your church may already have policies in place when you arrive. Be sure to review these documents to insure your agreement and work out any differences with the church. For example, one church's wedding policy stated that if a disagreement arose between the minister and a couple about some element of the wedding, then the deacons would make the final decision. What a terrible policy! No minister should submit his personal convictions to others, including the deacons. To minimize conflict, resolve such issues before a specific situation arises. Once personalities are involved, the problem becomes much more complex.

Common aspects of wedding policies include the following:

Who Can Perform Weddings? Will the church only allow its pastor and ministerial staff to perform weddings in its facilities? What about ministers of other churches of similar or dissimilar faith and order? What if the couple has a relative who is a minister but is not of the same faith? The policies should consider the kinds of situations that might come up and address each clearly.

Sometimes, the couple may wish a former pastor (possibly the pastor under whom they were saved or grew up) to conduct the wedding. Former youth or college ministers also tend to be requested as officiants. Unless the couple asks for a minister of a different faith or order from that of your church, this issue seems to be more one of church preference and policy.

Who Can Use the Church Facilities? The safest approach restricts the use of church facilities to church members and their families. Certainly, the church should not be used merely as a community center for anyone wanting a nice place to hold a wedding. The types of considerations related to officiants (above) can offer guidance regarding use of facilities.

Some churches require payment for use of the facilities. Church members may rightfully resent having to pay for use of their own church. Their tithes and offerings support the church. At the same time, extra costs for custodial service, musicians, sound technicians, and other expenses should reasonably be the responsibility of the couple or their families.

How to schedule weddings should be outlined in the policies. No one should be allowed to schedule a wedding without the approval of the pastor or his designee. To prevent putting the church secretary in the unenviable position of having to decide who can or cannot have a wedding, the policy should contain a wedding application form, which should offer the details of the wedding request. The pastor and staff can then review the application, perhaps after meeting with the couple, and approve (or disapprove) calendaring of the event.

Will You Use a Wedding Coordinator? Wedding coordinators can save the minister much grief and time. Inevitably, many of the details of the wedding become points of contention between family members, and sometimes the minister. A coordinator (either volunteer or paid) can help the couple work out the wedding plans, keeping in mind the church's policies and the pastor's preferences.

Will Premarital Counseling Be Required? Who Can Do Counseling? Wise ministers require couples to undergo premarital counseling. Some pastors counsel couples, while others delegate the counseling to others. When the couple lives a distance away (at college, for example), the pastor may enlist a trustworthy minister closer to the couple. Ministers who conduct the weddings for their own adult children also do well to have someone else do the premarital counseling.

Music Approval

Young Brides sometimes choose music based on sentiment rather than Scriptures. They may have a favorite secular song that has special meaning to them, yet it may be inappropriate for the worship service that comprises a wedding. Church policies should contain a method by which the couple submits prospective music to the pastor or the

Minister of Music for approval. A reasonable deadline should be set in advance of the wedding so musicians can be prepared.

Musicians: Church or Other? Paid?

Part of the discussion should involve who will provide music for the wedding. Members of smaller churches (and some larger churches) may expect the church accompanists to perform for the wedding, often without regard to remuneration. The policies should stipulate that enlisting the musicians (accompanists or singers) is the responsibility of the couple. A set fee schedule should be listed.

Florist and Photographer Issues

Florists need clear guidelines about what they can and cannot do in decorating a church facility for the wedding. Details should include prohibitions against use of nails, staple guns, or other instruments that would deface the church property. Candles should be placed so as not to drip on carpets or furniture. Use of rice (preferably birdseed or bubbles) should be limited to the area outside the church.

Similarly, policies should outline expectations for photographers and videographers. Most pastors do not like flash photography during weddings (not only by professional photographers, but also by guests). Movement by photographers or videographers during the ceremony can be distracting and should be avoided. Other guidelines should clearly delineate what they should and should not do.

Reception

While some couples host after-wedding receptions at a restaurant or country club, most families rely on the church facilities. Policies should address the availability of the kitchen and fellowship hall, expectations for caterers, and guidelines for cooking and clean up. Church policies should be clear if the church has prohibitions regarding smoking and the use of alcoholic beverages.

3. Conduct Meaningful Premarital Counseling

Couples whose marriages endure often comment about the value of solid premarital counseling. Requiring at least three or more sessions of counseling before the wedding can save many hours of marriage counseling after the wedding and prevent many heartaches along the way. Premarital counseling is not an opportunity for the pastor to deliver a series of mini-sermons; it should involve thoughtful discussions of specific issues.

While space does not allow a full instruction manual for effective premarital counseling, the following will offer a few tips. For further study, among the best resources for premarital counseling is Norman Wright's *Premarital Counseling Handbook*. Another resource is *Preparing for Marriage God's Way* by Wayne Mack.

My personal pattern for premarital counseling follows a three-session pattern. If additional issues emerge, we schedule more sessions to cover potential problems adequately. Following are the general outline of topics. Keep in mind, counseling is a discussion, not a sermon.

Session One

Relationship with Jesus Christ. Nothing is more important than the couple's relationship with Jesus. As mentioned previously in this chapter, the man and woman should be Christians. Unsaved people can become one physically, emotionally, and financially, but in the deepest aspect of human nature—the spirit—they can become one only if they have been born again, experiencing the regeneration of their spirit.

Marriage is challenging at best. Humans cannot succeed alone. Scripture declares, "Except the LORD build the house, they labor in vain that build it: . . ." (Psalm 127:1). The couple not only needs to be saved but walking with the Lord daily. Their dependence on God, shown in prayer and devotion, allows Him to empower and guide them in their interpersonal relationship, in raising children, managing a home, and other aspects of life.

Ask about their church involvement. If they come from different religious backgrounds, talk about theological differences based on scriptural truth. They need to commit to a solid, Bible-teaching church for personal growth, worship, and service.

Commitment to the Marriage. Ask, "Under what circumstances would you ever consider divorce?" While this may seem like a strange question for premarital counseling, you are establishing the level of commitment to the marriage. Unless each person is willing to make biblical commitments to one another, the relationship will begin on shaky ground. Do not wait until the statement of vows during the ceremony. Lead the couple to make their commitment to one another unequivocally. Share what the Bible has to say about marriage and the sacred nature of the home. If their commitments are based on their firm relationship with Christ, they will be more successful as they encounter challenges during the course of marriage.

Expectations. Norman Wright has a good section in his book, *Premarital Counseling Handbook*, concerning expectations the man and woman bring to their marriage.[3] In any relationship, unmet expectations provide the basis for most conflict. The husband may have trouble if he expects his wife to be a stereotypical housewife, raising children and cooking meals, while he goes out with his pals three nights a week and plays golf or hunts every weekend. Conversely, the wife may anticipate having a career of her own. She may imagine her husband and her coming home from work and sitting in front of the fireplace while chatting about the day's events. Likely, such a couple is destined for disappointment. Talk about their expectations of each other, the way they want to be treated, the manner of home they will have, career choices, habits, and other issues that might affect their home.

Session Two

Relationships with Parents. Never underestimate the importance of the couple's relationship with their mothers and fathers. Not only should each person have a good relationship with their potential in-laws but they benefit from positive backgrounds with their own parents. How a man's father treated his mother provides the role model, which will likely guide how he interacts with his wife. Similarly, a woman may have certain expectations for her husband, based on her experience with her father.

Communication and conflict resolution are two of the primary issues often passed down from generation to generation. If the husband-to-be comes from a family that did not talk much, especially about serious matters, he may have difficulty sharing deeply felt emotions. If the wife-to-be grew up in a family that enjoyed constant casual conversations, she may become frustrated with a husband who is more quiet and reserved.

Another issue involves parental approval of the marriage. While some cultures place more importance on the parents' involvement in choosing a husband or wife, every marriage is stronger when parents give their blessing. Respect for parents bears benefits in receiving encouragement and support for the new home being established.

Personality Issues. During courtship, men and women tend to be on their best behavior. Some personality traits emerge before marriage; however, the constant interaction of married life is a crucible that exposes the best and worst of human character. Pastors can help the couple recognize both good and bad personality tendencies in their lives. Ministers may use personality inventories, such as the DISC Personality Profile[4] to help the couple discover aspects of their natures and how they will interact with one another. (Several versions of this inventory can be found on the Internet. However, you should receive solid training in order to use the instrument responsibly.) At the same time, neither party should use such profiles as excuses for poor behavior. Remind them that they should yield to the Holy Spirit and allow His fruit to be expressed in their relationship.

Often, husbands and wives will have very different personality traits. While such differences may seem cute at first, they may get on each other's nerves over time. Particularly in times of stress, the negatives of personalities tend to emerge, often resulting in conflict. Help them to understand that God created them with each other in mind. Each has traits needed by the other. A task-oriented husband needs a people-focused wife to help him balance his interactions. A reserved wife may need an outgoing husband to help her expand her relationships.

Financial Management. Most young couples have no idea about what it takes to maintain a home. They think two can live more cheaply together than separately. Actually, marriage creates elevated expectations about the kind of home and lifestyle they will share. They may need help estimating costs of insurance, furnishings, utilities, start-up needs (someone has to buy the toilet paper!), and other items. A good homework assignment is for the couple to create a budget. If they have not lived on their own previously, they may need input from parents or married friends. You may have church members qualified to offer sound financial counseling so the couple does not create a debt-ridden, materialistic lifestyle.

Teach the value of the tithe. Demonstrate the biblical basis for honoring God with the tithe. Both Old Testament and New Testament clearly address the importance of giving in general and bringing the tithe into God's storehouse (the church). (See Genesis 14:20, Leviticus 27:30, Malachi 3:8–10, and Matthew 23:23.)

Discuss who will pay the bills and balance the checkbook. How much can each person spend without discussing the expenditure with the spouse? This question is not about who controls the money but establishes a mutual commitment for financial responsibility. Likely you will deal with dual income couples. If they see money as belonging to both of them, rather than "his and hers," they will have a more stable relationship as they manage finances.

Session Three

Decision Making. Scriptures plainly give the husband responsibility for being the spiritual leader of the home. However, if he uses this position to rule his wife rather than lead his family, he misunderstands God's plan. As the husband and wife submit to one another in Christ, the man will sacrificially love his wife as Christ loved the church, and the woman will submit to her husband in the Lord (Ephesians 5:21–25). They will discuss decisions in light of scriptural principles, not personal preferences. Prayerfully, they will seek God's guidance rather than blindly lurching about in their own desires.

> *As the husband and wife submit to one another in Christ, the man will sacrificially love his wife as Christ loved the church, and the woman will submit to her husband in the Lord (Ephesians 5:21–25).*

Sexual Relations. Most couples will have some level of knowledge regarding the intimate relationship between a husband and wife. However, pastoral counselors should not assume they possess a biblical or practical understanding of sex. Your job is not to provide sexual instruction, although you might refer them to helpful resources such as Tim and Beverly LaHaye's book *The Act of Marriage* or *Biblical Principles of Sex* by Robert Smith. Focus on teaching them what God's Word has to say about sex. They may be surprised that God gives principles regarding how husbands and wives can meet one another's physical needs.

4. Prepare the Wedding Ceremony

Identify Elements to Be Included in the Service

During the final stages of premarital counseling, discuss specific parts of the ceremony that you believe are nonnegotiables. The couple needs to understand that the minister is ultimately responsible to the Lord for conducting a worship service known as the Christian wedding. At the same time, encourage the Bride and Groom to share elements they would want; after all, it is their wedding. Approach their ideas with an open mind and try to accommodate them as long as their ideas do not conflict with Christian decorum or doctrine. Help them to imagine how each part of the service will flow into the next and decide what helps accomplish the goal of blessing them and honoring God.

Weddings may involve several elements: prelude; musical presentations; the giving of the Bride; testimonies; a charge to family and friends; the wedding sermon; prayers; songs; lighting a unity candle or, increasingly common in contemporary weddings, pouring a flask of unity sand, mingling colors as if mingling lives and hearts; declaring the couple to be husband and wife; the ceremonial kiss; recessional.

Ministers should discuss each with the couple, including giving special attention to the following:

Involvement of Family Members. Contemporary weddings increasingly involve blended families. Discuss the Bride and Groom's family issues to determine who will be present at the wedding, where each set of parents and grandparents will sit, and what roles various family members may have in the service. For example, if the Bride was raised by a stepfather and her biological father is present at the wedding, which man will walk her down the aisle?

In traditional weddings, the Father of the Bride participates in the giving of the Bride. In more contemporary ceremonies, both sets of parents sometimes participate in the giving of the Bride. Which option does the Bride prefer?

Music. Couples sometimes forget the religious nature of the wedding ceremony. They often want to include music that is not appropriate for a Christian service. Songs may be romantic and convey special meaning to the Bride and Groom, but they may not be conducive to worship and the Lord's House. Church policies should spell out the procedures for submitting vocal and instrumental music for approval well in advance of the wedding.

Vows. Increasingly, contemporary couples want to write their own vows. While each minister will develop his own approach, personally developed vows can be very meaningful. Still, the Bride and Groom should submit their vows (or anything else they want to include) to the minister so he can advise any changes and approve the final product. Allow the couple some freedom at this point, but then insist on inclusion of additional vows that spell out specific commitments important to a lasting marriage. Certainly lacking originality, these promises have a solid history in Christian weddings: "_____, do you receive _____ as a gift from God and do you promise to love, honor, trust, and serve him/her in sickness and health, in adversity and prosperity, and to be true and faithful to each other for as long as you both shall live?" I prefer the word "serve" to the word "obey" since it conveys the biblical relationship more properly.

Should You Include the Lord's Supper? One problematic trend in contemporary weddings involves including the Lord's Supper as part of the wedding. The Lord's Supper is a church ordinance (ordained by Christ Himself) that symbolizes His death—broken body, shed blood. It is shared by the church specifically to remember the Lord's death until He returns (1 Corinthians 11:25–26).

When incorporated into a wedding, the meaning morphs into a quasi-sacrament or diminishes into a representation of the couple's union with each other. The Lord's Supper is not a proper element for weddings. Leave the Lord's Supper to its proper role in the church, and let the wedding ceremony focus on the union of a new family in Christ.

Develop the Wedding Sermon

The minister must develop a sermon that complements the overall service. During premarital counseling, the pastor will learn much about the couple, if he does not already have a strong relational base. His sermon should be personal to this Bride and Groom, not merely a boilerplate, cookie-cutter, one-size-fits-all standard message. Begin with Scripture and bring forth the beauty of the marriage relationship, its love and commitments, that God's Word details. Now is not the time to preach about the wife submitting to the husband; if you have not already dealt with this important issue (and the husband's sacrificial love for his wife) in the premarital counseling, it's too late now! Still, the sermon can certainly include reminders of the commitments represented in the wedding vows, which "end honorably in the sight of God only by death."

Ministers may find plenty of useful Scriptures from Genesis' first marriage in the Garden to Revelation at the wedding feast of the Lamb. First Corinthians 13 is a wonderful text for a wedding sermon. Examples of godly marriages weave their ways throughout both Testaments and provide ample sermon fodder for the conscientious preacher.

Illustrations can range from beautiful poetry to lessons from life but should be appropriate in every instance. One contemporary problem is a trend of some young pastors to use illustrations or language with an element of crudeness. Perhaps they think being edgy adds to their image of being cool, but in reality their lack of respect to the Lord's office, house, and people reveals insensitive, unholy hearts. Others may simply employ language they have habitually used in common conversation, a problem in itself. In any case, ministers of the Gospel represent their Lord in wedding worship. Everything they say and do should glorify Him.

Often, Christian couples will want the Gospel presented in the wedding ceremony, perhaps even sharing their testimonies as a witness for Christ to family and friends, many of whom will be lost and in need of Jesus. Even if they do not specify the Gospel element, ministers can find appropriate ways to share the Good News in the course of the sermon and ceremony at large. Keeping in mind the nature of the service is a wedding not a revival, the wise pastor will clearly show that "if the Lord build not the house, they labor in vain who build it" (Psalm 127:1).

Conducting the Wedding Rehearsal

Blessed is the minister who has a wedding coordinator or an associate pastor who can manage the wedding rehearsal for him. However, most pastors will have to perform this responsibility themselves. A general outline for an effective wedding rehearsal might follow this pattern:

- Have a list of participants in advance.
- The Bride and Groom have the responsibility of insisting that everyone involved in the wedding be present and on time for the rehearsal and the wedding.
- Have the groom give you the wedding license at rehearsal.
- Ask everyone to be seated and explain the procedures of the rehearsal and the wedding. Go over the order of service for the wedding. Everyone should have a printed copy.
- Instruct musicians, ushers, and candle lighters of their responsibilities.
    o Musicians should be ready, dressed appropriately, and in place well in advance of the beginning of the service. Music is timed so that the Bride enters at the time advertised for the start of the wedding.
    o Ushers should know how to guide and seat guests. Friends and family of the Bride generally are seated in the left side of the sanctuary (left side as you face the platform), while the Groom's guests sit on the right side. When the time is right, ushers will

seat the Groom's grandparents, then the Bride's grandparents, then the parents of the Groom, and, finally, the Mother of the Bride. No one is seated after the Bride's mother takes her seat.

o   Candle lighters usually will have long instruments of brass to use in lighting candles. They should carry small lighters in their jacket pockets in case their instrument's flame is extinguished. If the ceremony employs a unity candle, candle lighters will stand at the front of the sanctuary and give their instruments first to the parents of the Groom, who light the single candle on the right of the unity candelabra, then to the parents of the Bride who light the single candle on the left. (Following which, the Father of the Bride exits in order to walk his daughter forward in the bridal march.)

- Position all the participants as they will stand when the processional is completed (as the wedding party faces the minister).

o   The minister will stand front and center between the stage and the pews.

o   The Groom stands in front of the minister's left hand. The Best Man is the Groom's right.

o   The Groomsmen will take positions from floor to stage on the right side of the platform (as the congregation faces the stage).

o   The Bridesmaids will enter (either alone or with the groomsmen) and take places on the left side of the platform.

o   The Maid or Matron of Honor will enter and stand to the minister's right.

o   The Ring Bearer will enter bearing symbolic rings (not the actual rings) tied to a pillow.

o   The Flower Girl will enter prior to the Bride.

o   If the Ring Bearer and/or Flower Girl are very young, they will do better having a seat with a parent on the front row of seats after they complete the processional.

o   The Father of the Bride will enter with the Bride on his left arm. He will stop directly in front of the minister, with the Groom to his right hand.

o   At this point, some contemporary weddings have both sets of parents join the couple for the giving of the Bride, for really, these parents give their children to the Lord Who gives them to each other as His good and perfect gifts.

o   After the minister asks, "Who gives this woman to be married to this man," or a similar statement, the Father of the Bride (or in modern cases both families) will respond.

- o Some ministers include a charge to the family and friends at this point. They remind the audience of their responsibility to support and pray for this new family being created in their presence.
- o After a prayer, the father (or families) takes a seat and the minister leads the couple, Best Man, and Maid/Matron of Honor to the center of the platform.
- Walk through wedding service from that point to the recessional. Include prayers, songs, candle lighting or sand pouring, sermon and vows (without having the couple actually saying "I do" or actually pronouncing them to be man and wife).

Note the **position of a kneeling bench**, if used. A single kneeling bench generally is positioned so the kneeling Bride and Groom have their backs to the audience. The minister may stand behind the bench during the entire ceremony. This position can appear awkward and can be solved by using two kneeling benches facing each other. In this way, a kneeling Bride and Groom face each other, with their profiles toward the audience.

At the end of the rehearsed ceremony, have the wedding party exit as if in recessional. The minister remains on the platform until everyone in the party (including parents and grandparents of the Bride and Groom) exit the sanctuary. In the actual service, at this point he may thank the audience for their attendance and invite them to the reception, urging them to proceed to the reception area where they family will join them after brief photos.

Line everyone up and rehearse the entrance as if in processional. Do not repeat the ceremony rehearsal, but walk through the recessional again. Inform the wedding party and the parents and grandparents of the couple that after the actual recessional, the wedding party should go to a side room and wait for guests to go to reception hall so the wedding party can get back into sanctuary quickly for photographs. (Do as many photos before the ceremony as possible.)

The Ceremony

While preparations leading up to the actual ceremony may seem hectic at times, if everyone fulfills responsibilities competently, the wedding day should flow graciously. If the church has a wedding coordinator (paid or volunteer), she will manage many of the details related to positioning and preparing the wedding party, musicians, ushers, candle lighters, and others. The minister's responsibilities may be outlined as follows:

- Make sure the custodian has the church open on time for the day of the wedding for florist, caterers, wedding party, etc.
- Show up. Show up early. Greet people, but don't get in the way.
- Dress appropriately. A dark suit with conservative tie or a ministerial robe is generally preferred to a tuxedo, depending on the couple's wishes. If they want you to wear a tuxedo, the groom should bear the expense of providing a rental.
- Shine your shoes. Get a haircut. Watch your personal grooming, giving special attention to your breath.
- Make sure you have the marriage license and the sermon with you.
- Candle lighters begin lighting candles fifteen minutes before the start of the ceremony (with the start of music).
- Ushers seat guests as they arrive. Just before the ceremony begins, ushers seat the Groom's grandparents, then Bride's grandparents, then Groom's parents, then Mother of the Bride. No one is seated by an usher after this time. If a unity candle is present, the parents of the Groom and the parents of the Bride will light the appropriate single candles upon their entrance and prior to being seated.
- On cue, lead the Groom, Best Man, and Groomsmen into the sanctuary.
- Stand before the center of the platform on the ground level. The groom will be at the minister's left hand. The Best Man will be to Groom's right hand (as the wedding party faces the minister). Groomsmen will stand on stairs to the minister's left.
- At the processional, Bridesmaids will enter center aisle or aisle to the minister's right and proceed to their places on the stairs. Maid/Matron of Honor will stand to the minister's right opposite the Best Man. The Flower Girl and Ring Bearer will enter and then be seated with their parents. (By the way, never, never, never put the real rings on the Ring Bearer's pillow. They may end up lost!)
- At the first measure of "Bridal March," the Mother of Bride stands, followed by the congregation. The Bride's father (or other escort) enters with Bride on his left arm. They stop in front of the minister for the giving of the Bride. After giving of the Bride, the minister may give a charge to the family and friends and/or offer a prayer.
- Proceed up the stairs to the stage for ceremony.
- If a single kneeling bench is used, stand behind the bench. If a double bench is used, stand in front of bench during ceremony and move behind it for prayers.

The Wedding Sermon

Don't be very long, but don't be too short. About fifteen to twenty minutes for a message is good. Be personal. Make each ceremony unique to each couple. Include information about their Christian testimonies.

Exchanging Vows

Whether the couple writes their own vows or uses the minister's choice of vows, they generally do better repeating the vows a phrase at a time, led by the minister. Even the brightest Bride and Groom can forget memorized vows in the stress of the moment.

Exchanging Rings

The Best Man will have the Bride's ring; the Maid/Matron of Honor will have Groom's ring. At this point, the Bride will hand her bouquet to the Maid/Matron of Honor, meaning the latter has two bouquets and a ring to handle. Ask for the Bride's ring first. Speak about the meaning of the rings. A typical statement found in many ministers' manuals reads: "The purity of the metal symbolizes the purity of their love for each other. The unending circle represents the vows and commitments they have made to each other which end honorably in the sight of God only by death." Hand the ring to the Groom and have him repeat vows as he places it on the Bride's ring finger. Repeat with Groom's ring.

Unity Candle or Sand Globes

After the exchange of vows and rings, the minister usually will pray. Afterward, during a song, the couple moves to the unity candle. Each takes the appropriate candle, lights the unity candle, and blows out the individual candles. If sand globes are used, the Bride and Groom take the globes with the different colored sand and mix them together in the common globe at the center of the arrangement. At that point, the couple returns to kneeling bench and kneels in prayer until the song concludes.

Bible Presentation

The church may wish to buy a nice family Bible for the couple. The minister can present it at the kneeling bench (having placed it there before the service.) The Bible is left on the bench until after the service.

Pronouncement

After leading in a final prayer, the minister makes the pronouncement, "Upon your having made these vows and exchanged these rings as indication of your vows, by the authority of God and the state of _____, I now pronounce you husband and wife. What God has joined together, let no one put asunder. You may kiss your Bride." At end of ceremony, move to the side of the Groom (Minister-Groom-Bride) and introduce the new couple: "It is my pleasure to introduce to you for the first time, Mr. and Mrs. _____."

The Recessional

Upon the pronouncement, the instrumentalist will begin the recessional music.

- As the recessional is played, the Groom and Bride exit, followed by the Best Man and Maid/Matron of Honor arm in arm, followed by pairs of Groomsmen and Bridesmaids who come to the center of the platform, descend the stairs together, and exit.
- Ushers escort the Mother of Bride out of the sanctuary first, followed by the Groom's parents, the Bride's grandparents, and the Groom's grandparents.
- The minister remains at the front of the stage after everyone has exited. On behalf of the family, he thanks the guests for coming and gives them instructions about exiting to the reception.
- After the congregation has gone, the minister escorts the wedding party back into the auditorium for pictures. Prior to the service, the couple should work with the photographer and videographer to insure the post-wedding photography does not take very much time so the family can join the reception promptly.
- If the marriage license requires signatures of witnesses, have predetermined persons sign at this time.

After the Wedding

- ***BE SURE TO SIGN AND SEND BACK TO THE CLERK OF COURT ALL NECESSARY PAPERS (signed marriage license) ON TIME.*** Most courts require the signed document be submitted within ten days of the ceremony. Check the document for the due date and the place where it should be sent. You may want to make a photocopy of the signed document in case the original is lost in the mail.

- Do not look for or ask for an honorarium. If the minister is offered a gift, accept it graciously. You may want to give any wedding honoraria to your wife and let her use it for something in the house or use it to take her out to dinner. This is a nice gesture since she has given up two of her nights with you away from home.
- Two or three weeks after the couple returns from their honeymoon, the minister and his wife should visit them in their home or have them to your home.
- Help the couple adjust to life and church as marrieds. Remember, many of their friends may still be in the singles' Bible study or Sunday School groups. They may need help integrating into their new roles, make additional friends, and begin service in the church together.

Weddings should provide great joy to everyone involved. While some difficulties inevitably occur, at the end of the day the minister will sense a feeling of fulfillment for his role in creating a new home.

Chapter 13

CONDUCTING CHURCH ORDINANCES

The Bible describes two rituals we call ordinances of the church. Unlike the term *sacrament*, which suggests God's grace is bestowed through the ritual, we use the word *ordinance* because Jesus ordained the church observe them. Scripture includes two ordinances: baptism and the Lord's Supper.

Baptism

"And Jesus, when he was baptized, went up straightway out of the water: and the heavens were opened unto him, and he saw the Spirit of God descending like a dove, and lighting upon him: And a voice from heaven, saying, This is my beloved Son, in whom I am well pleased" (Matthew 3:16–17).

The New Testament details two kinds of baptism: the baptism of John the Baptist and baptism associated with the New Testament Church. John's baptism represented repentance. When Pharisees and others desired John to baptize them, he demanded evidence suitable for repentance (Matthew 3:8). On the other hand, when Jesus requested baptism, John said Jesus did not need his baptism (Matthew 3:13–17).

The Meaning

Jesus' death, burial, and resurrection changed the nature of baptism for the Christian Church. Paul described baptism in this way: "Therefore we are buried with Him (Christ) by baptism into death: that like as Christ was raised up from the dead by the glory of the Father, even so we also should walk in newness of life" (Romans 6:4).

We are not saved by baptism. The thief crucified beside Jesus was not baptized, but Jesus assured him that as the man had expressed faith in Jesus, he would join Christ in paradise that very day (Luke 23:43). Baptism does not wash away sin; only the blood of Jesus cleanses us from sin (1 John 1:7; Hebrews 9:13–14). Baptism symbolically portrays our identification with and acceptance of Jesus' death, burial, and resurrection. It also represents our own death to an old way of life and resurrection in Christ to a new way of life.

The Method

Consequently, the method of baptism is immersion. In fact, the Greek word translated as *baptize* literally means "to immerse." Some of the Protestant Reformers continued the practice of sprinkling or pouring as methods of baptism as an accommodation, but such methods do not describe death, burial, and resurrection.

The Candidate

Since baptism represents a person's salvation through the death and resurrection of Christ, the candidate for baptism must be someone who has been saved. An infant should never be baptized because an infant cannot repent of sin and believe on Jesus (Acts 3:19; John 3:16). The idea that baptism replaced circumcision as the sign of covenantal inclusion has absolutely no foundation in Scripture. Allusions to family members being saved (such as that of the Philippian jailer in Acts 16:30–34) are spurious because the text includes no evidence that the jailer's household included an infant. In fact, Acts 16:32 describes Paul speaking the Word of the Lord not only to the jailer but to the entire household, which would have included the servants as well as his family. When they were baptized, all had repented and placed their faith in Christ. Paul would not have participated in anything contrary to his clear teachings on baptism in other Scriptures.

What about People Who Desire to Be Rebaptized?

Sometimes you will have people who have already been baptized ask to be rebaptized. Biblical baptism of believers by immersion is appropriate if the persons were not saved when previously baptized. Also, if they had not been baptized by in biblical manner (infant baptism, sprinkling, pouring), proper baptism is appropriate. Such is not rebaptism since the previous acts were not biblical baptisms. In addition, if persons were baptized in a church of a different faith and order in which the meaning of baptism and salvation are different from your church, then biblical baptism would be proper. Such cases might include baptism in churches that believe baptism is part of salvation or churches that believe you can lose your salvation.

Some people desire rebaptism for the wrong reasons. Often someone who has been saved, but has sinned greatly, will desire baptism. Such an individual misunderstands its meaning. Help the person realize the need is not for baptism but for repentance and a renewed walk with Jesus.

Some people may want to be rebaptized to show unity with a family member who has been saved and is being baptized. Teach them that their support can be shown in other ways. Do not change the meaning of the ordinance for sentimental reasons.

Maintain the high meaning of baptism. Believers in closed countries risk their lives in order to follow Christ in baptism. Do not demean such sacrifice by lowering the standards or special nature of obedience to Jesus in baptism.

Practical Issues

- Have a Baptismal Committee prepare the baptistery. Arrange the changing rooms and prepare the candidates. Have towels and robes available.
- Have private changing areas for males and females.
- Have adequate robes or extra clothing for the minister. Many ministers wear baptismal waders underneath their robes so they don't have to change clothes after baptism.
- Instruct candidates on the meaning and method of the baptism. Demonstrate how the procedure will be conducted. Assure persons who are afraid of water.
- Candidates should bring change of clothing and a handkerchief. Have extras on hand.
- Have a family member present with minor children.
- Include a way for the candidate to make a public statement of faith, either by answering a question or by preparing a recording of the candidate's faith story.
- Baptize females first. It takes longer for their hair to dry.
- Invest in a baptismal bench. This simple fiberglass seat will save years of back pain.
- Do not "dunk" candidates; bury them slowly, gently, under the water.
- Scheduling baptism at the beginning of the service encourages others who may be considering their need for salvation and are concerned about baptism.
- Include an introduction and conclusion in order to share the meaning of baptism and encourage others to be saved and follow Jesus in baptism.

The Lord's Supper

"For I have received of the Lord that which also I delivered unto you, that the Lord Jesus the same night in which He was betrayed took bread: And when He had given thanks, He broke it, and said, 'Take, eat: this is my body, which is broken for you: this do in remembrance of me.' After the same manner also He took the cup, when He had supped, saying, 'This cup is the new testament in my blood: this do, as often as you drink it, in remembrance of me.' For as often as you eat this bread, and drink this cup, you show the Lord's death till he come"
(1 Corinthians 11:23–26).

You cannot understand the Lord's Supper without studying the Passover. On the night Jesus instituted the ceremony we know as the Lord's Supper, He and the disciples were celebrating the Passover. Passover began in the prelude to the Exodus from Egypt. God decreed that the firstborn of every household of the Egypt would die. Only those homes displaying the blood of a sacrificed lamb would be spared. When the angel of the Lord saw the blood on the door lintels, he passed over those homes (Exodus 12).

After Israel escaped Egypt, God instituted the Passover feast (also known as the Feast of Unleavened Bread). The feast forever reminded the Jewish people of God's miraculous and gracious deliverance. However, they did not understand that God's greatest salvation was not from Egypt but from sin. This salvation also came at the price of the blood of a Lamb—the Lamb of God, which takes away the sin of the world (John 1:29).

Passover included a meal whose components represented various aspects of the Exodus experience. For a fuller explanation, see presentations of Christ in the Passover through such websites as Jews for Jesus, Friends of Israel, or other organizations such as Chaim.

When the meal was over, Jesus took a piece of the unleavened bread, broke it, and gave it to the disciples to eat. He said it represented His body, broken for them. This bread was not simply food for the supper. It bore special significance. Called the "afikomen" today, it was one of three pieces of unleavened bread used in the Passover meal. Even today, Jews see the afikomen as representing the Lamb. It is not eaten during the Passover feast but is set aside "for Messiah." Jewish tradition teaches Messiah would come during a Passover celebration.

So, what bread was left over at the end of the Passover? What bread did Jesus take and break, representing His body? It was that which was set aside for the Messiah. In using this piece of bread (matzo), Jesus was declaring Himself to be the Messiah.[1] The broken bread represented His body that would be broken for our salvation.

Jesus also took a cup of the "fruit of the vine" and gave it to the disciples. This wine could not have been fermented since no yeast (leaven) was allowed inside the house during Passover. What cup was it? A series of cups was used during the supper. The final cup is the cup of redemption. Modern Jews employ a fifth cup, called the cup of Elijah, but whether four or five, the element of redemption through the Messiah is present. Jesus took up the last cup, the cup of redemption, and said, "This is my blood of the new testament, which is shed for many for the remission of sins" (Matthew 26:28). He was introducing another part of this object lesson we call the Lord's Supper—His blood established a new covenant as He redeemed us through His blood.[2]

The Meaning of the Lord's Supper

The Catholic Church teaches a doctrine called transubstantiation. They believe when the priest speaks certain words, the bread and wine are transformed into the literal body and blood of Jesus, bestowing grace to whoever eats it. Martin Luther introduced a variation of this idea, which he called consubstantiation. He believed that while the elements did not become the physical flesh and blood of Christ, the blood and body of Jesus become literally present alongside the bread and wine.

> *Nowhere in Scripture does God indicate grace comes through communion. It was not the cup, but Jesus' blood that was given for the remission of sins.*

However, the Lord's Supper is an ordinance, not a sacrament. Nowhere in Scripture does God indicate grace comes through communion. It was not the cup, but Jesus' blood that was given for the remission of sins. The Lord's Supper, then, is symbolic, representing Jesus' broken body and shed blood, His sacrifice, which makes salvation/redemption possible. Paul referred to Jesus as "our Passover," clearly indicating Jesus fulfilled the Passover (1 Corinthians 5:7).

Who Can Participate in the Lord's Supper?

Through this Supper, Jesus commanded His followers to celebrate a remembrance of His death until He comes again (1 Corinthians 11:23–26). Since it is symbolic of salvation and memorial in nature, only believers should partake of the Supper. Some churches practice "closed communion," allowing only members of each church to participate. Other churches accept "open communion," allowing any baptized believer in Christ to join in the Supper. Still other congregations follow "close communion" in which participation is limited to persons baptized in churches of like faith and order (whose doctrines follow their own).

A few people may decline to participate because they do not feel worthy. They read Paul's admonition to the Corinthians (who were abusing the Supper) to examine themselves lest they take of the Supper "unworthily" (1 Corinthians 11:28). The word *unworthily* describes the manner in which the Supper is received. In other words, we should not partake of the symbols of Christ's body and blood in a flippant, casual manner. Remind people that none of us are worthy of Christ's sacrifice. He gave Himself as our substitute on the cross strictly because of His loving grace and mercy.

The Method of Celebrating the Lord's Supper

While a few churches include the Lord's Supper in every worship service, the Bible does not specify the frequency or occasion of its celebration. Jesus merely said, "When you . . ." assuming they would but not commanding when they would observe the Supper. Many churches have the Lord's Supper every three months, often alternating between Sunday morning and Sunday evening services.

Whenever you observe the Supper, do not merely add it to the end of a worship service without thought or planning. Elevate the Supper by making it central to the service. Select music and other elements of worship that focus people's hearts on Jesus and His sacrifice for our salvation. Preach strong messages about sin and salvation, lifting up our Redeemer Jesus! Explain the elements within the context of the Passover so believers can understand Christ's fulfillment of all prophecy regarding the sacrificial atonement.

Practical Suggestions

- Have a committee of deacons purchase and arrange the elements prior to the service. You may use prepared wafers purchased from a Christian bookstore, or you might use actual matzo available in the Jewish food section of many grocery stores.
- Train the deacons how to distribute the elements. In larger churches, servers may be assigned to certain sections to expedite distribution.
- The pastor and other worship leaders should work together to plan a cohesive worship experience featuring the Supper.
- If distributing the bread and cup separately, follow Jesus' example of asking God's blessing prior to each distribution. Remind people what each element represents.
- Throughout the service, maintain the dignity demanded by the solemn observance.
- Congregations typically end the service by imitating the disciples' singing of a hymn (Matthew 26:30).
- Following the service, the committee may dispose of leftover bread and juice. They should not be concerned that they are throwing away holy elements. Remember, these elements are symbols, not sacraments.

Chapter 14

FEEDING THE FLOCK:
YOUR TEACHING AND PREACHING MINISTRY

"Preach the word; be instant in season, out of season;
reprove, rebuke, exhort with all longsuffering and doctrine" (2 Timothy 4:2).

Are there prophets in the land today? Is there anyone who can respond when people cry out for a Word from the Lord? To hear modern pundits and ecclesiastical critics, you might think the role of preacher/prophet has no place in this society. Dialogues and dramas parade in the guise of proclamation in pulpits across America. Too many ministers think preaching belongs to the nineteenth century, not the twenty-first.

Some pastors think of themselves as communicators instead of preachers. They believe people prefer talks rather than sermons. Your self-concept greatly affects the way you go about the holy business of speaking to God's people. Do your people perceive you as a herald of God or simply as a source of nice ideas gathered from the latest self-help books? Do you begin with perceived needs in the audience or Spirit-directed Scripture? Do you use the Bible only as a starting place to give credibility to your personal thoughts about the topic of the week, or does your message resound with "Thus saith the Lord" because the message comes from His Word?

John R. Stott claimed, "Preaching is indispensable to Christianity," in spite of contemporary objections due to an "anti-authoritarian mood" in postmodern society, the revolution of information and media, and a seeming "loss of confidence" in the Gospel by the world and, in some cases, by churches and their ministers.[1]

Now more than ever, our world needs men of God who will "stir up the gift" and preach God's Word with conviction (2 Timothy 1:6). As James S. Stewart declared, "Surely in this immensely critical hour, when millions of human hearts are besieged by fierce perplexities, when so many established landmarks of the spirit are gone, old securities wrecked, . . . when the soul is destined to meet, amid the crash of old beliefs, the ruthless challenge and assault of doubt and disillusionment; when history itself is being cleft in twain, and no man can forecast the shape of things to come—the Church needs men who, knowing the world around them, and knowing the Christ above them and within, will set the trumpet of the Gospel to their lips, and proclaim His sovereignty and all-sufficiency. . . . Preach Christ today in the total challenge of His high, imperious claim. Some will be scared, and some offended; but some, and them the most worth winning, will kneel in homage at His feet."[2]

Power for Preaching

The best preacher cannot create power for preaching. Bryan Chapell eloquently states, "No amount of homiletical skill will substitute for the Spirit's work. . . . Sermons succeed when the Holy Spirit works beyond human craft to perform His purposes. However, only the most arrogant servant will impose on the Master's goodness by anticipating blessing for shoddy work. We serve best when we not only depend on the Holy Spirit to empower our words, but also craft them so as to honor Him."[3] We are dependent on the Holy Spirit to illuminate the Scripture, anoint the preacher, proclaim Christ, convict the hearer, and glorify the Father.

> *We are dependent on the Holy Spirit to illuminate the Scripture, anoint the preacher, proclaim Christ, convict the hearer, and glorify the Father.*

The Holy Spirit Aids Sermon Preparation

Misconceptions about the role of the Holy Spirit abound. Some preachers think dependence on the Spirit conflicts with personal preparation in advance of preaching. They rely on Matthew 10:19b–20: ". . . Take no thought how or what you shall speak: for it shall be given you in that same hour what ye shall speak. For it is not you that speaks, but the Spirit of your Father which speaks in you." However, the context for this passage relates not to preaching, but persecution. Note the previous verses: (17–19a): "But beware of men: for they will deliver you up to the councils and they will scourge you in their synagogues; and ye shall be brought before governors and kings for my sake, for a testimony against them and the Gentiles. But when they deliver you up . . ."

Certainly, without the power of the Holy Spirit, our words fall to the level of nice advice at best. Only the Holy Spirit can convict the hearers of sin, righteousness, and judgment. Only the Holy Spirit can guide pulpit and pew into truth. Only the Holy Spirit can infuse the preacher with God's anointing and create of him a herald of God. Even the mighty Paul confessed his absolute dependence on the Holy Spirit: "And my speech and my preaching were not with enticing words of man's wisdom, but in demonstration of the Spirit and of power: that your faith should not stand in the wisdom of men, but in the power of God" (1 Corinthians. 2:4–5).

The Holy Spirit Anoints the Spirit-Filled Preacher

As Jesus began His ministry, He claimed the anointing of God's Spirit. "The Spirit of the Lord GOD is upon me; because the LORD hath anointed me to preach good tidings unto the meek; . . ." (Isaiah 61:1). As Jesus preached, people recognized He spoke with power and authority, unlike the scribes and Pharisees (Mark 1:22).

While no one can be anointed in the same way as Christ, the Anointed One, every preacher should seek God's power before preaching. Jerry Vines described the anointing of the Holy Spirit as "the spiritual fervor that flows through a man in the preaching event. . . .He preaches with inspiration and fullness of thought. He has both freedom and simplicity of utterance."[4]

No truly effective preaching takes place aside from the presence and power of the Holy Spirit. Homiletical orators can stir minds and emotions, but only the Holy Spirit can convict people of "sin, and righteousness, and judgment" (John 16:8). Theologically astute pulpiteers may instruct congregations regarding biblical truths, but only the Spirit of truth will guide them into all truth (John 16:13). Preachers may inspire listeners with dramatic stories of their experiences, but only the Holy Spirit can bring Jesus to bear on their hearts as He testifies of Christ alone (John 15:26). Evangelists can use persuasive techniques to move audiences to action, but only the Holy Spirit can draw the lost to salvation through Christ (John 6:44).

> *No truly effective preaching takes place aside from the presence and power of the Holy Spirit.*

The Power of God and Prayer

Paul asked believers to pray for him that "utterance may be given to me, that I may open my mouth boldly, to make known the mystery of the gospel, for which I am an ambassador in bonds: that therein I may speak boldly, as I ought to speak" (Ephesians 6:18b–20).

We not only depend on others' prayers for us, but we recognize that powerful preaching needs a praying preacher. If our prayers lack passion and perseverance, they will lack power. We begin by making prayer a priority in our personal lives. Schedule appointments with God, beginning early in the morning. Be consistent in your time with the Lord, resisting intrusions by other good, but less important activities. May we desire God's power for God's people through powerful, persistent prayer that He might be honored and His people touched with His Spirit.

Preparation for Preaching

"Study (be diligent) to show yourself approved unto God, a workman that need not be ashamed, rightly dividing (correctly interpreting) the Word of Truth" (2 Timothy 2:15).

Did Isaiah spend twenty hours a week preparing each sermon? How many books did Amos have in his library? Did Paul write manuscript sermons and memorize them or did he preach extemporaneously. (I wonder what he might have done if he had a word processor?)

The demands of a changing world offer temptations to today's prophets that Micah never knew. Endless hours are required for administration, visitation, and civic responsibilities. Combined with the voluminous publications of sermons and study resources, these duties form a strong lure to attract the preacher from diligent preparation of messages.

Beside the obviously unethical practice of plagiarizing sermons, some ministers simply rob the flock of an effective presentation of God's Word through a lack of personal preparation. Proper groundwork for preaching goes far beyond a Saturday night perusal of one's favorite commentary. More pointedly, preparation for approaching the pulpit supersedes the mere study required for any one sermon!

Pray that men of God would halt before the pulpit until they have brought their hearts before the purging fire of the Spirit and been cleansed by Christ's blood of any matter that offends the Herald of Truth.

Haddon Robinson recalled William Quayle's definition of preaching. When asked if the art of preaching was not found in the making of a sermon and delivering it, Quayle responded, "No, that is not preaching. Preaching is the art of making a preacher and delivering that."[5] Declaring a Word from God requires a man of God who knows the Lord, walks with Him, listens to Him, and faithfully shares what he has heard from Him.

Preaching begins with the personal preparation of the minister spiritually, intellectually, emotionally, and physically. Without diligence in this discipline, the herald of God not only will disappoint his hearers but he will fail the One Who commissioned him to speak.

Preparation begins by **confession of personal sin**. To stand before people who wait for a touch of the Holy while harboring sin within one's heart is the deadliest of endeavors. Many pastors confess to being convicted by their own sermons about some sin that had been passed over in their lives. People in the pews usually can tell when the pastor is not speaking in the fullness of the Holy Spirit. Not only does the preacher falter in his words, but his message loses its divine impetus and the holy mantle falls aside.

I heard it said of D. L. Moody that he hesitated while crossing a street one day and would not move until he had prayed, confessing a sin that had brought a shadow between him and the Most Holy. Pray that men of God would halt before the pulpit until they have brought their hearts before the purging fire of the Spirit and been cleansed by Christ's blood of any matter that offends the Herald of Truth.

The problem for some ministers is not overt sin but a shortage of **prayer**. They rush from task to task and then into the worship hour without taking time for deep communion with the Father. Prayer is imperative if the preacher is to receive a Word from God week to week. Prayer is also required to prepare the congregation to accept the Word. Meditation on the scriptural text helps expose the meaning and application of the Word to the preacher. Intercession for the hearers opens their hearts, plowing and breaking up fallow, hardened ground so the precious seed may be planted successfully. May the prayerless preacher find repentance for his sake and that of his congregation before another Sunday passes!

Personal preparation also includes the **intelligent study of the Word**. Notice I did not say *intellectual* study. Many of God's prophets are not great scholars. Yet God blesses even simple minds with the ability to study the Scriptures intelligently so they might "rightly divide the word of truth" (2 Timothy 2:15).

Enough helps are available even to poorer preachers that none should lack the tools to examine the Word thoroughly. Bible software, lexicons, concordances, word studies, commentaries, and other resources abound. They can help trained and untrained preachers to understand scriptural meaning. Nothing will substitute for personal wrestling with the text, and books cannot eliminate the necessity of the illuminating work of the Holy Spirit. Still, the Spirit can lead the preacher to utilize such tools in exploring the truth of God's Word.

The effective preacher devotes significant preparation to **the sermon itself**. Some homiletics experts strongly believe that a sermon should be written out, memorized, and delivered. Others feel an outline is sufficient to have on paper if the message itself has been fleshed out in the preacher's mind. Extemporaneous preachers prefer the free-flowing stream of conscience preaching from a simple text and a basic idea.

The anointing work of the Holy Spirit is not limited by advance preparation. In fact, while He occasionally leads a preacher away from his prepared message, the Spirit can just as easily inspire the pastor while he prepares. If the truth is known, many pulpiteers who boast of their lack of preparation "so the Spirit can have His way" are merely excusing laziness in preparation. This practice demonstrates a low view of inspiration, an attitude of indifference toward the Scriptures, and a lack of respect for the people.

Stuart Briscoe writes, "Slothful sermonizing begins with haphazard exegesis of the Scripture—reading a verse or two and stating the obvious. When we only circle our subject, our lack of preparation shows." He adds, "Laziness also manifests itself in careless content. Little illustration and vague application convey that there's been little preparation."[6]

167

> *Faithful is the minister who has such high regard for God that he prepares his own spirit, who has such a love for the people that he intercedes for them to receive the Master's instructions, who has such a respect for the Scriptures that he will use every available tool to study the Word and prepare the sermon, and who has such an understanding of his own limitations that he will set personal priorities in order to be at his physical, mental, and spiritual best when he stands before the congregation as a herald of God.*

A final area of preparation is the **physical condition of the pastor.** Homileticians are unanimous in their concern for the physical dimension of preaching. If a man comes to Sunday with a hoarse throat because he spent Saturday yelling for his favorite sports team, if he comes to the pulpit tired because he stayed up late the night before with worldly entertainment, if he cannot come within arm's length of his sermon notes because of gluttonous eating habits, that preacher is less able to be used of God.

Faithful is the minister who has such high regard for God that he prepares his own spirit, who has such a love for the people that he intercedes for them to receive the Master's instructions, who has such a respect for the Scriptures that he will use every available tool to study the Word and prepare the sermon, and who has such an understanding of his own limitations that he will set personal priorities in order to be at his physical, mental, and spiritual best when he stands before the congregation as a herald of God.

Sermon Planning

The Holy Spirit not only guides the preacher in the preparation of a sermon but He leads in preparation of a series of sermons. Sometimes the Lord may give His herald one message at a time. At other times, He lays out a longer plan for preaching. Ministers who prayerfully think through God's leading in advance will find greater freedom in preaching as they give the Holy Spirit more time to lead them into His truth.

Some pastors of larger churches take two or three weeks in the summer to plan an entire year's worth of sermons. Most preachers do not have such luxury. They fight for time to serve the needs of a congregation with limited resources or staff. However, most ministers discover that planned preaching actually saves time.

Sermon series, particularly expository preaching through various Bible books, tends to expedite preparation. You do not have to research biblical context and backgrounds every week if you are preaching through the same biblical book for several Sundays at a time. Time is also saved in deciding what to preach each week since you have already planned the sermon series under the leadership of God's Holy Spirit.

Planning may begin by noting special days in the calendar. If the preacher is working through Leviticus, the people expect him to focus on Christ's birthday at Christmas, the resurrection on Easter, and the value of godly motherhood on Mother's Day. Sometimes the sermon series can coincide nicely with special days. At other times, a one-week diversion from the regular series takes advantage of special emphases. Knowing when these days occur helps the pastor plan his preaching.

Prayerfully consider the broad needs of the congregation as you choose a text. You may not know all that is going on with the people, but the Holy Spirit does. This approach does not devolve into needs-centered preaching; it simply means you are aware of the audience as you seek the Spirit's guidance in deciding on which Scripture to focus.

Develop a Sermon Garden. Andrew Blackwood urged preachers to develop a sermon garden.[7] Whenever you run across Scripture passages that capture your attention, write down your preliminary thoughts. The full sermon may not be germane to the current season of preaching or the complete thought may not be ripe for picking. The sermon garden contains several sermons in various stages of development but handily available for the preacher to return from time to time and cultivate along the way. They will be ready when the time for delivery comes.

The Substance of Preaching

"Preach the Word" (2 Timothy 4:2).

How do you decide what to preach? Human needs? Current interests? Where do you start? The congregation? Yourself? God? What is your source? Your own ideas? Books? Other people's sermons? What is your subject? Contemporary issues or God? Is all preaching really preaching? Paul declared, "We preach not ourselves, but Christ Jesus the Lord . . ." (2 Corinthians 4:5).

Some seeker-sensitive pastors depend on **topical preaching**. In this style, the sermon is built around a subject. The idea may come from the Bible or elsewhere. The problem with topical or needs-based preaching is it assumes the preacher knows more about what the people need than God, that his ideas are superior to the Word of the Almighty. Some topical sermons sound good, but they generally follow the speaker's thoughts rather than the biblical text.

Here is an example of a topical sermon:

The Power of God
- God's Power Is Greater than Any Other Power
- God's Power Is More Glorious than Any Other Power
- God's Power Is More Giving than Any Other Power

While the outline is good and the points are true, they do not reflect the contextual truth of Scripture.

Other preachers prefer the **textual sermon**, which is based on one or two verses. The main theme and divisions come from the text. The sermon expounds what the text says. However, by using only one or two verses, you risk using texts taken out of context. Consider this example:

The Power of the Lord (Luke 5:17)
- God's Power Is Present
- God's Power Is Potent
- God's Power Is Persuasive

In this brief outline, you can identify several ideas connected with the text but miss much depth contained in the context (Luke 5:16–26). In another example, many sermons have been preached about Philippians 4:13, generally encouraging people they can do anything through Christ. Actually, the text is part of a larger context (Philippians 4:10–19). Paul was emphasizing how he learned to be content whether in prison or palaces, in want or in abundance, because Christ enabled him to do so. While textual sermons can be approached from an exegetical methodology, they often miss the larger truth of scriptural context and, thus, misinterpret the meaning of the text itself.

Next-Gen ministers increasingly have been embracing **expository preaching**. David Platt, Matt Chandler, and Steve Gaines are examples of pastors who start with the scriptural text and fully explain its context and meaning while making practical application to their hearers' lives. God calls us to preach the Word, carefully handling the Word of truth (2 Timothy 2:15). Expository preaching insures the sermon remains true to the intent of the human writers and the divine Author.

> *The main point of expository preaching is that the source is the Word of God, which is opened to the people with clarity, order, and integrity.*

Some people push back against expository preaching. However, most objections are not really toward expository preaching but bad expository preaching that lacks practical application, prefers old stories to living illustrations, or gets bogged down in unnecessary detail.

Sidney Greidanus says, "At heart, expository preaching is not just a method, but a commitment, a view of the essence of preaching, a homiletical approach to preach the Scriptures."[8] The primary issue is not the form of the sermon (points and subpoints or the use of alliteration) or the length of the text. The main point of expository preaching is that the source is the Word of God, which is opened to the people with clarity, order, and integrity.

Robinson defines expository preaching as: "the communication of a biblical concept derived from and transmitted through an historical, grammatical, literary study of a passage in its context, which the Holy Spirit first makes vital in the personality of the preacher, and then through him applies accurately to the experience of the congregation. As a result the congregation has an experience with God through the accurate application of the Word energized by the Holy Spirit which conforms them more to the image of Christ."[9]

God warned people not to listen to prophets who did not speak His Word. "Do not listen to the words of the prophets who prophesy to you, filling you with vain hopes; they speak visions of their own minds, not from the mouth of the Lord. . . . **Let him who has my word speak my word faithfully**" (Jeremiah 23:16, 28; cf. 27:14, 16, emphasis added).

Sydney Greidanus reminds us, "The prophets were keenly aware of the fact that the word was God's word not theirs. God . . . put His words in their mouths" (Jeremiah 1:9).[10] Similarly, in the New Testament, Paul wrote, "And we also thank God constantly for this, that when you received the Word of God which you heard from us, you accepted it not as the word of men, but as what it really is, the word of God, which is at work in you believers" (1 Thessalonians 2:13).

Pastors who seek to expose the Word of God faithfully must consider various factors of biblical interpretation to insure each statement reflects the intended meaning. Stephen Olford urged preachers to stay true to biblical preaching that is accurate historically, contextually, grammatically, linguistically, and doctrinally.[11]

Take a look at a brief example of the main points of a short expository outline:

The Power of the Lord (Luke 5:16–26)

1. The instrumentation of power is prayer, v. 16
   - Jesus prayed intimately (by Himself)
   - Jesus prayed intensely (in wilderness)
   - Jesus prayed intentionally (before the need arose)

2. The Source of power is the Lord, v. 17a
   - Power comes from Him (of)
   - Power belongs to Him (of)

3. The result of power is redemption, vv. 17b–25a
   - Jesus redeemed the man spiritually (he was forgiven), v. 20
   - Jesus redeemed the man physically (he was healed), v. 24
   - Jesus redeemed the faith of those who believed, v. 20

4. The goal of power is God's glory, vv. 21–22, 24, 25b–26.
   - In the midst of faith, there are those who doubt, vv. 21-22
   - In the midst of doubt, Jesus demonstrates faith's power, v. 24
   - In the midst of faith's power, God is glorified, vv. 25b–26

In this sample, each idea comes from the text. Moreover, the complete context of the biblical narrative is included. In fleshing out this outline, each point would derive substance from exposition/explanation of the various verses, application of the truth to the hearers, and illustrations that would shed light on each. In addition, each major point could be expanded in several ways, following the intention of the text and the application to life.

Excellent expository preaching uses the details of the text to derive deeper understanding of the truth. Details should not distract the preacher from the main point. Life application and living illustrations help hearers understand how to apply the biblical truths personally.

Preaching through Bible Books

Not all expository preaching requires preaching through books of the Bible. A stand-alone sermon based on a reasonable pericope (scriptural thought block) can be the basis of an expository sermon as long as the message comes from the text. Still, preaching the whole counsel of God requires systematically guiding the congregation through God's Word.

While preaching through Joshua in a series on leadership and change, I wrestled with the Holy Spirit as the story of Rahab approached. What did a prostitute's narrative have to do with the topic? Surrendering to God's direction, I delivered a message that showed how God used Rahab to protect His servants, and also how, as a result, God blessed this former harlot and made her part of the Messiah's ancestry. He is the God of the second chance. After the sermon, a young woman tearfully approached and said, "I am Rahab. Tonight I learned God might be able to use someone like me." I had no knowledge of her background, but God knew her need and directed the sermon for her if for no one else.

Can you grow a church preaching through Bible books, especially outside the Bible Belt? Vance Pittman was a young church planter with a freshly minted seminary degree when he moved to Las Vegas to begin a new church. He believed in preaching through Bible books while making strong applications relevant to his people's lives. Beginning with seventeen people, his church attendance grew to over 1,700 in just a few years.

If you choose to preach through a book of the Bible, **read the book repeatedly**. Make it your friend. Then **study the book thoroughly**. Harold Bryson recommends answering several questions about the Bible book, including the following: "Who wrote this book? To whom was this book written? When was the book written? From where was the book written? What literary genre did the book follow?"[12] (By the way, his book, *Expository Preaching*, remains the best work on preaching through books of the Bible.)

Think about each of these questions:

1. **Who wrote the book** (on a human level)? What was he like? Can you find information about his personal history and personality? What was his relationship with God and with the people to whom he wrote? Get to know this person as an individual, not merely a historical name. The more you understand the author, the better you will be able to interpret his writing.

2. **When was this book written?** What's happening in world at this time? The Bible was not written in a cultural vacuum. Get a history book and study the world scene during this period. Comprehend the influences of events that impacted the writer and his audience.

3. **Where was the book written?** What was this place like? Get sufficient information about this place (culture, geography, politics, spiritual dimensions) to understand the environment in which the writer penned the book.

4. **Why was this book written?** What prompted the author to set pen to papyrus (or parchment)? What was his purpose? What did the Holy Spirit want to accomplish? Remember, while each Bible book had a specific audience, God's ultimate intention was to speak to His people throughout the ages. Consider the eternal truths within each section of Scripture. Note application to yourself and your people as well as to the people of the biblical era.

5. **What kind of book is this?** Hermeneutical guidelines for interpreting poetry will be different from historical books. Epistles (letters) vary from apocalyptic writings. Understanding figurative language, such as in the Psalms or the Revelation, requires study of symbolism common in the writer's culture.

6. **Who are the people who read this book first?** Where did they live? What's going on with them? Until you know something about the people who received the Scriptures, you likely will not be able to make the transition of applying scriptural truth to your congregation today.

7. **What other Bible books relate to this one?** If you are studying Kings, you should also read Chronicles. Understanding an epistle like Philippians requires reading about Paul's involvement in Philippi as recorded in Acts.

8. **What are the issues in this book?** Pastor and Evangelist Bob Pitman[13] uses a notepad with several columns to help him study a Bible book. Each column details specific information from the text:

- **People**—Note the names of people mentioned in the text. Use the immediate context and other biblical references to learn as much as possible about these people. Commentaries can help at this point. Try to relate aspects of these people to contemporary culture. Do you know anyone like Barnabus? Diotrophes? David?

- **Places**—Jot down places that are mentioned. Look them up on a map from the biblical era. Consider the geography (By the Sea of Galilee? On a trade route? Rural or urban? Hebrew, Greek, or Roman?) Ask, "What about this place helps us understand the people?"

- **Events**—What events are going on? Passover? Wars? Ask, "How do these events help us understand how the people interact with God?"

- **Key Words/Phrases**—While you may include familiar passages (such as "With God nothing is impossible") avoid taking phrases out of context. Ask, "What do these words mean in the original setting and how do they relate to people today?"

Divide the Bible book into sections comprising complete thoughts. Haddon Robinson recommends dividing the book into thought blocks (pericopes) and sections.[14] Too often, preachers launch forth through a book without considering where they are going or how long it will take to preach through the book. Expository preaching does not involve simply stopping at whatever verse hits twelve o'clock one week and beginning with the next verse the following week. Expository preaching requires thoughtful deliberation of the entire book as a whole. It views sermons from each pericope as independent messages, yet at the same time each discourse should be integrated into the complete series.

Stages in the Preparation of an Expository Sermon

Most pastors love to preach. A few love to prepare. Without thorough preparation, your preaching will be shallow at best. Paul advised his preacher-boy Timothy: "Study to show yourself approved unto God, a workman that needs not be ashamed, rightly dividing the word of truth" (2 Timothy 2:15). The word *study* means "to be careful or diligent." Preaching is work. Properly declaring the Word of Truth requires comprehensive investigation of the text, proper definition of your purpose, and dynamic proclamation of the message.

Sermon development rarely follows a static series of steps. Like any living thing, it is organic, growing in your heart and mind until it is mature. Still, having a plan helps any preacher work through the biblical text and fashion a message worthy of hearing. The following stages lay out a typical path of preparation.

Stage One: Spend Time with God in Prayer and Private Devotion

We cannot overemphasize the preacher's dependence on prayer. Someone might develop personal communication skills that enthrall eager listeners, but only the Lord can transform sinners into sons and daughters of God.

Pray to connect with God.

Pray for cleansing. Invite Him to reveal your heart. Join David in praying: "Search me, O God, and know my heart: try me, and know my thoughts: And see if there be any wicked way in me, and lead me in the way everlasting" (Psalm 139:23–24).

Pray for clarity. Trying to understand ancient texts can be challenging. The Holy Spirit will guide you into truth (John 16:13). Ask Him for wisdom, and He will give it freely (James 1:5).

Pray for the congregation. Interceding for the people is not only a basic responsibility of a good shepherd but it helps the preacher study the text with specific individuals in mind.

Stage Two: Determine the Text

If preaching through a Bible book, the plan you developed for the series of sermons will guide your choice of text. Otherwise, you must decide week by week what text should be the source for each message. Beware of starting with an idea and then searching for a text to support your own thoughts. Biblical preaching starts with God's Word. Let the Holy Spirit draw the truth from the text and guide you into the key idea for each sermon.

The text must be large enough to include the complete thought block and immediate context. At the same time, if the pericope is too large, the congregation and the preacher can become lost in information overload. Some narrative texts are long by necessity. However, the focus for this specific sermon may be selected verses within the larger text, allowing the preacher to tell the story while concentrating on specific truths along the way.

Stage Three: Investigate the Text

Study the Context

If a sermon involves a single verse, or part of a verse, the text stands in danger of being misinterpreted. One preacher used Philippians 4:13 to develop a sermon about having a positive mental attitude that leads to visionary action. While this idea is nice and worthy, it does not represent the meaning of the text. The context of the verse involved the apostle Paul's ability through Christ to live contentedly in whatever state he found himself, whether abundance or adversity.

Begin your study of the text by considering its **broad context**. If you are preaching through a Bible book, you will have already considered the issues of who wrote the book, to whom it was written, and when, where, and why it was written. If you are preaching a single sermon separated from a series, consider the questions mentioned by Harold Bryson in the previous section. Put faces to the people. Understand what kind of personalities they were. Consider the geography, architecture, and customs that affect your comprehension of the biblical setting.

Study the **immediate context**—the thought block or pericope containing the sermonic text. Notice specific emphases. Watch for the flow of ideas. The more you can observe about the text, the deeper you can delve into its truth.

Refer to any **corollary contexts**. If you are preaching from Matthew, are there other Gospel writers who chronicle the same narrative from different points of view? What additional details of the account can be found in related passages? For example, if preaching from Psalms, find historical accounts in Samuel's writings that help you understand the background and context of the particular Psalm in your sermon.

Study the Parts of the Passage

Examine each word. Be careful not to overlook the small words (prepositions, conjunctions, adjectives, and adverbs). Often modifiers and connectors dramatically transform the meaning of a passage.

What kind of language did the writer employ (Literal? Figurative?) What specific Greek or Hebrew or Aramaic word did the author use? If you have not studied the languages, a good Bible software that keys individual words to Strong's Exhaustive Concordance can help you identify the original word within the passage. Use word study books or Bible software to investigate the term's meaning in this particular verse. Vine's *Expository Dictionary of Old and New Testament Words*, Robertson's *Word Pictures in the New Testament*, and the *Theological Wordbook of the Old Testament* are only a few of the many resources available to a serious student of the Word.

Analyze the Structure of the Passage

Structural analysis cannot easily be used for narrative passages but offers wonderful aid in understanding the meaning of a didactic text and identifying component ideas of the passage. Notice how words relate to each other. How did the writer express certain ideas in relation to other ideas? Are there comparisons or contrasts? Can you see lists of qualities, actions, names, or other items?

As you place the passage in analytical form, each word or phrase relates to the other words in the sentences. Stephen Olford's *Anointed Expository Preaching* and other homiletics books offer good examples of structural analysis. This format helps you visually identify word relationships, lists of modifiers or explanatory phrases, and other key ideas. When reading Scripture in paragraph form, you might overlook related ideas in the long flow of words, particularly in Pauline passages. Putting the text into an analytical structure allows ideas to explode off the page.

Beside the analysis, write down definitions of words, identification of persons and places, and sermonic ideas that emerge along the way. Later, as you develop the body of the sermon, word groupings may form the various points and subpoints. If preaching narratively, you may employ ideas gleaned from the analysis as descriptors of characters in the story, action in the plot, or observation about the development.

Stage Four: Develop the Idea

Once you accurately understand the text, determine and develop the idea for the sermon. A sermon may have two expressions of the central idea: the **textual idea** and the **sermonic idea**.

The **textual idea** is the timeless truth found in the biblical thought block you are studying for each sermon. Haddon Robinson called it *The Big Idea*. Jerry Vines and Jim Shaddix referred to the CIT—Central Idea of the Text. Harold Bryson used the term ETS—Essence of the Text in a Sentence. The important point is that you clearly understand the primary idea that the text expresses. If you cannot express this concept in a single, clear, concise sentence, you probably need to spend more time analyzing the passage.

The **sermonic idea** refers to how you plan to address the eternal truth of the textual idea. How will you approach this particular idea in this particular sermon for this particular congregation on this particular day? A single text can find thousands of means for expression. You can approach different parts of the text with varying emphases. The sermonic idea is the homiletical hook on which you will hang the elements of the message.

Some Next-Gen preachers build their sermons around innovative object lessons or interesting illustrations. Be careful not to fall into the trap of making the message fit the idea rather than deriving the idea from the text. The sermonic idea cannot simply be cute or unique; it must appropriately represent the sentiment of the text.

The sermon may contain additional **supportive ideas**, but these points develop the primary idea. If you have many ideas, no one will understand what you are trying to say. Each point and subpoint, every illustration, all application, and the textual exposition should center on the single key idea for this sermon.

Stage Five: Determine the Proposition and Objective

Formalize the textual idea into a **proposition**. Communicators who embrace postmodern philosophy dislike propositional truth. They prefer to tell a story and let the listeners deduce whatever application suits them. Preachers of the Word recognize God has something to say to every generation. "His truth endures to all generations" (Psalm 100:5).

Every Scripture and every sermon contains an idea the speaker wants the hearer to understand, believe, and act upon. That timeless idea is the **proposition** and the action to be taken based on that truth is the **objective**. Clearly state the proposition in a single sentence. As you develop various points and subpoints, you simply are laying out what the text says about the main idea (proposition). Every aspect of the sermon explains, amplifies, proves, or describes the primary proposition.

The **objective** is a simple statement as to what you want the listeners to DO about the main idea. Your objective may include a knowledge goal ("I want my people to know Jesus rose from the dead"), but information alone is insufficient. What action do you want them to take as a result of that knowledge? ("I want my people to live with hope because Jesus rose from the dead.")

Your objective must be consistent with the proposition. With the proposition in mind as you begin and with the objective in mind as you work toward the conclusion and decision, each part of the sermon will develop harmoniously and effectively. Sermonic unity emerges from focusing on that specific proposition for this text and this sermon with a view toward accomplishing a particular objective.

Stage Six: Design the Structure

Most preachers are accustomed to the idea of sermonic points—having several main points and a few subpoints for each main point. Remember, the sermon should have ONE key point, which is the proposition. The main points should all support the key point. If the various ideas are not integrally related to each other and to the key idea, the people will not follow you and exit the sanctuary confused about what you want them to do. Similarly, any subpoints should support those main points to which they relate.

Craft each point and subpoint in simple, memorable ways. Some preachers like to alliterate the points to aid memory. However, do not feel like you must alliterate. If you use alliteration, do not force an inappropriate word just to find an alliterated sound. People in the pew are more interested in understanding what you have to say than in the cleverness with which you say it.

How you present the message may be the difference in people hearing and heeding the message or not. Consider what type of body development best accomplishes the sermon's objective. The text itself offers the best guide. Some passages immediately suggest a **listing** style. For example, Colossians 1:12–20 might focus on **reasons for giving thanks to God**:

1. He made us to be partakers of the saints' inheritance
2. He has delivered us from the power of darkness
3. He has translated us into the Kingdom of His Son
4. He has redeemed us through Christ's blood
5. He has made peace through the blood of the cross
6. He has reconciled us to Himself through Christ

Another approach to the same passage might concentrate on reasons why Jesus should be preeminent in all things:

1. Jesus is God's dear Son
2. Jesus is our Redeemer
3. Jesus is the Image of the invisible God
4. Jesus is the Firstborn of every creature
5. Jesus is the Creator of all
6. Jesus is the Head of the Church
7. Jesus is the Firstborn of the dead
8. Jesus is the fullness of God

On the other hand, a passage like Ephesians 2:1–22 lends itself to a **comparison/contrast** style of development:

We Were	We Are
Dead in trespasses and sins (v. 1)	Made alive in Christ (v. 5)
Walking according to the world (v. 2)	Sitting in heaven with Christ (v. 6)
Fulfilling lusts of the flesh (v. 3)	Created in Christ unto good works (v. 10)
By nature children of wrath (v. 3)	Reconciled by God's peace (vv. 14–16)
Far off, without Christ (vv. 11–12)	Brought near through Christ's blood (v. 13)
Aliens from the covenants of God (v. 12)	Fellow citizens with the saints (v. 19)

Other types of development include two-point sermons such as problem–solution or question–answer. These forms can also be combined using a listing style for the main points and a two-point style for subpoints.

Whatever style of development you choose should follow the natural flow of the text. Do not force the text into three points and nine subpoints, each alliterated. If the sermon lends itself to beginning points with the same letter or sound (alliteration), that is fine. However, some preachers choose ill-fitting, confusing terms simply to achieve a certain style.

Stage Seven: Expose the Text, Apply the Truth, and Illustrate Both

Develop the Exposition

Truth for life comes from the biblical text. The words are the very Word of God. Don't rush into a sermon based on a quick glance at the surface meaning. Dig deep. Ask the Holy Spirit of Truth to guide you as you consider the parts of each sentence. Be careful not to base your interpretation on individual words or phrases apart from their relationships in the sentences and the sentences in each paragraph and each paragraph in each pericope.

Word studies conducted in the investigation stage are helpful not only in understanding the meaning of the text but in conveying that meaning to your listeners. Many terms are word pictures in the original languages. They paint portraits full of scenes, characters, and concepts. However, words undergo a change of meaning depending on how they are used. Combine your explanation of the words, ideas, people, places, events, and other aspects of the text as you develop the sermonic points.

Word pictures, such as metaphors and similes, aid visualization of the scene and the emotional response of the hearer. Jesus used both narrative and imagery in His preaching. Drawing upon familiar scenes and experiences from everyday life, Jesus related profound spiritual truth in understandable, relevant ways. For example, He likened the Kingdom of God to a sower, to a fisherman, to a field with hidden treasure, to a field with various types of soil, to a pearl of great price, and to a tiny seed that grows into a great plant.

Effective sermons use **imagery, illustration, and application** that capture the hearers' imagination and emotions. People who listen to well-told stories visualize the characters and action. They enter the story and experience multisensory aspects of the biblical account. If the preacher refers to "the stench of the garbage dump that was Golgotha," people not only hear what is said, but they remember what a garbage dump smells like, which triggers a response as if experiencing the smell again. They envision the nasty nature of the site where Christ was crucified, enhancing their revulsion of His humiliation.

Each point and subpoint and every application and idea must emerge from the foundation of textual exposition. Otherwise, you are merely sharing human ideas rather than proclaiming God's Word. Resist the temptation to rush into application before developing a firm basis from the text.

Direct the Application and Exhortation

Understanding the biblical truth provides the foundation for your next stop along the sermonic journey. People need to know what to do with that truth. How does this text impact their lives? How can they apply this principle in their homes, workplaces, schools, and everyday life?

Today's audiences value experiential truth. They want to see, hear, touch, and taste it. John wrote that what he shared about Christ was not an esoteric concept, but "That which was from the beginning, which we have heard, which we have seen with our eyes, which we have looked upon, and our hands have handled, of the Word of life; . . . declare we unto you, . . ." (1 John 1:1–3).

Next-Gen preachers may lean toward passages that easily find practical application in life. They commonly develop series of sermons on marriage and family, financial stewardship, success in business, and overcoming worry and stress. However, every biblical truth, all of the biblical text, is practical, applicable, and experiential. The challenge for the preacher is to show the congregation HOW it applies.

Some preachers excuse their resistance to doctrinal preaching because they do not see how various doctrines find practical expression in the average person's life. Does the preacher genuinely think God's truth is not practical? Or that the roles and gifts of the Holy Spirit cannot be applied to life? Does the biblical teaching about Christ, the cross, atonement, salvation, resurrection, and imminent return not impact believers in real life?

The key to developing strong application from each text is to discover the timeless truth presented by the text. The preacher then considers the question: what difference does this truth make in my life? If he can't answer that inquiry for himself, he certainly cannot do so for his people.

Exhortation makes the difference between teaching and preaching. Both approaches involve applying the truth, but the preacher goes further to exhort listeners to follow through with action. It is not enough for hearers to understand how a truth may apply to their lives; they need to actualize the truth. Exhortation is an **urgent appeal** for people *to accept* what the text requires. Exhortation is a **sincere encouragement** that people *can do* what the text requires. Exhortation is an **earnest incitement** of the heart and mind, motivating people *to put the application into practice*.

Exhortation is emotional, mental, and, most of all, spiritual. It not only employs the emotional dynamic of the speaker but (as with Aristotle's *pathos*) moves the emotions of the hearers. Yet, exhortation is not solely an exercise of the emotions. People's emotions wane with time. In addition, their minds must understand and accept the application as true and appropriate for their lives. Still, reasoning alone will not change a person's life.

Mental and emotional appeals undergird the primary appeal, which is spiritual. Only when people's hearts are moved will substantial change occur. The Bible uses the term *heart* to include not only the human's mind and emotions but the spirit as well. (See 2 Timothy 2:22, Hebrews 3:10, and 1 Thessalonians 3:13.) Ultimately, the Holy Spirit works in the preaching event to convict the hearer's spirit and moves the person to apply God's truth to life.

Describe Exposition and Application with Illustrations[15]

(Part of this section originally appeared in *Preaching* magazine under the title "The Curious Case of the Illusive Illustration." Copyright 2009. *Preaching*. The content was written by Dr. Jere Phillips. Used by permission.)

Creative preachers might employ object lessons, videos, skits, and other techniques to illustrate a message. Many pastors rely on personal experiences, church history tales from seminary, or Scripture passages to illustrate their sermons. Some desperate clergy cling to "10,001 Illustrations from the Annals of the Dead Preachers Society" or search Internet sites filled with tired old retreads or spurious stories of doubtful veracity. No wonder congregations cringe whenever the new pastor begins a tale they have heard time and again. They politely laugh at the right time to make him feel better, but privately they wish he would be more original.

How do you build a resource base of illustrations that are powerful, appropriate, and living? Too many preachers spend hours at the last minute tracking down illustrations rather than enjoying the fruit of a garden that has been tended through the years. How can you maximize your sermon illustration resources? Here are a few tips:

Begin with a database. Contemporary preachers use a plethora of electronic gadgets to keep up with e-mails, text messages, Internet resources, and daily appointments. Yet they fail to employ the most basic tools to store and retrieve vital illustrations, leaving them to a Saturday-night search through old *Reader's Digests* for last-minute material.

While Microsoft Access, Logos software, or other databases are excellent tools for categorizing sermons and illustrations, many pastors need something simpler and easier. Microsoft Excel is a fine alternative. It is simple, easy to use, and highly efficient. Excel uses rows and columns of cells into which any amount of text can be applied.

When you find a good illustration, determine which topic it describes. Type the topic into a cell in the first column of an Excel worksheet. Excel allows selected sets of cells to be alphabetized. Being able to sort illustrations by topics in alphabetical order puts all your material into easily accessible order.

Into the cell of the second column, type the name of the speaker. Record the source of the illustration with bibliographical information in the third cell. The fourth column allows you to note the date you found the illustration so you can cull old illustrations from your database.

The illustration itself goes in the fifth column. It can be typed or copied and pasted from another location, website, e-mail, or document. (*Hint*: Paste copied data into the active cell of the formula bar to avoid having information placed in multiple cells.) The illustration can be as large as you need without unduly distorting the appearance of the worksheet. Simply format the cell to "wrap text." If the height of the row becomes unwieldy, format the row height to "13."

Hyperlinks provide another option for larger illustrations, scans of magazine articles, sections of books, maps, or pictures. Simply save the scan, jpeg picture, or other material into a Word document or other file. Right-click on the active cell into which you want to create the hyperlink, and click on "hyperlink" in the drop-down menu. This simple box allows you to hyperlink the cell to the document saved elsewhere on your computer.

Put the date and place you use the illustration into the sixth cell. You may want to use the illustration again, but not at the same church. People may forget your sermons, but they will remember good illustrations. Finally, if you want to associate this illustration with a particular biblical text, type the textual reference into the seventh column.

As you add rows of illustrations, you can find illustrations by alphabetized topic or by searching for specific words within an illustration. Using the edit function of Excel, click on "find" and simply type the key word you are hunting.

You can view the entire illustration by clicking on the active cell. The formula bar will open a box with the whole text available for viewing, editing, or copying and pasting into a Word document containing your sermon outline.

Develop Strong Illustrations

1. **Personal illustrations** can be powerful if used with discretion. People are touched by the transparency of a preacher who is not afraid to be vulnerable. However, no congregation wants to hear about the preacher and his family every week. Also, no minister's family likes being the source of sermon fodder Sunday after Sunday. Try depersonalizing and universalizing personal experiences. Instead of saying, "Last weekend my son and I were on a hunting trip and . . . ," try this: "Have you ever been on a hunting trip with your son and . . ." You are able to translate the personal experience into a common life situation with which many of your people can relate. The anecdote becomes their story, not just your story, evoking memories and emotions.

2. **Historical illustrations** can be useful provided they do not require contextual knowledge. Any reference to a historical event or character should be self-contained if possible, making the point whether the hearer knows the historical context or not. Preachers wanting to connect with postmodern hearers will not limit themselves to church history, since most listeners will not be familiar with pages from seminary textbooks.

3. **Biblical illustrations** are useful, but are best if self-explanatory. A biblically illiterate congregation may not understand references to Hagar or Haggai. If you use Gomer in trying to describe unconditional love, some of your people may wonder who you're talking about. If you must explain the biblical illustration's context, you may divert attention from the primary text of the sermon.

Keep Your Antenna Up for Other Sources of Illustrations from Day to Day

1. **Newspapers and magazines.** Look for human-interest stories that move you emotionally. Identify the story with a particular topic or issue common to people's everyday experiences—love, hate, sin, grace, family, jealousy, kindness, etc. Watch for statistics of all types, but be sure to date the source. Statistics change quickly. You do not want to use numbers from 1973 in a contemporary sermon! Don't overlook anything, even the obituaries.

2. **Television and movies.** News stories may contain stories that connect with your listeners, though you should avoid using specific names. You might occasionally refer to characters in a television show, but be careful to choose films that are appropriate for children. In addition, such references should be self-contained; don't assume everyone is watching the same show. Movies and movie clips can help tell a story, but only if you don't have to retell the movie plot in order for hearers to understand the point. Also, avoid any movie with a rating that would raise eyebrows or lower respect. If you use clips, be sure to have permission. A church can obtain a license for using video clips.

3. **Internet and e-mails.** Do a search of stories, quotations, or statistics related to the topics or ideas contained in the scriptural text. Double check the validity of anything you choose to use. Widen

the scope of your search. I discovered testimonies by educators at a secular university in the West. The school had given Christian professors a page on which they could record their thoughts. Six months later, I used one testimony in a message to college students. Many electronic newsletters can give you valuable information for illustrations. Be wary of forwarded e-mail material, since it often is spurious or inaccurate.

4. **Everyday life.** Watch people around you. If you really want to connect, next time you are at the mall, go to the food court and spend an hour people watching. Take a notebook because what you see and hear will be priceless. Observe signs on billboards, trucks, and bumper stickers as you drive, but wait till you are at home to record the illustration.

Spend time with people of all ages; listening to them will provide wonderful insight into human nature, build deeper relationships, and (with their permission) possibly yield additional anecdotes for future sermons. Be on the lookout for appropriate metaphors. Postmodern listeners perk their ears to well-formed metaphors or similes.

However you discover and file your illustrations, remember that the primary point is the Bible and its application to your people's lives. Illustrations are not the main thing; they merely help us understand the main thing. A well-balanced sermon has solid exposition of the biblical text, practical application to the lives of real people in the pews, and powerful illustrations that connect with your congregation.

Stage Eight: Develop the Conclusion and Invitation to Correspond with the Objective

Too many sermons end abruptly with "Let's pray." Draw your message to a strong conclusion. Go back to your original objective. What did you want people to do as a result of this sermon? Look at what you have said about the text's timeless truth. Do those ideas bring the listener along to understand, accept, and act? If so, draw the various points together in a short paragraph that summarizes, reiterates, or illustrates the primary concept. Avoid re-preaching the sermon, but help the hearers arrive at the "Aha" moment when they not only "get it," but want to do something about it.

Develop a natural transition from the conclusion to an invitation to action. Not all churches offer a public invitation at the end of sermons. Some offer optional methods of response, from filling out a card, to meeting the minister after the service, to raising a hand for prayer. Preachers who present an invitation to respond to the Holy Spirit's wooing as part of the sermon can be more effective by observing a few key principles:

Be True to the Sermon

If your sermon deals with husbands and wives loving one another (from Ephesians 5 for example), offer some way for couples to respond to God and to each other. They may come forward, recommitting themselves to one another and to the Lord. They may remain in their seats but simply take each other's hand and signify by doing so that they want to express godly love and commitment afresh.

Be True to the Gospel

Every sermon has a Gospel foundation and implication. A strong marriage, as exampled above, only finds its security in the Gospel of Christ. "Except the LORD build the house, they labor in vain that build it: except the LORD keep the city, the watchman wakes but in vain" (Psalm 127:1). If preaching on tithing, one might conclude by admitting that giving 10 percent of one's income to the church makes no sense without a saving relationship with Christ. Every topic can be brought back to the Gospel. After offering a way people can respond to the specific objective of the sermon, use this transition to share a simple Gospel presentation and give an opportunity for people to receive Christ.

Qualities of a Good Invitation

You can find several good books to help you deliver a good invitation, including *65 Ways to Give Evangelistic Invitations* by F. D. Whitesell, *Giving a Good Invitation* by Roy Fish, and *The Effective Invitation* by R. Alan Streett. Among the many qualities of good invitations, these authors and other homileticians agree your invitation should be clear, concise, and compelling.

Clear: People need to understand exactly what you want them to do and why they should do it. General statements like "Respond as the Lord leads" does not give the average person enough information. Imagine yourself as an unchurched person sitting in the pew. What do you need to know about the Gospel to be saved? What do you need to know about the response—why should you come forward—in order to feel confident you are responding appropriately? Give enough theological and practical information for the people to know what to do.

Concise: Don't preach the sermon all over again. Many preachers actually discourage decisions by dragging out the invitation too long. Certainly, you should allow time for the Holy Spirit to move in people's hearts. Still, by continuing on and on and on, you may hinder people's response. Share the invitation, turn it over to the Spirit, and get out of the way. Don't keep talking over the singing. Be quiet and let God work. If you need to add something as the Spirit leads, have the music cease while you share another word or two, but keep it short and to the point.

Compelling: Boldly declare the Good News of Jesus and encourage people to respond to Him. You need not be afraid of overpowering the will of people (providing you don't manipulate decisions). Help your listeners know that their response to the message and to the Gospel is vital for them and their families.

Be Honest in Persuasion

From the standpoint of the world, a massive ego is required to stand before a group of people and seek to persuade them to accept a certain point of view, course of action, or new lifestyle. Yet, persuasion is a common activity among people of all cultures worldwide. It is not unique to the activity of Christian preaching or personal evangelism. Nevertheless, the question is raised more often in the context of religious activity than in any other persuasive process.

Preaching is persuasion. You will preach many types of sermons—expository, topical, doctrinal, inspirational evangelistic—but all are persuasive by nature. Robert Coleman declares, "Preaching must move the will if it is to change lives through the grace of God. For this reason, the final test of any sermon is what people do about it. The content of the message is prevented from degenerating into mere rationalism on one hand, and mere emotionalism on the other hand, by the way it is linked with commitment. Truth by its very nature demands a verdict."[16]

Ministers who use unethical means of moving their people lose the one, indispensable commodity that makes them effective—credibility. Without integrity, the preacher becomes unbelievable and without people who will believe him, he has no congregation. The flock of God is not sheep-like in this respect. When they are abused, church people will remove the shepherd rather than continually suffer at his hand.

Congregations in general are not really opposed to persuasion in preaching. They want a preacher who can move them to do something different or to be something new. Their hearts beat faster for a prophet who will stir their souls with passion to serve God in a greater way. However, they will balk and rebel against any unscrupulous pulpiteer who uses dishonest means to do seemingly godly deeds.

Stage Nine: With the End in Mind, Develop an Introduction and Title

Why not write your introduction at the beginning of sermon development? How can you introduce something you have not yet prepared? Only after working through the entire sermon can you best determine how to begin. In the classic movie, *The Wizard of Oz*, Dorothy could only begin after she set her destination. To get to The Emerald City, she had to follow the Yellow Brick Road. The introduction helps place your listeners on the Yellow Brick Road to the ultimate objective—whatever it is you want them to do at the conclusion of the message.

You only have a few minutes to seize people's attention and make them want to hear what you have to say. Avoid using a joke or anecdote simply because it is funny or interesting. The introduction sets the spiritual, emotional, and intellectual direction for the following thirty minutes. Make sure that whatever you use helps put the audience onto the right path to end well.

Using a variety of introductions helps insure sermons will be fresh each week. Questions that help listeners related to the biblical text engage their minds from the beginning. True stories or testimonies can grip hearers' hearts and emotionally tie them to the outcome of the message. An effective method for using anecdotes is to tell part of the narrative in the introduction but waiting until the conclusion to complete the story, maintaining emotional tension to the end.

Titles should entice people to want to hear what is being said. They should not merely be a cute motto on the one hand or a dry statement on the other. Some churches place the sermon title on the church marquee so passersby can see what to expect on Sunday. More commonly, the sermon title is not revealed prior to its preaching, unless listed in a sermon series through a church publication.

Titles should be interesting, short, and relevant to people's lives. Avoid silly titles that make no sense to the average person. Observe titles of books, articles, and media to get some ideas of the types of titles people find attractive.

The preacher should not introduce his sermon by stating: "My sermon today is entitled . . ." Rather, the title printed in the Sunday bulletin or stated in some other way is sufficient to give people a reference to this message as opposed to the one preached last week.

Stage Ten: Refinement

Pray, pray, pray, edit, edit, edit.

Invest the time to make the sermon the best it can be. Consider your particular audience for this specific sermon. Will the illustrations and applications connect strongly enough to move them? Will they understand the biblical and theological exposition? Does the sermon have enough information so the hearers will comprehend the timeless truths, or conversely does the sermon have so much content it will take an hour to deliver? Does each part of the sermon advance the hearer toward the accomplishment of the sermonic objective? Are there better ways of communicating these ideas?

Do not hold your sermon so tightly that you are not willing to change it. Let go of even good ideas in favor of the best ideas. If the sermon is too long, divide it into two or more parts and develop it into a sermon series. Think through how the sermon will come across with your congregation. Preach it through mentally, adjusting the sermon as you go along. You may perform this exercise several times until it is just right, until you say to yourself, "That's it!"

Stage Eleven: Prepare the Sermon for Delivery

If you use a manuscript, write it out completely, but please don't read it from the pulpit. People need your eye contact to establish that you really believe what you are saying and you care that they do also. Write out your pulpit notes in outline format. Include only what you absolutely need to stay on track during the sermon. Preach through the sermon verbally or mentally several times before preaching it to your people. Master the ideas, not being slavish to memorize specific phrases unless they are important to the sermon.

Integrity

Heralds of God must maintain integrity as they proclaim the Gospel. The prophet may not dilute the authority of his office through inadequate or inappropriate delivery. To maintain integrity in the proclamation of a sermon, the preacher must first allow the impact of the preaching moment to empower and energize the delivery.

Dr. Wilbur Swartz, longtime professor of preaching at the New Orleans Baptist Theological Seminary, used to tell his homiletics students to experience what they preached as they preached it. Preaching can never be unemotional or detached. Real preaching is always personal.

Authenticity

Authenticity is another standard of effective sermon delivery. Phillips Brooks' famous definition of preaching as "truth through personality" implies that the message must be channeled through a genuine persona. For a preacher to speak for God using a false or affected voice or mannerisms is to demean the message and its Source. Still, many preachers set aside their true personalities at the church door and assume the identity of their favorite pulpiteer. Not only are they unaided by these thin disguises, their messages lose the respect of a knowing congregation.

The authentic prophet can speak in normal tones of voice with natural body language. If the sermon calls for intensity of emotion, he can rise to the need. Should quiet thoughtfulness be required, the preacher can speak in hushed tones, which command the attention of even large congregations.

Finally, to paraphrase Alistair Begg: pray yourself hot, then preach yourself empty.[17]

Preaching and Worship

Preaching has always been the center of true worship. During the Dark Ages, preaching lost its place in favor of church rituals. It was hard for an unbelieving clergy to preach the Bible, so they depended on worship that deemphasized or eliminated the sermon altogether. However, when Scripture came again to the forefront of church life in the Reformation, preaching regained its prominence.

In the next chapter, we will discuss worship more thoroughly. Suffice it here to acknowledge that while people worship through music, prayers, giving, and other participative acts during the corporate service, preaching should lift people to the throne of God in worship.

Contemporary generations enjoy experience over spectating. They want to be involved. They want to feel something. Consequently, people tend to think about worship as whatever they can do to participate in the service. Unfortunately, they can mistake emotional release for biblical worship, and feelings can become more important than biblical foundations for life.

Next-Gen pastors must master the art of crafting sermons in such a way that people enter the biblical experience of the biblical message. Excellent exposition forces the preacher to go deep into the biblical context and use sound homiletical techniques to bring that context to life. The great preachers of history used word pictures to help people see, hear, feel, and otherwise sense the places, people, and events of the Bible. Employing metaphors, similes, narratives, and parables, they enlivened timeless doctrinal truths.

Today's preachers must not only experience their sermons in the midst of delivery, but they must also bring their audience into the experience of living out the biblical message as well. Touching people's hearts, minds, and spirits with Scripture is not a mechanism of manipulation but a loving and living encounter made possible by God's Spirit speaking through God's man as he faithfully and fully opens God's Word.

Preaching as worship requires much in the way of prayer and preparation, much more so than merely "getting up a sermon." It means the pastor must work diligently through the text with his people in mind. It means the pastor must involve other worship leaders, such as the Minister of Music, in planning worship services that are coordinated around the biblical theme. It means the pastor must experience worship for himself as he prepares his message, for only from a position prostrate before the throne of God can he call people to join him in worship.

Creative Styles of Sermon Development

Narrative Preaching

If you are preaching a biblical narrative, you can use a type of development that enhances the presentation of both textual truth and practical application. Narrative preaching often follows a story/application format that appeals to people of all ages.

Narrative preaching has often been the victim of bad press and poor use. Some conservative preachers identify narrative preaching with narrative theology, a mistaken premise. Narrative theology employs a liberal approach to biblical interpretation in which the historical veracity of the story is not as important as the moral of the story. Obviously, once a preacher disregards whether a biblical account actually occurred, he undercuts the authority of Scripture and, with it, surrenders credibility for his sermon.

The word *narrative* simply refers to a story. Most of the Bible is written in narrative format. Scriptural stories can be preached using deductive propositional structures, but a more natural approach would be to employ a style similar to that of the text. Narrative preaching simply employs the techniques of storytelling into the development and delivery of the sermon.

One of the most conservative, expository preachers of modern American history was R. G. Lee. Yet his most famous sermon was "Payday Someday," which he preached over a thousand times. Lee used a **third-person narrative** style to set up scenes, introduce characters, describe the plot and action, and make application to his congregations. He presented the story as if he were the narrator, looking in from the outside.

African-American pulpiteer E. K. Bailey used **first-person narrative** in preaching through the book of Hosea. Taking on the role of Hosea, he told the story of God's redeeming love through the eyes of a prophet who was ordered by God to marry a prostitute. Mixing humor and piercing application, Bailey invited the listener to join him as Hosea shared how God worked to change his heart so he might declare God's relentless love to an adulterous nation.

In both sermons, the preachers maintain **the integrity of the text**. The historicity of the narrative enhances the value of its truth and defines the authenticity of its application. For example, if someone tells you a fictional story, regardless of clever word crafting, its moral (the application of the story) lacks the power of a well-told narrative that actually happened.

The narrative sermon requires studying not only the biblical text, but cultural, historical, and interpersonal aspects of the scene and its characters. The more **details** one can use, the better the audience is able to see the story in their minds.

Narrative preaching takes more time in preparation and requires a degree of imagination and creativity, as well as a command of language. The average preacher will not likely employ this style weekly. However, if well-crafted and dynamically delivered, a narrative sermon can be a powerful addition to the minister's homiletical toolkit.

Imagery is not limited to narrative preaching. Every sermon can be more effective when the preacher uses word pictures that help listeners see, understand, and relate to spiritual truth.

Inductive Preaching

Inductive preaching can be one of the more effective approaches to preaching in the next generation. A deductive sermon presents the primary proposition or idea at the beginning of the sermon and proceeds to explain or prove the central point. The problem is the nature of human beings, which questions what they hear. When the preacher sets up his premise at the beginning of the messages, some people engage in a mental debate as to whether or not what the speaker is saying is true.

When Peter preached at Pentecost, if he had begun with his primary point—that Jesus of Nazareth was the Christ—many of his hearers would have cut him off (likely literally!). The Holy Spirit inspired Peter to begin with the matter that held the people's attention—the strange behavior of the disciples under the influence of the Spirit. Peter introduced a primary Scripture from Joel for the basis of his statements. He followed with several arguments and support Scripture that led the listeners further along the path to the final conclusion, that God had made this same Jesus both Christ and Lord (Acts 2:14–36). Without doubt, Peter did not deliberate on what type of sermon he would preach, much less did he think about inductive development. Still, isn't it interesting that the first sermon of the Christian Church would be inductive?

An inductive sermon simply helps the audience walk through the text as the preacher has done so himself, beginning with a life question related to a specific text, making the discoveries of truth along the way before arriving at the "Aha" moment of truth at the end.

In presenting the message deductively, you start with the general proposition as stated in the introduction and then elaborate or expand on that truth or provide specific proofs for the truth. In presenting the message inductively, you begin with the text and a question about the text that relates to the lives of the hearers. Work through the text, revealing as you go the specific points, proofs, applications, and illustrations, arriving in the conclusion with the general propositional truth while carrying the audience through the process with you. Their mental defenses never rise up because they are engaged with you in discovering where the trail of evidence leads. When you and they arrive at the conclusion, the validity of the primary point is powerfully obvious.

Authority

One problem inductive preaching has encountered through the years is the unfortunate identification it has had with writers who deny the authority of the preacher and elevate the audience to a point that the preacher may not feel qualified to state an authoritative, "Thus saith the Lord."

Expository inductive preaching shows appreciation for the audience, and involves the audience in the discovery of truth. Still, the preacher must speak with the authority of the Word of God, the authority of his calling, and the authority of the Holy Spirit.

The Starting Place

Some advocates of inductive preaching focus on topical preaching that starts with life needs of the congregation rather than the Scriptures. Biblical inductive preaching starts with the Scriptures, sees in application of the exposition how the Scripture relates to people and their lives, then uses the life situation discovered from the Scripture to raise a life question in the introduction that finds its answer from the exposition of the text.

The Destination

Improper inductive preaching leaves the listeners to come to their own conclusions, failing or refusing to draw the specific points together in a general principle. True inductive preaching is not complete until the specific points, proofs, or observations are drawn together in a general principle at the end of the message. That general principle is the propositional truth toward which the entire sermon is directed and to which the audience arrives.

One last word about preaching . . .

Prophets are alive today. They quietly enter pulpits across the land each week and boldly proclaim the *kerygma*, which has the power to change lives. The effective prophets, the ones who last, the ones who wear the mantle of Elijah, are those who maintain diligence in preparing themselves and their messages, who experience their own sermons in order to preserve integrity in their proclamation, and who steadfastly adhere to honesty in their persuasion of God's people.

Chapter 15

BIBLICAL WORSHIP
IN A CONTEMPORARY WORLD

*"God is a Spirit: and they that worship him must worship him
in spirit and in truth" (John 4:23–24).*

Human beings have no higher endeavor than worship. Ministers have no greater responsibility than leading worship in a way that glorifies God. Inherent in the heart of every believer rests the need to worship, to praise, to sing, to pray, to give, to be edified through biblical sermons—all to the glory of God. Referring to Jesus' use of Isaiah 29:13 to describe the problem with the Pharisees, John Piper observes, ". . . the essence of all worship is the act of honoring God." Based on this idea, Piper defines worship as "an act of reflecting back to God in praise the glories emanating from his presence."[1]

Vibrant worship is vital to growing churches in an increasingly secularized society. Nearly every list of steps to church growth highlights the importance of a worship that is personal, exciting, and inspiring. Sincere ministers sometimes find themselves choosing between contemporary expectations and the expression of what they consider to be biblical worship.

> *Human beings have no higher endeavor than worship.*
>
> *Ministers have no greater responsibility than leading worship in a way that glorifies God.*

To worship biblically cannot mean simply imitating the rituals of ancient Israel. The bloodletting ended when the Jesus, the Lamb of God, was slain and His blood symbolically poured upon the heavenly mercy seat (Hebrews 9:23–28). Neither can scriptural worship merely copy the practices of house churches in Acts. While house churches are certainly valid, their use in the anti-Christian environment of Roman and Jewish societies of the first century does not invalidate worshipping as part of larger congregations today.

Biblical worship transcends human traditions. To worship in spirit and truth is to express authenticity and integrity as one approaches God. Leaving a sacrifice at the altar in order to repair a relationship with a brother restores horizontal relationships before encountering a vertical one. Offering praise in hymns and psalms and spiritual songs employs the melody of the spirit in the adoration of the Most High. Proclaiming the kerygma declares the wonders of God's grace. Each act of worship should focus on the ultimate purpose of glorifying God, whether it be through personal worship, family worship, or congregational worship.

The Worship Leader

Many churches identify the worship leader, or worship pastor, as the person who leads in music. Consequently, we confuse worship as only being the musical part of the worship service. Certainly, music fulfills a vital role in worship. Musical worship lifts our soul and allows us to express our love and adoration for the Lord. Whether through congregational singing or hearing an individual or group, quality music is one way we worship in spirit and truth. The person who leads musical worship and guides the corporate worship services is certainly a worship leader, but he is not the only one.

Who leads worship and what acts we perform in worship are immaterial if we do not focus worship on God, lifting His name in praise, holding Him in adoration, and yielding to Him in humble obedience.

Worship involves prayers, giving, preaching, celebrating the ordinances, music, and much more. The pastor should be seen as the worship leader, although the music leader may coordinate many of the elements of a worship service. Such responsibility means the pastor and other ministers involved in worship services meet regularly to plan each element and insure cohesion. Having upbeat, celebratory music just before a sermon about hell not only is incongruous, it is distracting. Coordination, timing, and flow of service elements aid the congregation's participation in worship.

Unfortunately, too many pastors simply tell the music leader to "handle it" (meaning the service planning) and just leave him time to preach. Effective pastors do not abdicate responsibility for working with other worship leaders to insure a worship expression that honors God and brings worshippers to His throne.

However, who leads worship and what acts we perform in worship are immaterial if we do not focus worship on God, lifting His name in praise, holding Him in adoration, and yielding to Him in humble obedience.

Handling the Holy

Before the priests were allowed to present sacrifices of worship, they offered cleansing for their own souls (Exodus 29:15–29; Leviticus 16:11). Jesus told His followers to correct any difficulty they might have with a brother before they offered an act of worship (Matthew 5:24). Both admonitions refer to the care that worshippers and worship leaders must give to preparation for handling the holy.

Can the prophet speak with authority when he has not yielded his own life to God in worship? Can the priest bring people before a holy God when he himself has not removed his sandals upon holy ground? Can one lead in public prayer who has not worn the carpet in his own prayer closet?

The most dangerous aspect of ministry is becoming so accustomed to handling the holy that we may take it for granted.

The most dangerous aspect of ministry is becoming so accustomed to handling the holy that we may take it for granted. The sons of Eli the priest grew up around the temple. Instead of recognizing their high privilege, they took advantage of their positions to abuse people who came to worship (1 Samuel 2: 22–25). We should be careful to maintain a high awe of the holy things of God, lest we fall into their error and suffer their fate.

In every generation, the pressure on the minister to produce a continual stream of spirituality week after week, sermon after sermon, prayer after prayer, and lesson after lesson can make it difficult for his personal well to be filled.

If the priest is presumptuous enough to stand before a congregation without personal spiritual preparation, his pretense will soon be discovered. If, on the other hand, the minister has allowed the Spirit of God to search his heart and cleanse him, if he has known the pains of the heavenly confessional and the joys of its absolution, then the pastor is ready to offer public intercession for his people.

The minister begins preparation for worship leadership by examining his personal spiritual life. Is there unconfessed sin? Bring it to the One Whose blood cleanses all iniquity. Is there a relationship problem with a brother or sister in the congregation? Go and make matters right, restoring your relationship with one whom you can see before you attempt to bring him to the One you cannot see. Is there a lack of faith? Freely admit it to the Giver of the faith by which you first believed.

God will not begrudge His servant who comes contritely to confess and repent of his failures, but woe is the priest who attempts to hide his sin and presume to bear the holiness of worship. Like Uzzah, whose irreverence in touching the ark of covenant cost him his life, the hypocritical worship leader places himself in jeopardy (2 Samuel 6:6–7).

Avoiding Worship Wars

Next-Gen pastors and church staff ministers, as well as younger members of the congregation, enjoy the experiential aspect of worshipping through music. Their style of music varies but often reflects the language, melody, and tempo of their culture. Because their personal expression of worship through contemporary music is so powerful, some Next-Gen ministers may impose their style of worship on a congregation, while eliminating more traditional hymns and instruments enjoyed by some segments of the church. Drastic change without consideration of the values of all the people is a sure way to launch a worship war.

Every age group loves the music of its younger days. The Builder Generation cherishes the old hymns. The Boomers trend toward the praise songs introduced when they were in the church youth choir. Millennials have invented their own brand of musical worship. Each style has been contemporary in its own generation. All styles must have room for expression in a congregation that includes more than one age group.

Every age group loves the music of its younger days.

Ed Stetzer's study of comeback churches indicates that no single style of music provides successful turnaround toward church growth. Rather, the most important factors involved having music that is appropriate to the context of the congregation and the vitality with which worship is engaged.[2]

Avoiding wars over worship involves blending all types of music into a dynamic opportunity of worship for all the people and educating the congregation in understanding true worship involves much more than music. Younger people need to respect and care for the older members of the congregation by learning some of the grand old hymns of the faith. Older people need to encourage the younger generations by giving them some flexibility of expression through newer songs. All people need to focus not on what they personally enjoy but on glorifying God through their musical worship.

Planning Worship Services

Quality worship services require prayer and time as ministers seek the Holy Spirit's direction, consider worship elements, and plan each service. Music ministers cannot adequately prepare choirs or other musical groups with only a few days' notice. Preachers offer better sermons when given sufficient time to prepare. Committees responsible for baptism or the Lord's Supper require sufficient notice to have materials ready and in place.

Smaller churches tend to follow a similar plan of service from week to week. The songs may be chosen as late as Sunday morning. The pastor may prepare messages during the last days of the week. Bivocational pastors especially find time constraints that force them to struggle with sermon preparation. Most musicians and other staff ministers are bivocational also. Neither group has the luxury of days in the church office devoted to preparation. These problems provide an even greater need for coordinated, intentional planning. Giving regular time for worship planning makes weekly execution much easier and requires less time for weekly preparation.

Long-Range Planning

Worship emphases, preaching plans, musical presentations, and special events can best be planned well in advance. Effective worship teams schedule several hours annually and quarterly to pray together about God's direction for the coming months. They consider congregational needs, special occasions such as Christmas or Easter, and other issues that might impact the plans. Usually, the pastor initiates planning as he lays out what he believes is God's leading regarding sermons, either in series or individually. The music leader contributes ideas about music, pageantry, and any special elements that might enhance the scriptural themes suggested by the preaching plans. The church staff may offer input regarding upcoming events, service concepts, or other elements for services.

Quarterly planning meetings become more specific with sermon titles and texts, musical selections, and enlistment of persons to lead in prayer and other specific parts of the service. Outside groups, such as committees responsible for the ordinances, are notified so they may be ready to execute their duties.

Weekly Planning

Based on adjustments to the long-range plans made in quarterly meetings, the church staff will meet each week to pray together and to finalize details. Quality teams look several weeks in advance, even in the weekly planning meetings, so each part of every service is well considered and each contingency anticipated. They will clarify themes for the upcoming Sunday and the month ahead. The team will construct the final worship outline and distribute it to everyone involved in the services.

Sound and light technicians need written plans for the services in order to have technical equipment ready. Ushers must know when and how they should receive the offering, distribute visitors cards, seat guests, or handle other responsibilities. Persons responsible for preparation of visual aids, such as Media Shout or PowerPoint, need specifics regarding sermon outline, musical lyrics, announcements, and other content, along with the arrangement of presentations.

Elements of Worship

Public worship services may contain a wide variety of elements:

Scripture Reading

Formal reading of Scriptures elevates the Bible as the basis of scriptural worship. The pastor or someone else might read a passage that may include the text of the sermon or may simply support the worship theme. Responsive readings help involve the congregation as the leader reads one verse and the congregation reads the next verse in unison, alternating through a single text or a selection of several texts.

Music

Musical selections include congregational music (including hymns/choruses/praise songs, instrumental music, special musical presentations, preludes, and postludes).

Prayers

Some prayers are led by ministers, others by lay participants. Do not call on someone to pray without knowing that person is comfortable with praying in public. Also, be careful that people pray and not engage in preaching through prayer.

Fellowship

Many congregations enjoy an opportunity to greet one another during an early part of the service. Generally, larger churches give shorter time to this part of the service.

Acknowledging Guests

Churches have a variety of ways to acknowledge visitors. Seeker-sensitive churches may be cautious about doing so in a way that makes guests feel uncomfortable. Some means of registering visitors' names and contact information should be offered so the church can follow up later.

Announcements

Announcements generally work best when kept to those issues that affect the entire church. The worship service is not the best way to announce committee meetings and other small group activities. Scheduling announcements at the end of the service make them more memorable and take less time from the primary acts of worship.

Ordinances

Position the ordinances in the service to take advantage of the maximum benefit of each. For example, having baptism at the beginning of a service may encourage other people who are considering coming to Christ and being baptized.

Special Elements

Drama, video clips, and other elements can help illustrate worship themes or specific points of the sermon.

The Sermon

Preaching is an act of worship. The sermon can instruct about worship, but it should be more than an educational instrument. Proclaiming God's Word puts people in touch with the Lord. His Spirit illuminates the Word, inspires the preacher, and elicits a response from the people.

The Invitation

Most services should include an opportunity to respond. A formal invitation to respond at the conclusion of the sermon can be very helpful in confirming individuals' decisions, offering opportunity for counseling, and encouraging other people to respond. The invitation should be true to the sermon (giving a specific way of acting on the sermonic objective) and true to the Gospel (giving a complete, but concise presentation of the Gospel and an opportunity to be saved). Have counselors trained to help respondents. Decision counseling may be done in the worship center or, better yet, in nearby rooms. Staff or trained lay counselors can help people clarify their decisions and follow through appropriately for baptism, church membership, or other options.

The Offering

Worshipping with tithes and offerings may happen early in the service or later. Scheduling it after the invitation provides extra time for decision counseling, especially if your church presents respondents at the end of the service.

Some churches deemphasize the offering, thinking any emphasis on money is negative, especially for guests. Leaders may even specifically state that visitors should not give, since members bear responsibility for supporting the church programs. This approach shows a lack of understanding regarding the offering. The offering is not a method of collecting money; it is a vital part of worship. Our tithes and other financial gifts are not contributions or donations, but are the "firstfruits," holy to the Lord. Giving is an act of worship of God.

If church members see the offering merely as supporting the needs of the church, but does not like some aspect of the church's ministry, they may no longer feel obligated to give. On the other hand, if we give as unto the Lord, then we give consistently, whether or not we agree with some issue in the church. We give because it is an integral part of worship.

The second error is the denial of a blessing to visitors. Yes, visitors should not feel pressured to give. However, by defining the offering as anything less than a worship experience, visitors are given the impression that the offering is not for them. Every person who enters the house of God should feel encouraged to participate in all parts of the worship experience, including worship through giving to the Lord.

Timing

Musical leaders should be sensitive to time requirements for all songs, including introductions and set-up time. With the average service lasting sixty to seventy-five minutes, the pastor will need at least thirty minutes for the sermon plus time for the invitation. Consider all the elements of the service and set accurate time expectations for each part.

Details

Ministers responsible for each part of the services should plan each element thoroughly. Excellence is in the details. Participants not only should be enlisted but given sufficient instructions so their roles flow smoothly with all other participants. Do not assume everyone knows what to do.

Family and Personal Worship

Worship began on an individual basis, expanded to include families, and later included the congregation. Churches can help people worship God outside the corporate services by educating them about the benefits and methods of personal worship. Some churches provide family worship guides on Sundays to help members worship at home during the week. Websites can offer online suggestions, devotionals, and links to worship songs (through sites such as GodTube or YouTube). Vibrant personal worship leads to more vital public worship.

Families can draw closer to one another as they approach God together in family worship. Having a specified time for family worship as well as a plan helps improve consistency. Family worship needs planning, just as does corporate worship. As the spiritual leader, the father has the primary responsibility for initiating family worship, but the entire family should be given opportunities to initiate ideas as well as participate through prayer, Scripture reading, sharing, singing, and other ways.

Worship is the one eternal act in which we participate on earth. Personally, by families, and as congregations, we join now with the heavenly refrain heard throughout ages to come, "And every creature which is in heaven, and on the earth, and under the earth, and such as are in the sea, and all that are in them, heard I saying, 'Blessing, and honor, and glory, and power, be unto him that sits upon the throne, and unto the Lamb for ever and ever'" (Revelation 5:13).

> *Worship is the one eternal act in which we participate on earth.*

Chapter 16

FULFILLING THE GREAT COMMISSION: LEADING EVANGELISM AND MISSIONS

"And he gave some . . . evangelists . . ." (Ephesians 4:11).
". . . do the work of an evangelist, make full proof of thy ministry" (2 Timothy 4:5).

What is evangelism, a gift and calling of the Spirit for only some disciples or a job for every pastor (and every believer)? Each minister has had some shy saint offer a lack of giftedness as an excuse for avoiding personal evangelism. Some clergy share that reluctance.

Certainly, the role of vocational evangelism blesses the church. However, the local pastor cannot dismiss his personal responsibility to lead in soul winning. Every church that successfully reaches the unreached with the Gospel features a pastor who is an effective soul winner. The man of God does not limit his evangelistic efforts to his pulpit ministry but loves engaging people individually with the Good News of Jesus. As a good shepherd, the minister's compassion for the lost sheep motivates him to search until the wanderer is secure in the fold (Luke 15:4–7). This work of evangelism is at the heart of the Master who came "to seek and save that which was lost" (Luke 19:10).

The role of the pastor as evangelist includes, but goes beyond, his personal involvement in soul winning. He sets the spiritual tone for the church's mission and momentum. His example leads the church into witness involvement. He may facilitate actual evangelism activities or he may delegate organization and administration to another. Yet, he cannot delegate his role as prime model and pace setter.

Another aspect of the pastor as evangelist involves his preaching ministry. Today's preacher is pulled between the need for growth sermons and the desire to win souls from the pulpit. Every biblical passage has application for sanctification but also builds a bridge for salvation. Exposing scriptural truth brings hearers into confrontation with a holy, loving God. As the preacher works through God's Word, he leads people to repent of sin and receive Christ as Savior and, then, to grow as His disciples.

Leading the Church in Evangelism[1]

"What are you doing to reach people?" That question is commonly heard by pastors of growing churches. With a large percentage of churches being plateaued or declining, ministers are constantly searching for something that works. However, a study of churches who consistently lead in baptisms reveals a diversity of methodology. Churches wanting to model their ministries after success stories will not find a one-size-fits-all, cookie-cutter mold.

In a study of churches from various sizes, locations, backgrounds, and traditions, the author discovered many different approaches. The investigation involved a selection of churches among the top fifty churches in baptisms (either numerically or in comparison to membership) in the Southern Baptist Convention.

Three Surprises

Interestingly, only two pastors mentioned a contemporary style of music or informal clothing as being connected to their success in reaching people. While both factors possibly are involved in many of the churches, when asked "what helps you reach people?" most leaders did not include either issue as a direct help in evangelism.

Another surprise from the study was the diversity of approaches. A few churches have regular visitation weekly. Others emphasize the constant "as you go" impact of believers on people in the community. Overall, every church had its own methodology for reaching people for Christ.

A third unexpected result was that while few of these churches use typical evangelistic revivals, all employ evangelistic events to varying degrees. This finding does not support the idea of discontinuing revivals. A recent study of the North American Mission Board of the SBC showed that churches that have evangelistic revivals using vocational evangelists tend to baptize more people annually than those churches who do not use revivals.

Two Commonalities

Intentionality

Every leader interviewed stressed that the church makes an intentional effort to reach the lost for Christ. Every program, ministry, activity, sermon, and group has as its goal the touching of people's lives with the Gospel. In addition, the corporate culture encourages members to share Christ as a lifestyle and to bring friends to church.

Pastor Initiated

Every pastor sets the tone for the staff and congregation. From sermons to organizational plans, to staff agendas, to ministry activities, these leaders model and mold evangelism into the corporate DNA of the church. While staff ministers may administrate evangelistic efforts, none can replace the pastor in creating a commitment to evangelism. Although each pastor had differing personal styles and organizational approaches, the common quality of a focus on reaching people started with the Senior Pastor.

Varying Approaches

Relationships

Most of these congregations stress the importance of healthy relationships among members, but they also focus on developing relationships with friends, family, and neighbors. Reaching a primarily Mormon community in Utah, one church works to create a family atmosphere of people who reach out in love to their friends.

In the more traditional setting of Tennessee, another congregation also emphasizes lifestyle evangelism. Leaders successfully encourage members to build relationships and to ask people to come to church with them.

Similarly, the leaders at a church in North Carolina work constantly to instill a bridge-building culture into its congregation. One study has revealed that most unchurched people will attend a church when invited by a friend to participate WITH them. Too many church members invite people to church but have no intention of developing a personal relationship with them. Successful evangelistic relationships are **genuine**, extending outside the church hours, and **intentional**, designed to bring people to faith in Christ.

Transformational Testimonies

The testimonies of people who have been dramatically transformed impact friends who observe believers' changed lives. A Hawaiian congregation celebrates people rescued by Christ from backgrounds of alcohol, broken marriages, and other life tragedies. The pastor observed that as the people live out their Christianity and demonstrate their love for God, other people are attracted to the Gospel.

Biblical Preaching

Another common focus for evangelistic pastors is the use of strong, biblical preaching to influence people for Christ. At one church in Bowling Green, Kentucky, the most likely baptismal candidate is an adult man over the age of forty. The associate pastor suggested that the strong combination of the members' witnessing and the pastor's preaching were responsible for this remarkable result. This congregation has grown from 30 to over 3500 primarily through decisions at worship services.

Modeled after the *Simple Church* approach, a church in Albuquerque emphasizes weekend activities. The pastor demonstrates his heart for evangelism through strongly evangelistic preaching.

The Gospel Invitation

The various pastors use a variety of approaches to drawing the evangelistic net at the conclusion of the sermon. Most have a typical invitation in which seekers are invited to come forward to receive Christ at the end of a sermon. Pastors regularly offer a strongly evangelistic message followed by an intense call for decisions, resulting in healthy responses.

Raising the Visibility of Baptism

A large church in Houston stresses immediate baptism. At many of its events, helpers are ready with baptismal clothes for people who receive Christ to be baptized immediately. Another church, in Orlando, also elevates baptism as a celebration—both at its regular baptism services and at special services by the lake, at the beach, or at times in baptism troughs placed on the stage. A congregation in Orange Beach, Alabama, often baptizes on the beach, an activity that attracts onlookers who ask for baptism on the spot.

Event Evangelism

Many, though not all, of these churches employed attractional events to one degree or another. One congregation emphasizes jail and beach ministries, gospel concerts, and disaster relief benefits to reach people. Another church uses strategic one-day events, coupled with multiday events (such as Next-Generation student camp) and traditional activities like Vacation Bible School.

Community Ministry

Several churches use community ministry to demonstrate Christ's love and to provide opportunities to share the Gospel. A congregation in Alabama has offered health fairs and parish nursing to minister to people and provide an opportunity for them to hear the Gospel. This church often has up to a thousand volunteers for its "2nd Saturday" community ministry—partnering with various nonprofit ministries to touch human needs.

Technology

One African-American church in Chicago uses a teleministry system, which places ten thousand phone calls a week. Teams trained in soul-winning techniques visit three days a week, following up on people who respond.

Other churches typically employ well-designed websites to share information about the church. Most websites include a Gospel presentation, along with the opportunity for seekers to initiate contact with the church for follow-up. Technology also aids outreach, follow-up, and assimilation through church information software systems.

Small Groups

Some churches have traditional Sunday Schools or connect groups, but also include numerous groups meetings on multiple days/nights of the week. Each group is intentionally evangelistic, built around teaching God's Word and reaching people with the Gospel. The connect group leaders at one church in North Carolina understand their purpose is to grow and multiply. The church constantly starts new classes, some at the church and others in homes.

Multisite Approaches

Several larger churches have satellite campuses in multiple locations. Each campus has a pastor and staff for each site, but the Senior Pastor of the main campus is seen as the primary pastor of the entire church. Other "global" pastors help lead coordinated approaches to student ministries and other activities. By offering opportunities in areas that are experiencing population growth, these churches are able to reach more people in younger demographics, who typically are more open to the Gospel.

Retention Rates

With the various methods of evangelism and the strong emphases on baptism, a reasonable question may be asked about retention rates. A survey of these churches revealed retention rates from 50 percent to 80 percent. Those churches with the higher retention rate were more intentional in follow-up, discipleship, and assimilation.

Conclusion

Some people say that you can't argue with success and each of the churches studied have succeeded in reaching people evangelistically in record numbers. Their baptismal records rank among the top fifty congregations in the nation. Each of these churches insist on being biblical while, at the same time, being effective. Their methodologies are extremely varied—some using formal programs such as Evangelism

Explosion, while others focus primarily on building evangelistic relationships. Events and other attractional programs are balanced with small group and individual discipleship emphases.

A legitimate question relates to retention. Most churches studied showed a 50–80 percent retention rate. A few demonstrated a lower rate and acknowledged the need to help assimilate new members more effectively. This writer's observation is that churches lacking an effective Sunday morning Bible study program, such as the Sunday School or connect groups, have a more difficult time assimilating new believers.

What Can Churches Take Away from This Study?

First, recognize that what works in one church does not necessarily work in another. Each congregation must seek to incarnate the Gospel in its own culture.

Second, successful churches are committed to biblical consistency. These congregations know their methods are only ways to support people's encounter with God through His Word.

Third, to reach people, the pastors must lead the way. The congregation will follow what the pastor models. If the pastor's heart is to win people to Christ, the people will likely do the same.

Fourth, whatever methods a church adopts, the congregation must be intentional in forming its strategy to focus on the result—people coming to faith in Christ in such a way that helps them live the Christ life consistently in their daily setting.

Developing a Church Outreach System

Effective churches develop church-wide systems designed to involve the entire congregation in reaching the unreached. The diagram (below) illustrates a system for church outreach that incorporates the pastoral staff, deacons, Sunday School/Bible study group leaders, and the entire congregation. It describes a plan developed at Germantown Baptist Church in Germantown, Tennessee. W. A. Criswell described a similar program of Sunday deacon visitation in his book, *Criswell's Guidebook for Pastors*.[2]

The funnel represents data gathered about visitors and other unreached persons from whatever means possible. Every organization and event should have a system for registering visitors and recommending prospects. Worship services, Sunday School/ Connect Groups, recreational centers, special events (such as Vacation Bible Schools, Fall Festivals, musical presentations, etc.), and all other opportunities need easy-to-use forms for getting names and contact information. All of these forms should come into a central collection point for input by an administrative assistant in the church computer database.

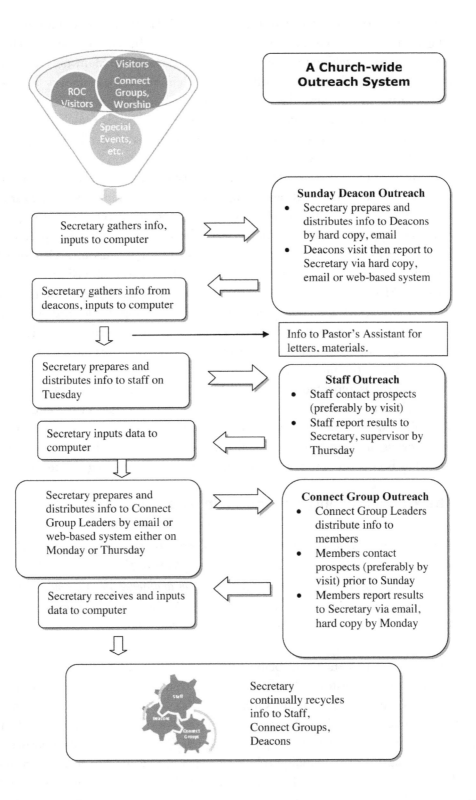

A Church-wide Outreach System

Secretary gathers info, inputs to computer

Sunday Deacon Outreach
- Secretary prepares and distributes info to Deacons by hard copy, email
- Deacons visit then report to Secretary via hard copy, email or web-based system

Secretary gathers info from deacons, inputs to computer

Info to Pastor's Assistant for letters, materials.

Secretary prepares and distributes info to staff on Tuesday

Staff Outreach
- Staff contact prospects (preferably by visit)
- Staff report results to Secretary, supervisor by Thursday

Secretary inputs data to computer

Secretary prepares and distributes info to Connect Group Leaders by email or web-based system either on Monday or Thursday

Connect Group Outreach
- Connect Group Leaders distribute info to members
- Members contact prospects (preferably by visit) prior to Sunday
- Members report results to Secretary via email, hard copy by Monday

Secretary receives and inputs data to computer

Secretary continually recycles info to Staff, Connect Groups, Deacons

The first use of this information could be a Sunday afternoon visitation program by rotating teams of deacons or other volunteers. One church sustained much of its growth by having teams taking turns visiting visitors on Sundays. Many new members of one church commented that a prime influence on their decision to join was the personal visit by laypersons on the same day that they had visited the church. Following visits, teams turn in a response form indicating data discovered in the visit, such as other family members not mentioned on previous forms, special interests of family members (music, sports, missions, etc.), and other information.

On Monday, the outreach administrative assistant takes the visitation reports and updates the computer files (in this case using software from Shelby Systems). During the Monday morning staff meeting, ministers receive assignments from the visitor/prospect files. They make appointments and contact each family during the week, preferably by personal visit. After their contacts, the ministers report back to the outreach assistant for further computer updates. The pastor may also send letters to each visitor.

Also on Monday, the outreach assistant sends prospect information to outreach leaders related to each of the Sunday School/Connect Group/Bible study classes. The outreach leaders assign names to various class members who in turn make visits or other contacts with the prospects. Again, persons making contacts report back to the outreach assistant who updates the files again.

The process is repeated each week. Usually prospects need repeated contacts of various kinds over many weeks before they make decisions about the church. Many of these families will contain lost persons who may be evangelized during the visits. Relationship evangelism and personal soul winning go hand in hand through such a system. The key is consistency, persistence, and the desire to build genuine friendships.

To All The World: Leading the Church in Missions

"And Jesus came and spake unto them, saying, All power is given unto me in heaven and in earth. Go ye therefore, and teach all nations, baptizing them in the name of the Father, and of the Son, and of the Holy Ghost: Teaching them to observe all things whatsoever I have commanded you: and, lo, I am with you alway, even unto the end of the world" (Matthew 28:18–20).

Next-Gen ministers value being missional. I've been impressed by the high percentage of younger pastors who are visionary and passionate in their desire to reach unchurched people. Following Jesus' Great Commission to the church, they lead their congregations to carry the Good News from their backyards to the backwoods of distant lands. Local, regional, national, and international missions resonate with their hearts.

Pastors have a responsibility to help their people respond to Jesus' Commission and fulfill their purpose as churches. Since the parishoners will go only as far as their pastor, he has the blessed opportunity to demonstrate a heart and habit for personal soul winning (evangelism) and missions. Several ways you can build a missional church include the following:

1. Preach and Teach

Open God's Word to the people with biblical examples and admonitions regarding God's desire to reach every person with His saving love through Christ. Rather than motivating through guilt, inspire the people with the wondrous prospect of being a co-laborer with Christ in fulfilling His purpose. Show them how they can be part of life-changing ministry for people in their communities and around the world.

2. Connect

Build regular connections between your congregation and missionaries across the nation and in distant lands. Your missionary board (like the International Mission Board and the North American Mission Board of the Southern Baptist Convention) can put you in touch with missionaries and provide information about the people groups with whom they are working. If your church does not provide a missions organization for children, help the children's ministries connect your young people with children of missionaries. Prayer needs can be discovered from such resources as www.IMB.org. Their newsletters contain actual prayer requests from missionaries overseas.

3. Pray

Lead various groups and individuals of the church to pray for missionaries. Some organizations provide lists of missionary birthdays so you can pray for them on their birthdays. Use special missions emphases (such as Christmas and Easter missions offerings) to highlight specific mission needs and individual missionaries who are reaching people around the world.

4. Give

Show me your budget, and I'll tell you your values. A church that does not give a substantial part of its regular budget to missionary support is not missional. Special missions offerings give people the opportunity to give over and above their tithes, either at designated times like Christmas and Easter or throughout the year.

5. Cooperate

Many denominations support career missionaries who have invested their lives in an international ministry. They have moved their families, learned the language, and, in some cases, risked their lives to serve in a foreign land. Southern Baptists support ten thousand missionaries across the United States and around the world through their Cooperative Program and the special offerings at Christmas and Easter. Such a powerful, ongoing missions effort is only possible because thousands of churches, large and small, give to their joint channel of funding.

> *Few churches can support a missionary family, but through the Cooperative Program, every church can participate in the ministries of thousands of missionaries having a global impact for Christ.*

Few churches can support a missionary family, but through the Cooperative Program, every church can participate in the ministries of thousands of missionaries having a global impact for Christ. Cooperate with your denomination. Learn how it supports missionaries. Lead your church to give sacrificially to make their work possible. Pray for the missionaries regularly. Educate your people about the ministries their missionaries are doing and share the results at every opportunity. Host a missions conference and invite a missionary who is on home assignment (furlough) to speak. Adopt a missionary and a mission field. Working together with other churches within your denomination, you can accomplish much good for the Kingdom.

6. Go

Few activities will generate passion for missions like being part of missionary work. Short-term mission trips give you and your people the opportunity to partner with career missionaries in reaching people in places you have never been before. While short-term missions groups can never replace career missionaries who learn the languages and live year round with their target people groups, they can be valuable supplements for the missionary's ministry. Equip the people with information about cross-cultural relationships and appropriate communication with people of different backgrounds. Be well prepared for the trip. Help your people understand their purpose is to help the missionary rather than constantly demanding the missionary serve the group. While the short-term group may experience some tourist-oriented activities, their primary purpose is not to see the sights or buy souvenirs, but to reach people for Jesus!

Chapter 17

DEVELOPING THE FLOCK: ASSIMILATING NEW MEMBERS/MAKING DISCIPLES

"Teaching them to observe all things whatsoever I have commanded you: . . ."
(Matthew 28:20).

Having reached people with the Gospel, churches have a responsibility to help them integrate into the fellowship of the church and grow as disciples of Jesus. How terrible it would be for a mother to set her newborn baby on a city sidewalk and merely walk away. It should be equally incredible that a newborn child of God would be left on his own. His spiritual skills in self-preservation and personal growth are little more than a babe regardless of his chronological age. The new Christian needs nurture, love, instruction, and protection. More mature believers who join a church also depend on their new congregation to take the initiative in helping them assimilate into the Body.

Many churches assume people will find their place in the church. They expect people to grow into responsible followers of Christ simply by attending Bible study and worship. Such churches may be aggressive in reaching people but passive in retaining them. They place the responsibility on the new members for settling in to their new church home. Unless the newcomers are remarkably outgoing, they often sit back uninvolved, unrelated, and unloved. We should not be surprised that they eventually join another church or simply drop out altogether.

If I invite people into my home, I make sure they are comfortable. If other guests are present, I introduce them and help them get acquainted. I don't just say, "Make yourself at home" and expect them to raid the refrigerator and cook their own dinner. My invitation obligates me to be hospitable, to take the initiative in developing the friendship, and to insure my guest wants to come back! We should do no less with new church members.

John Mark Terry observes two keys to retaining members: "a sense of belonging and a sense of involvement." He adds, "We need to make new members feel accepted and we need to get them involved in a meaningful way in the church."[1]

Next-Gen pastors value relationships and are passionate about making disciples. How can you take deliberate action to assimilate new believers and new members? What processes aid your priority in developing disciples? Responsibility for making disciples and helping new members become involved in the congregation does not rest solely on the shoulders of the pastor. The pastor employs other mature believers and various ministry organizations and systems to help achieve this vital goal. Church ministers should be personally involved in helping people grow in the image of Christ.

Providing Follow-Up/Assimilation

Second Baptist Church of Houston, Texas, regularly leads the nation in evangelism and baptisms. It equally emphasizes assimilating and developing new believers. The church uses a six-tier approach to assimilation. (The following six-point outline was shared in a telephone interview with a senior staff minister. The narrative for each point is the author's.)

- **Attract**—The church employs various events to draw people to a place where they can hear the Gospel. This plan not only includes activities at the church (worship, Bible study groups, age group programs, etc.), but at other venues as well. These events are designed to help attendees meet church members who initiate relationships with them. They also have deliberate plans for sharing the Good News of Jesus and the way to salvation. Gospel presentations include a variety of ways for people to make decisions for Christ.
- **Attach**—The church immediately offers baptism, Bible study groups, and discipleship for people who respond. Church ministers do not passively sit by, hoping people will find their way into church involvement and spiritual growth.
- **Assimilate**—Second Baptist makes a priority of involving all members, especially new believers, in Bible classes. While worship services have become the new front door of evangelism and outreach, small Bible study groups remain the most effective ways to offer fellowship and discipleship.
- **Advance**—Church leaders help believers grow through discipleship in small groups. Discipleship means more than learning biblical facts; it requires application of biblical principles to life as people become more like Jesus in everyday life.
- **Activate**—The church systematically involves people in various ministries based on spiritual giftedness. Everyone can do something. People who are active in serving Christ will be more committed to the church than persons who merely attend, spectate, and go home as soon as possible.

- **Affirm**—The congregation believes in constantly encouraging believers at each stage of their spiritual journey. When people join a church, they will be at different levels of maturity. Some new members need more help than others. All require affirmation. Effective churches are intentional in finding and implementing ways of encouraging their members.

Maximizing the Educational Ministry

Objectives for assimilation and discipleship can be accomplished through the church educational ministry. Often this ministry involves several organizations and opportunities, including small-group Bible study, either in a typical Sunday School (whether by that name or others, such as Connect Groups) or home cell groups. Many churches also have Discipleship Training programs and ministries for various age groups, including men's and women's ministries, youth and children's ministries, Children's Church, missions' organizations, and others.

Some church planters and Next-Gen pastors lean toward using home cell groups rather than traditional Sunday Schools. Newly birthed churches may not have the physical facilities to provide for a Sunday morning Bible study program, leading them to use homes for small-group ministry.

What are the advantages or disadvantages of each system?

Participation

The most successful home group system that I have found has an attendance of 40 percent of Sunday morning worship attendance. On the other hand, the average Sunday School reaches 80 percent of worship participation. One reason is **accessibility**. People who come for worship are already committed to being at church on Sunday morning. Coming an hour or so early for Bible study is easier than going to someone's home on another evening of the week.

Developmental Considerations

Home cell groups generally are oriented for adults. Often older adults choose not to participate due to physical limitations of getting out on another night, traveling to someone's home, having a lack of handicapped accessibility, and other problems. Teenagers tend not to participate in cell group Bible studies, although they enjoy social activities in homes. Another challenge is provision for child care for preschool and elementary children. Many young parents will not enlist babysitters or drop off their children at another location in order to go to someone's home for the Bible study.

Acceptability by Unchurched Persons

Unchurched people are more likely to come to the home of a friend or neighbor than to a church building, making home groups an effective evangelistic tool. However, studies have shown that a high percentage of lost persons are also open to coming to church if invited by friends to go with them. The key is having genuine personal invitations to participate in the church alongside someone they know. Simply urging people to attend the church without the accompanying relationship is less effective.

Purpose

Home groups by their nature are more informal, tend to remain small in attendance, and lean toward social engagement. All three characteristics have positive benefits but also can be counterproductive in achieving the purpose of evangelism, growth, and discipleship. On the other hand, traditional Sunday morning groups that focus solely on teaching a lesson can lack meaningful fellowship, omit practical application of Bible principles, and become introspective as members are satisfied with their group and not be motivated to reach unchurched people. The best qualities of each venue should be developed to maximize effectiveness.

The simple answer is to offer both—Sunday morning Bible study groups (Sunday School, etc.) as well as home fellowship groups. In either ministry, to be effective they need a clear purpose, well-trained leader/teachers, streamlined organization, biblical curriculum, an atmosphere conducive for fellowship, and opportunities for ministry.

Principles for Effective Small Groups

Clear Purpose—Win People to Christ and Make Disciples

Without a clear purpose embraced by members, small groups will wander into whatever is the primary interest of the leader. Healthy groups have emphases on several activities but will center on a single purpose. Activities will include gaining Bible knowledge, learning to apply biblical principles in practical experience, mutual support through prayer and encouragement, fellowship and social interaction, ministry events, and others. However, all activities should intentionally help to accomplish the singular purpose of making disciples. The purpose of the Sunday School or Bible class is not merely to teach the lesson, but to use the lesson and other activities to make disciples.

Teacher Training

Some classes will develop around a few master teachers, people who are gifted with the ability to study and exposit Scriptures with biblical depth and practical application.

Most classes, however, are led by well-intentioned people who have little background or qualifications needed for their positions. They need training in how to study the Bible, develop lesson plans, employ effective teaching methods, and understand group dynamics, disciple making, and other skills. The pastor may not do all of the training, but he must insure training occurs, not only for teachers but for all leaders.

Biblical Curriculum

Content for Bible study groups is available from many publishing companies. Some Bible teachers develop their own lessons, based on personal study or following a book written by someone they respect. The problem, particularly with the latter method, includes the fact that most teachers lack theological foundations, have insufficient study resources, and have not been taught in proper hermeneutical techniques. Without a check and balance, teachers can teach unbiblical ideas, however unwittingly.

Using a sound curriculum, such as the various series offered by LifeWay Christian Resources, overcomes most of these difficulties. Each lesson is the product of writers who have been trained in lesson development. Editors have checked the lessons for theological and biblical accuracy. Teacher aids provide lesson plans and methods that enhance class experiences. Printed study books do not eliminate the necessity of teachers doing good preparatory work, but they do make instruction more efficient.

Fellowship

Strong small groups offer a warm atmosphere for fellowship both within the class time and at other occasions. The schedule, arrangement of chairs and other furniture, availability of simple refreshments, and other aspects of the class experience should allow people to interact socially with one another. In addition, classes can offer fellowship opportunities in members' homes, at appropriate restaurants, or in other venues.

Prayer

Developing relationships includes praying for one another. Time for prayer should not be superficial or perfunctory. Members benefit by genuinely offering intercession. Paul urged the believers to pray for one another: "Praying always with all prayer and supplication in the Spirit, and watching thereunto with all perseverance and supplication for all saints; . . ." (Ephesians 6:18).

The class my wife and I attend has a prayer leader who collects prayer needs and shares them by e-mail with class members. Naturally, such sharing must not allow prayer requests to degenerate into gossip. As we have experienced various needs, we've felt a stronger connection and love from our class as they have prayed for us and we have prayed for them.

Ministry

God gives pastors and teachers to equip the saints for the work of ministry (Ephesians 4:12). Gaining Bible knowledge is not an end in itself; it enables us to know and serve God. We minister to the Lord by ministering to His people (Matthew 25:45). Small groups should be sensitive to members' needs and provide ministry to serve one another. They also are blessed by serving other people in the church and community. By engaging in ministry, individually and as a group, members will grow in spiritual maturity as disciples of Jesus.

Integrating New Members into Ministry

Every new member comes into the church with spiritual gifts, interests, abilities, and experience that God intends for the benefit of others in the Body of Christ. They also have a need to express those gifts in service. While the entry level of some new members focuses on their need for fellowship and having the church minister to them and their families, God has built into each believer the desire to have significant roles in ministry. Successful churches develop intentional systems to discover the people's interests and abilities and to give them opportunities to serve God. As people participate in ministries within and outside the church, they find satisfaction in fulfilling God's purpose. The greater their involvement, the stronger their commitment to the church. At the same time, beware of overloading good workers to the point they burn out or get discouraged.

Maintaining an Effective System for Follow-Up

Member care cannot be left to informal happenstance. Effective churches develop intentional systems for following up with members' spiritual growth and involvement in the congregation. Consider where individuals are in the various stages of disciplenships and what needs to happen for them to reach the next level. Build into the natural relationships and organizational activities of the congregation such activities and expectations that aid assimilation and growth. Help the entire congregation understand the importance of each member giving attention to one another. Encourage them to reach out to persons to build relationships, to help with various needs, and to serve through informal ministry.

Chapter 18

WORKING WITH DEACONS

"Wherefore, brethren, look ye out among you seven men of honest report, full of the Holy Ghost and wisdom, whom we may appoint over this business" (Acts 6:3).

"And let these also first be proved; then let them use the office of a deacon, being found blameless" (1 Timothy 3:10).

Pastors do not bear the ministry of pastoral care by themselves. The office of deacon provides godly men who can help in the ministry. Deacons were established by the first-century church at the recommendation of the pastors, who at that time were the apostles. The church was experiencing conflict over the administration of widow benevolence. The believers held things in common, giving to the church what they could, which in turn became part of the support of persons who lacked, especially as a result of persecution or economic deprivation. The church provided food regularly for Christian widows who lacked family support. The Greek-background Christians believed the Hebrew-background widows were getting preferential treatment to the neglect of Greek widows.

The matter came to the apostles' attention. Peter called the entire congregation together, which was a good example of congregational decision making since the disciples could have simply issued an edict if they exercised elder rule. Instead, Peter informed the people that the pastors' primary responsibilities were the ministry of the Word and prayer. His solution was that congregation should choose among themselves seven men of honest reputation and full of the Holy Spirit "whom we may place over this matter" (Acts 6:1–6).

This idea "seemed good to them," indicating the entire congregation was part of the deciding to establish the deaconate and was responsible for choosing the deacons, who were confirmed in their roles by the apostles/pastors through the laying on of hands.

The primary responsibility of the deacons was not simply "waiting on tables." They led a ministry. The word translated *deacon*, which is not used in Acts 6 but is clearly implied, simply means "minister." Deacons were not in authority over the pastors but served under the pastors' supervision. Their role was to take care of this ministry so the pastors would be free to concentrate on spiritual leadership and ministry.

Deacons were born out of church conflict. Unfortunately, today some ministers have a poor concept of deacons because of associations with deacon–pastor conflict. How pastors think about deacons and how deacons think about pastors depends on past history, personalities, power struggles, and personal traits, including spirituality and maturity.

> *The office of deacon was created to resolve church conflict, not be embroiled in it.*

Actually, the office of deacon was created to resolve church conflict, not be embroiled in it. Pastors and deacons should be best friends and effective co-laborers. Unfortunately, many ministers and deacons experience conflict, often due to **misunderstandings of their roles and relationships.**

Self-Concept: Some deacon bodies think of themselves as deacon boards. In fact, their churches also think of them in that fashion. Part of the history of such churches involves short-tenured pastors.

A pastor comes to the church, stays a short while (usually around twenty-four months) and then leaves before building the trust of the congregation. Often the church has interim leadership for six months to a year before calling another pastor. The church tends to depend on the leadership and decision making of the deacons as the only other elected group of ordained men. Deacons tend to have a higher profile of authority than committees due to their ordained status and biblical origin.

Pastors can help lead the church past such problems by staying longer, building trust, developing stronger relationships, and gradually educating the church and the deacons into a return to biblical paradigms.

Past Experiences: Relationships between deacons and pastors often get off to a wrong start not due to either party's actions, but in reaction to previous experiences. Churches may have had difficult experiences with previous pastors and look to the deacons to guide and somewhat control the new pastor. The new pastor may have had conflicts with deacons in previous churches and may see deacons as challenges to his authority and leadership. Pastors and deacons must be honest enough with each other to share their concern about past problems. They also need to work toward the future in love rather than remain bogged down in the past.

Control: Some pastors want to be in control. They think the pastor should be the CEO of the church. A few dislike basic pastoral ministry, such as visitation, pastoral care, hospital ministry, etc., so they try to delegate these responsibilities to the deacons, emphasizing the deacon's spiritual leadership. At the same time, these pastors deemphasize any administrative role by the deacons and assume more authority/ administration for themselves.

On the other hand, many deacon bodies exercise control over the church and the pastor. They think of themselves as a Board of Directors with authority over all the decisions in the church. Not only is this model unbiblical but it is unhealthy for the church, the pastor, and the deacons themselves.

A better option exists. If each party understands the biblical nature of their roles and relationship, and commits to loving each other and serving the church, a wonderful partnership can ensue.

In summary, what were the biblical roles and relationships of pastors and deacons?

1. Deacons were established by a joint decision of the pastor and the congregation, with each playing key roles in determining who would serve.
2. Deacons were placed under the supervision of the pastors. In turn, they exercised leadership over assigned aspects of ministry.
3. Deacons' functions focused on practical ministry to the congregation.
4. Pastors supervised the deacons, while the deacons supported the church by freeing the pastors from the details of certain ministries.
5. Instead of being the source of conflict, the deacons served to resolve conflict in the congregation as partners with the pastors.
6. While deacons do not supervise pastors, wise ministers will recognize the value of seeking the advice of these godly leaders. With the abundance of counselors, there is wisdom and safety (Proverbs 11:14). Only a foolish pastor tries to run roughshod over men to whom the church has entrusted the deacon ministry.

Qualifications for Deacons

Acts 6:1–4 and 1 Timothy 3:8–13 contain the basic requirements for a deacon.

1. Deacons were men. Having male deacons is not chauvinistic; it merely follows the biblical pattern.
2. Deacons were to have an honest reputation. Church members and people in the community should acknowledge them as trustworthy.
3. Deacons were to be full of the Holy Ghost. Being filled with the Holy Spirit meant they were fully surrendered to the Lordship of Christ and the leadership of the Spirit. True ministry can only be accomplished in the power of the Holy Spirit. Also, Spirit-filled deacons and ministers will not express the works of the flesh but will enjoy the fruit of the Spirit (Galatians 5:16–26).

4. Deacons were to be known for wisdom, not worldly wisdom but wisdom that comes through application of the Word of God.

5. Deacons should be grave, serious minded. This qualification does not mean a deacon should not have a sense of humor. Rather, they should not be flippant or frivolous.

6. Deacons should not be double tongued. They should speak honestly, consistently, and always with good intentions.

7. Deacons should not be "given to much wine." Some contemporary pastors (and deacons) debate the appropriateness of totally abstaining from using alcoholic beverages. Notice that Timothy had to get specific direction from Paul (who had the advice of Dr. Luke at hand) who told him to "drink no longer water (by itself—inferred), but take a little wine" for his stomach problems. This verse obviously demonstrates that Timothy's habit had been not to drink alcohol at all, not even the diluted form common to society of that day. An honest study of scriptural references to alcohol throughout Old and New Testament show the danger of using beverage alcohol. Anyone questioning this practice should ask themselves, am I seeking the glory of God or looking for an excuse for self-indulgence?

8. Deacons should not be greedy of "filthy lucre"—that is, they are not motivated by financial greed.

9. Deacons should hold "the mystery of the faith in a pure conscience." That is, they should single-mindedly be committed to the Gospel.

10. Deacons should be "proved," meaning new believers should not be set aside as deacons. Deacons need to be mature spiritually and experientially.

11. Deacons should be "husbands of one wife." Most conservative churches interpret this statement to mean the deacon should not have been divorced and remarried. Some scholars translate this phrase as "one woman man" and argue that, in an age of polygamy, the deacon simply should not be married to more than one woman at a time. However, polygamy was clearly not practiced among the church, so why have a special requirement that the deacon not be a polygamist? Obviously, the reference describes something else regarding the deacon's marital status. On the other hand, some readers question whether single men are eligible for deacon service since they are not "husbands of one wife." The text appears not to restrict the deaconate to married men but makes the point that if he is married, he should not be divorced.

12. Deacons, like pastors, should manage their households well, as demonstrated by the way they raise their children and treat their

wives. If deacons and ministers cannot lead their own households, they cannot be trusted with the church of God.

13. Deacons' wives also had to meet certain qualifications, being grave, not slanderers, sober, and faithful in all things. Thus, if a man's wife is a gossip, he is not qualified to serve as a deacon.

Most churches rightfully expect deacons to attend all regular Sunday and Wednesday church functions and deacons' meetings unless providentially hindered. Absence or failure to fulfill the duties of his office often initiates some level of accountability or counseling regarding whether the deacon should continue in service.

Deacons should support the ministers of the church, its mission, and programs. Support includes faithfulness in financial stewardship, including giving a tithe as the minimum of giving to the church. In addition, they should abstain from questionable forms of entertainment, such as gambling.

What Do Deacons Do?
Try the 4-10-30 Deacon Ministry Plan

Deacons minister in many ways. Some participate in hospital visitation, ministry to widows and widowers, grief ministry, and much more. One of the most effective methods of multiplying pastoral ministry is the Deacon Ministry Plan. Unfortunately, few churches have an effective ministry plan.

"We have tried Deacon Ministry Plan before and it just does not work, Pastor." Those words have greeted me more than once while serving as pastor or interim pastor. Rather than using the best plan devised for deacon ministry, many churches give up in frustration.

The usual problems involve shortage of time, ineffectiveness of organization, lack of accountability, and a perception that this is just not fun. Deacons, like everyone else, are pressed for time. Their work schedule, family needs, community groups, and church activities demand so much that they cringe whenever the chairman talks about adding the Deacon Ministry Flock.

Applying the 4/10/30 Plan solves each of these problems. The plan has four simple keys:

Key #1: Enlist a Leader

The deacon chairman or vice-chairman should be the leader of the Deacon Ministry Plan. If the chairman and vice-chairman have each other on their own deacon flocks, and divide the rest of the deacon body between them, they accomplish several important results:

1. By remembering that the deacons and their immediate families are in need of prayer and ministry just like all the other church families, the deacon chair lets them know he loves them as people, not just as cogs in the deacon ministry machine.
2. By calling them regularly and praying for their families' needs, the chairman sets an important example that his fellow deacons will follow. Leaders should not use the call as an opportunity to talk church business or to check up on them.
3. By having their own families in someone's flock, the chairman and vice-chairman do not miss out on their own needs being met by a caring deacon.

Key #2: Organize People by Affinity Groups

Too often, deacons already have groups for which they are responsible: Sunday School classes, sports teams, choir, or other ministry groups. Adding a separate Deacon Ministry Flock is like piling on at the end of the run in football. Someone ought to throw a flag! However, when you organize by affinity groups, you start with those groups to which the deacon is already committed. Those people become his deacon flock. Since he already has relationships with them, he is excited to enhance his ministry by being their deacon also.

If a deacon is a Sunday School teacher, his class and their families becomes his deacon flock. If his class is too large for one flock leader, he can divide the class between himself and one or two other flock leaders. If the teacher is not a deacon, a deacon who attends the class could take that class as his flock. Similarly, if a deacon is a coach, his flock is made of his team members and their families. Deacons who are in the music ministry can focus on their fellow singers in choir. One deacon exclaimed, "Since my fellow choir members have become my deacon flock, it's working out great! I get to see them and build on those relationships." Another shared, "Since I got a group that I'm more compatible with, I am much more involved and enjoying the flock ministry more."

Those persons not involved in any organization can be divided among the deacons much like a sports draft program. The names are read aloud and deacons who already have relationships with these people can claim them for their flocks. Church families that are left over are divided geographically so, at the least, the deacon lives nearby and does not have to drive a great distance to see them. In addition, such people may be inactive because they have not built relationships in the church. Having their own deacon for a neighbor may open the door for a friendship and reclaim the family for active involvement.

Key #3: Outline Expectations

Too often, deacons are hit with the maximum expectations rather than the baseline requirements. While not shying away from challenging deacons to do all they can in ministering to their families, the chairman should begin by offering a simple plan with the understanding that anyone serving as a deacon should commit to this as a minimum.

In the **4/10/30 Plan**, deacons contact four of their families each week. While personal visits are ideal, as a minimum the deacon should make a phone call to these four families. After introducing himself in the first call, he simply says, "I'm praying for several families in my ministry flock tonight, including yours. I just wanted to know, is there is anything for which you'd like me to pray?" Most phone calls will average about five minutes each. After the four calls, the deacon spends at least ten minutes in prayer for those families. The total time: thirty minutes. Four calls, ten minutes of prayer, thirty minutes.

Can this plan involve longer calls? More time in prayer? Additional ways of contacts? Absolutely. One participant shared, "When I call my people, I can't stop talking after just five minutes. I find myself enjoying a good long discussion." Another reported, "At first this one person I called was taken aback by the call and did not respond well, but later she called me back and asked for prayer." A third said, "One person opened up about some difficulties they were experiencing at work. We prayed. A couple of weeks later the problem was resolved and they called back to say thank you for having someone to talk to."

By starting with the minimum basic requirement of thirty minutes a week, no deacon can honestly say he does not have enough time. Deacons who choose to give more time receive even greater blessings. In the average church, if every deacon follows through, the entire church family can be contacted personally every four to six weeks.

If the people are not home, the deacon simply calls another family on his list, insuring four completed calls a week. If no contact is made after two or three weeks, a personal visit or a letter should follow. One deacon shared, "After I couldn't reach these people by phone, I wrote a letter letting them know I was praying for them and was available to them. They showed up at church the next week and have been there steadily four weeks in a row."

Key #4: Establish Accountability

Without a regular system of accountability, even the best-intentioned deacon may let his ministry slip into irregularity. The deacon chairman should give each member a simple report form on which the deacons list the families that are contacted each month, the types of contacts, any results that need to be known, and any prayer or ministry needs that should be shared. Obviously, any matters of confidence should not be written down or repeated but indicated as an "unspoken request" for prayer. With this focus, the deacons' meeting becomes a time of celebration, sharing, encouragement, and prayer.

Reports from one church's deacons included these comments:

- "Following our initial contact with this family, my wife and I visited and took a hot meal. The husband is in my Sunday School class, so I get to talk with him nearly every Sunday. The wife is ill and homebound. We prayed for the entire family."
- "The son in this family recently graduated from boot camp in the military and is being reassigned to a new base. The family asked that we pray for his safety."
- "This lady's brother is very ill in another state and asked that we pray for him."
- "One man was seventy years old, dying of cancer. We visited with him, and he prayed to receive Christ."
- "Before this, my wife didn't really want to be involved in my flock ministry, but following a phone contact with one widow, my wife went with me to visit her. The lady was elderly and needed help getting to the doctor's office, but she would not have felt comfortable asking me for help. My wife took her to the doctor and now calls the widow often to follow up."

What Are Some Benefits of the 4/10/30 Plan?

- *Needs Discovery*: A regular system of contacts insures that many needs within the congregation and community at large will be discovered. Most church members will not initiate a call to their deacon or the church staff to discuss their needs. However, few respond negatively to someone showing enough concern to call them and pray for them.

- *Troubleshooting: Prevention and Correction:* When the deacon calls, a family may discuss some problem they are having. The problem may be personal, or may affect the church, or may relate to family, job, or other type of issue. By knowing the need, the deacon may be able to handle it directly and easily. In more serious matters, he should call on the church ministers and refer the matter to them. Often issues that have not developed into major problems can be addressed at a much earlier stage, preventing the harm that might occur had the matter gone undetected.

- *The Feeling that Someone Cares:* A congregation with an active deacon ministry has a much healthier self-image because the people know that someone cares about them personally. Having deacons and ministers personally praying for them regularly can provide a much higher level of satisfaction and support for the church as a whole.

- *Reclamation of Inactive Members:* A perennial problem for most churches is the long list of inactive people on its membership rolls. When deacons, Sunday School teachers, ministers, or others constantly contact families who have dropped out for one reason or another, the result is often discouraging. However, when those same leaders contact inactive people and do not focus on trying to get them back in church, but rather focus on hearing them, loving them, and praying for them, the results can be very positive. As a deacon who tried this beamed, "Four of my families have been inactive for a long time. After two months of contacts, two of the four are regularly in church again."

- *Deacon Cohesion:* Deacons who minister together, share with one another, and pray for and with each other cannot avoid drawing closer together. Rather than being divided by administrative concerns, these deacons are focused on Kingdom issues. The deacons become more cohesive as a body and also as a bonding force within the congregation.

While every system has its advantages and disadvantages, the **4/10/30 Plan** succeeds in leading deacons to be more active in the Deacon Ministry Plan. As a friend of mine used to say, "God will bless something before He'll bless nothing." While a few phone calls a week are not the ultimate goal of the plan, they are a good starting place. As your deacons take these simple steps, the deeper ministry will lie just ahead in their path.

EPISCOPOS—BISHOP

Servant Leadership and Administration

Chapter 19

THE PASTOR'S OVERSIGHT: BEING A SPIRITUAL LEADER

While witnessing to a certain lady, I asked if she were a Christian. She replied, "Oh, yes. In fact, I want to marry a pastor. No, better than that, I want to marry a bishop!" Like many other people, she did not understand that a bishop and a pastor are one and the same. Every time you see the term *bishop* (episcopos) in Scripture, it refers to a pastor. The qualifications for a bishop are those for a pastor (1 Timothy 3; Titus 1).

The word *episcopos* is also translated "overseer," and in the verb form is rendered "to give oversight." Some people take that idea and have the idea that the pastor rules the church. To the contrary, the concept behind being an overseer means simply to provide spiritual leadership for God's congregation.

The apostle Peter described the way one provides oversight in terms of shepherding. In a passage in which he uses all three words (presbuteros, episcopos, and poimen), Peter tells the pastors to provide oversight by shepherding the flock of God:

"The elders (*presbuteros*) which are among you I exhort, who am also an elder, and a witness of the sufferings of Christ, and also a partaker of the glory that shall be revealed: Feed (*poimen*) the flock of God which is among you, taking the oversight (*episcopos*) thereof, not by constraint, but willingly; not for filthy lucre, but of a ready mind; Neither as being lords over God's heritage, but being ensamples to the flock. And when the chief Shepherd shall appear, ye shall receive a crown of glory that fades not away" (1 Peter 5:1–4).

The Nature of Spiritual Leadership

Having a formal role does not necessarily make you a good leader. If you expect people to do what you say, like the captain of a ship, simply because you are the pastor or minister-of-something-or-other, then you will not lead long nor well. However, if you will study the Scriptures and follow the example of the Good Shepherd, you can experience the blessing of your calling as a "good minister of Jesus Christ" (1 Timothy 4:6).

Jesus offered the example of servant leadership: "But Jesus called them *to him*, and said unto them, 'You know that they which are accounted to rule over the Gentiles exercise lordship over them; and their great ones exercise authority upon them. But so shall it not be among you: but whosoever will be great among you, shall be your minister: And whosoever of you will be the chief, shall be servant of all. For even the Son of man came not to be ministered unto, but to minister, and to give his life a ransom for many'" (Mark 10:42–45).

Next-Gen pastors serve in a postmodern generation. The concept of servant leadership appeals to many postmodernists who claim to be egalitarian, rejecting the idea of authority-based leadership. Purists point to arguments by Deridder and Foucault that all texts (biblical and other) are efforts to exercise power over other people. They purport to prefer group decisions by consensus. However, nearly all writers claiming postmodern philosophies exercise authority in promoting their positions. They do not recognize the hypocrisy of their position.

Some ministers prefer a laissez-faire type of leadership, in which they defer decision making to other people. As in the biblical days of Judges, people do what is right in their own eyes. Again, such an environment may be preferred by postmoderns influenced by relativity and perspectivism. In their view, no one person has a corner on truth; therefore, every person has the right of self-determination.

Neither of These Viewpoints Models Jesus' Concept of Leadership. Jesus exercised strong leadership. He spoke with authority (Mark 1:22). The question was not whether Jesus had authority but rather how He used authority. Many modern leaders, including some pastors, use positions of authority for personal goals, often using other people to achieve their agendas. Jesus, on the other hand, used authority to serve people by bringing them into right relationships with God.

Any biblical leadership or authority relies solely on our being disciples of Jesus. The apostle Paul understood this nature of leadership. He told the churches of his day, "Be ye followers (imitators) of me as I am of Christ" (1 Corinthians 11:1). He could only expect people to follow him as he followed Christ. So, my personal definition of leadership is simple: "A leader is someone who is following Christ and provides a model and manner for other people to follow Christ."

> A leader is someone who is following Christ and provides a model and manner for other people to follow Christ.

By following Christ and helping others do so, we exercise the highest form of servant leadership. Authority and power are not intended to elevate the pastor, achieve grand schemes and plans, or build personal kingdoms. By being under Christ's authority, we are empowered to make disciples of all people. Being a disciple means knowing and following Christ.

Biblical leaders do not want simply to influence followers; they want to develop other people as disciples of Christ who can lead others to follow Him. To help other people fulfill their potential is one of the great joys of leadership. Unfortunately, most churches do not develop Christian leaders but simply try to identify people with leadership skills and put them into appropriate places of service. In those few cases in which pastors focus on developing leaders in the church, they often concentrate simply on teaching individuals the specific skills needed for a job in the church (such as how to teach a Bible class, or how to be a decision counselor).

Without a holistic approach to leadership development, churches lose the opportunity to see potential leaders emerge not only for service in the church but also for impact on homes, business, and the community at large. True leadership, then, involves a vision of leadership multiplication as we equip believers to reproduce themselves not only in other new believers but in new believers who become Christian leaders.

The Character of Spiritual Leadership

Think of people who have influenced your life. Take a minute and write down a list of the top ten people you admire. What about these people appeals to you so strongly? Certainly, they may have certain competencies that impress you. All leaders have abilities, skills, talents, and gifts to do their work with excellence. Yet, other people have those same competencies and do not make your top ten list of leaders. So why did you include the people on your list?

Likely, you are thinking about aspects of character. Leadership more often rises and falls on personhood than the success of the organization, the skills of the individual, or the social endearment of personality. The wise writer of Proverbs advised, "Choose a good reputation over great riches, for being held in high esteem is better than having silver or gold" (Proverbs 22:1). If our definition of leadership is to serve others by helping them follow Christ, then the leader's character qualities ought to reflect those of Christ. In addition to those character qualities found earlier in our discussion of the character of the pastor, consider the following characteristics based on Jesus' teachings in the Beatitudes (Matthew 5:3–12).

- **Poor in Spirit:** Being poor in spirit seems to be the antithesis of leadership. We think of leaders as self-confident, commanding, and assured. Yet, Scripture exalts humility as blessed by God, while pride precedes destruction (Proverbs 16:18). Jesus offered His example of humility for us to follow: "Learn of me for I am meek and lowly of heart" (Matthew 11:29). The phrases "lowly of heart" and "poor in spirit" have a similar meaning. The truly humble person is not self-centered or self-sufficient but recognizes his need before God. Consequently, Jesus taught His disciples: "Whosoever therefore shall humble himself as this little child, the same is greatest in the kingdom of heaven" (Luke 9:46).

- **Mourn:** We have difficulty imagining Jesus mourning because we identify this quality with having a lack of peace. Yet, Jesus wept at the tomb of Lazarus (John 11:35), grieved over Jerusalem (Luke 13:34), and prayed with an "exceeding sorrowful" heart in the Garden (Matthew 26:38). Leaders feel deeply. The general commanding the greatest respect of his men is one who cares about their lives and grieves over their pain.

- **Meek:** Akin to being poor in spirit and lowly of heart, meekness portrays a gentle spirit as opposed to a rough, combative nature. Rather than being a symbol of weakness, meekness reflects genuine spiritual strength enabling a godly pastor to lead without having to bully people around. Moses was meeker than all the great men of the Old Testament (Numbers 12:3). Yet Moses was strong enough to lead Israel out of Egypt at eighty and spend the next forty years guiding them through their desert wanderings. He was strong enough to withstand criticism and opposition; yet he never sought his own honor, glory, or status. He served God by serving God's people, even when they rebelled against him and rejected his leadership.

- **Hunger and Thirst for Righteousness:** One area in which we cannot directly relate to Jesus' experience involves longing for righteousness. Jesus was entirely righteous. His core nature was righteous. Every action and attitude fulfilled righteousness. We only have such righteousness as He imputes to us when we are placed in Christ at salvation. The idea of righteousness in this verse carries the weight of rightness with God not only positionally (as saved people) but in daily life. This character quality reflects a desire for a right relationship with God, a yearning for communion with the Holy One.

- **Merciful:** Jesus' entire ministry built upon His quality of mercy. Old Testament psalms regale in God's mercy, which endures forever. Mercy does not excuse evil or error but provides a means of forgiveness. Jesus made mercy possible on the cross. Through His blood, we can experience God's forgiveness. Having received forgiveness, we can extend mercy and forgive others (Matthew 6:14–15; Ephesians 4:32).

- **Pure in Heart:** Jesus was absolutely pure in heart. Knowing sin, we cannot experience the purity of heart to the extent of Jesus. However, the word for pure is *katharos* from which we get *cathartic*, meaning to cleanse. A spiritual leader knows the deceptive nature of the human heart and depends on the cleansing power of Christ's blood to purify him and enable him to see (know, understand, and relate to) God. The idea of pure in heart also relates to single-mindedness as opposed to being duplicitous. The pure in heart does not say one thing and mean another but is straightforward in word and deed.

- **Peacemakers:** Jesus was the Prince of Peace. Yet, He said He came not to bring peace but a sword that would divide even members of a family (Matthew 10:34). Some leaders believe one conquers by dividing others. That concept is not what Jesus meant. Jesus was peaceful in nature and made peace between us and God. At the same time, Jesus became a dividing line between people who accept Him and those who reject Him. Our emulation of the Peacemaker is to sow reconciliation and love rather than division and hatred. Such produces our identity as the children of God.

- **Persecuted for Righteousness:** Jesus understood persecution for righteousness sake. He was "despised and rejected of men . . ." (Isaiah 3:3). "He came into His own and His own received Him not" (John 1:12). Jesus warned His disciples that evil people who rejected and persecuted Him would do the same to them (John 15:18–20). Paul advised a young preacher to expect to suffer persecution if he lived a godly life in Christ: "Yes, and all that will live godly in Christ Jesus shall suffer persecution" (2 Timothy 3:12).

Godly leaders exhibit a Christlike character that attracts the following of godly people. Skills and abilities can be learned, but godly character is developed. How do we ensure we continuously and consistently reflect godly character? Godly character comes not through human effort but by being transformed into Christ's image by the power of the indwelling Christ. This would be a good place to go back and read chapter 3 again, especially about how to develop Christlike character through communion with Jesus.

The Spiritual Leader's Competencies

In what competencies should a pastor excel? When asked what skills, abilities, and competencies a pastor should have, young ministers generally offer the same answers the average person might mention: preaching, teaching, counseling, pastoral care, and leadership in a general sense. Certainly, the pastor needs to develop each of these functions. However, as the leader of the corporate group known as the church, the minister needs specific leadership competencies. You will find numerous books on leadership to develop this idea more completely, but consider a few vital competences pastors need to be effective.

Establish the Agenda

While every church member has a role in fulfilling the church's mission, the specific agenda of any given congregation usually begins with the pastor. As pastors change, the corporate focus adjusts to the heartbeat of each new leader. Change usually occurs over time as the pastor gains the people's trust. A pastor who stays in a place for any length of time is responsible to a great degree for the direction of the congregation.

Develop the Organization

The wise pastor will work with skilled and experienced leaders within the congregation to organize the church's processes, programs, ministries, personnel, and other resources to fulfill its purpose. Most people in the congregation or on the church staff view the church from the perspective of personal interest. Only the pastor sees the complete picture and has full understanding of how all the parts fit together.

Cultivate the Church Culture

As important as the development of various functioning components of the church (ministries, committees, staffing structures, etc.), equally vital is the corporate culture. While all organizations have a particular ethos, sometimes the congregational culture is not healthy or is not conducive to achieving the desired goals. For Christian churches and businesses, it is vital that the overall culture reflect the nature of Christ and His Body. The leader is tasked with guiding the development of such culture into a dynamic, and authentically Christian, quality.

Set the Pace

The church will generally match the pace set by the pastor. Granted, in many cases, the pastor may want to move faster than the congregation; in a few situations, the opposite may be true. However, most pastors set the pace for advancement by their personal example. Congregations cannot be pushed, prodded, bullied, or shamed into moving forward for any length of time. Eventually, they will rebel. On the other hand, if the pastor leads from the front and guides them forward, most people will see the vision and follow. The essence of servant leadership is to demonstrate a personal commitment to whatever you are trying to get others to be and to do. Whether in work ethic, sacrifice, character, or other area of service, the leader (in both secular and sacred venues) must show the way.

Guide Problem Solving and Decision Making

All leaders engage in solving problems. Effective leaders guide the process of solving problems in such a way that bring other people into the process so they feel part of the solution. In addition, they help participants learn how to resolve issues on their own or within the organizations, committees, or ministries they serve.

While good leaders place decision making as close as possible to those persons responsible for the activity, they also face constant decisions themselves. Good leaders understand how to seek God's face and follow biblical principles in making decisions. Spiritual leaders know that the goal of decision making is not merely to advance the task, solve a problem, or accomplish goals. Decisions are made in such a way as to glorify God.

Provide Inspirational Motivation

The congregation looks to the pastor for inspiration. When the church goes through difficulties and challenges, the pastor can motivate the people to renew their enthusiasm and commitment. He inspires not only through preaching but also through his example, his presence, his personal enthusiasm, and his resilience. However, the pastor's source of inspiration rests not in himself but in his ability to connect people with God. Henry Blackaby asserts the best way the pastor can inspire people is helping them reflect on God's prior work in their lives and remind them God does not change. He will be with them in the future as He has in the past.[1]

Effective leaders are good in many areas. Different leaders will excel in different competencies. All must constantly work to enhance their gifts and abilities to grow with the church. The leader who believes he can coast because of past success will soon find himself being left behind as the needs of his congregation exceed his level of competence.

Be a life-long learner. Find godly role models who are willing to be a Paul to your Timothy. Do not be afraid to ask questions, not only of other pastors but of laypeople whose leadership in the church and in business has demonstrated biblical foundations.

Most of all, spend much time in prayer, seeking the face of your heavenly Father. He can enable you, guide you, and protect you through the many challenges of leadership.

Chapter 20

TIME MANAGEMENT: LEADING YOURSELF

Managing time is really managing oneself. When pastors or students tell me they don't have time for matters that should be priorities in their lives, they are revealing a lack of self-discipline. You cannot lead the church if you cannot lead yourself. Too many ministers eagerly instruct others in how to live and serve God but fail in personal discipline.

The apostle Paul recognized the danger of an undisciplined life. "But I keep under my body, and bring it into subjection: lest that by any means, when I have preached to others, I myself should be a castaway" (1 Corinthians 9:27). That interesting phrase, "keep under my body," literally means "to give myself the knockout blow." Giving our best to God means denying personal desires that take away from loving service to the Lord. Even the most demanding of ministries can be handled well if we follow certain principles.

Most ministers struggle with finding time to meet all the various demands each day. The average church member does not appreciate the minister's wide range of responsibilities. Preparing sermons, visitation in hospitals and homes, committee and staff meetings, counseling, planning and administration, funerals, and pastoral care are only a few time-consuming activities pastors encounter each week. No two weeks are the same, making a normal schedule nearly impossible to maintain.

Younger ministers may watch pastors neglect family and personal needs while trying to meet every need of every church member every week. Some go to the opposite extreme and try to maintain a forty-hour work week. When ministers refuse to take on additional tasks, church members may become resentful and conflict can ensue.

> *The key to balance is learning how to manage your time under the guidance of the Holy Spirit.*

What is a reasonable approach? Does a faithful minister have to choose between family and ministry? Can one find a solid balance in life and ministry? Adrian Rogers once said, "God gives each of us daily all the time we need to do graciously everything He wants us to do." Catch the two key phrases: "graciously," "all He wants us to do."

Ministers are called "workmen" and "co-laborers" (2 Timothy 2:15; 1 Corinthians 3:9). Both terms employ the idea that ministry involves effort. God does not intend for His ministers to exhaust themselves in never-ending activities simply to prove our faithfulness. Neither does He expect them to be lazy and indolent. The key to balance is learning how to manage your time under the guidance of the Holy Spirit.

Invest in Prayer

Prayer is never a waste of time. Begin each day by seeking the mind of God. He is not obligated to insure the success of our plans. "There are many devices (plans) in a man's heart; nevertheless the counsel of the LORD, that shall stand" (Proverbs 19:21). Only when we spend enough quality time with God can we begin to plan with His guidance. During his encounter with God on the mountain, Moses received God's plan for the tabernacle. The construction went smoothly as the people followed God's direction (Exodus 26:30).

Instead of seeing prayer as an interruption to your day, understand that time with Jesus is the reason for our day. In prayer, we abide in Christ, loving Him and experiencing His love for us. In prayer, we share our burdens and concerns with the One Who is able to bear our burdens and ease our hearts. In prayer, we submit to the Lordship of our heavenly Bishop Who guides us through life. In prayer, we gain perspective on what is really important in life and ministry. In prayer, we plug into God's power source and are better equipped for the tasks He gives us.

Set Priorities

Part of the problem lies in what someone called "the tyranny of the urgent." When a minister's schedule is ruled by everyone else's emergencies, what is important often gets pushed aside. If pastors simply add the latest demands to their "do list" without considering God's direction, they will never accomplish God's purposes.

While I disagree with Steven Covey's philosophy in many cases, he does offer a vital insight when he encourages leaders to schedule their priorities.[1] In other words, instead of taking all the various tasks each day and ordering them according to what is most urgent, begin your scheduling process with your primary priorities.

Your Priorities Demonstrate Your Values. What you believe is important in your life. Hyrum Smith argues that one of the primary causes of stress is conflict between what we do each day and what we believe to be important. He advocates that by bringing our values, priorities, and daily schedule into sync, we are more likely to live happily and productively.[2]

What has God given you as your main mission? Jesus said, "Seek first the kingdom of God and His righteousness . . ." (Matthew 6:33). **Our first priority is our relationship with God.** If we launch out each morning in our own strength, we will ultimately fail. Only by abiding, remaining, and residing in Christ can we do anything (John 15:5).

Many ministers excuse their lack of a regular quiet time on a busy schedule. They do not have a busy schedule; they have an undisciplined schedule. If time with the Lord is the basis for everything else, it should be our top priority. Keep a calendar (hard copy or phone reminder) and schedule your time with Jesus like any other appointment. Only move it if God brings something else from His agenda into your life. In that case, do not skip the appointment with God; simply adjust your calendar to have it at a different time.

After Time with God, a Minister's Family Has Priority in His Life. While true ministry emergencies occur, too often ministers make the mistake of interpreting every request as something that takes precedence over family needs.

A minister can control, at least to a degree, interruptions in his family time if he will make family a priority and schedule family activities on his calendar. A child's birthday is coming up? An anniversary celebration? A school event? Put them on the calendar as soon as you know about them. Then, if a committee chairman requests a meeting during one of those dates, simply reply, "I already have a commitment at that time," and suggest an alternative schedule. You do not have to say what the commitment is. Your layperson may not feel your daughter's basketball game is as important as his committee meeting. However, most reasonable people will work with you to schedule activities so that you can meet both needs in an unhurried, gracious manner.

Granted, a minister must be reasonable and not use his family as an excuse for laziness. One minister was discouraged because his new church plant was not succeeding. Discussing his weekly schedule, he said he maintained his study at home, so he was at home studying in the mornings. He wanted to be home when his children came home from school, so he was home by mid-afternoon. He did not want to be away from his family at night, so he scheduled no services on Sunday night. Other than a few lunch meetings, a couple of hours at the church after lunch, and two services a week, he was at home. No wonder his church did not grow!

When Scheduling Ministry Activities, Seek God's Priorities. One pastor believed discipling men in his church was a prime priority. So he scheduled a breakfast meeting with a group each week and interrupted that agenda for only the direst emergency.

Preparing to preach and teach obviously require undivided attention in prayer and study. Put it on the calendar or phone reminder list. Some pastors try to set aside every morning for study and do not allow anything to interrupt. Sadly, when they refuse to go to a hospital when someone is having major, life-threatening surgery, their members lose confidence in them. At the same time, ministers cannot allow minor interruptions to disrupt their study. If you let your people know that you study in the mornings, but assure them you are available in case of an emergency, they will generally avoid calling on you during that time unless they really need you.

Schedule White Space

In his book, *Margin*, Richard Swenson urges people to build white space into their lives. He observes that if every minute of the day is scheduled, you not only feel rushed, but you lack available time for inevitable interruptions. Tasks often take longer than planned. People call. Visitors stop by. Without some unscheduled white space in the calendar, one feels stressed either to get everything done or to constantly put off important matters.[3]

Sometimes the white space in life is brief, an extra fifteen minutes after a committee meeting in case the meeting goes longer than expected. Occasionally, the white space is longer, like a week-long vacation with the family. Rest is not a waste of time. Jesus urged His followers to "come apart" because the constant demands of their ministry did not give them even so much time as to eat (Mark 6:31). Even within a typical day, take time to pray, to reflect, to relax, and to think. Each increases overall productivity in the long run.

Plan the Work; Work the Plan

This familiar adage remains wise today. Proverbs teaches the principle of advance planning. "Go to the ant, you sluggard; consider her ways, and be wise: Which having no guide, overseer, or ruler, provides her meat in the summer, and gathers her food in the harvest" (Proverbs 6:6–8). Many ministers are so busy doing, they do not take time to think through what they are doing. Claiming they do not have time to plan, they waste much time redoing mistakes made because they failed to consider how to do the task most effectively. Planning is not a waste of time; it is crucial to success. Jesus taught that no one begins to build without first considering the cost (Luke 14:28–30). That requires planning!

- **Plan alone with God.** God begins revealing His plans as the pastor gets alone with God in prayer. Martin Luther said, "I have so much to do today, I must spend the first two hours in prayer."
- **Plan together with other leaders.** Where there is a multitude of counselors, there is wisdom (Proverbs 11:14). Other people bring additional experience and perspective to enhance planning and decision making. Also, by involving other people during the planning

of a project, they are more likely to be committed to implementing the work successfully.

- **Plan major events, emphases, and directions well in advance.** Do not try to initiate a major activity without proper prayer, planning, and preparation. Take time to do it right and to do it well. Allow your people time to understand what needs to be done and why. Build into your long-range plan whatever milestones you need to insure you are making progress in the right direction. Divide the larger events into various processes and break the procedures into smaller tasks. Schedule the tasks between the milestones to keep everyone together.

- **Make detailed plans as you get closer to the event.** End each quarter of the year by making more detailed plans for upcoming activities. End each month by going more specifically into details for the next month. End each week by planning the next week's schedule. End each day by adjusting plans for the following day.

Evaluate the Past Before Launching into the Future

In his book, *The Fifth Discipline*, Peter Senge describes a learning organization.[4] Successful individuals, corporations, ministers, and churches learn how to learn. People who simply rush into the future without learning from their past are doomed to repeat mistakes and waste time undoing and redoing. Determine what information you need to evaluate what has already been done. Bringing other leaders into the process can help discover and interpret information to adjust the plans for the next phase.

Use Small Chunks of Time

Often you will find yourself with short segments of free time. You finish a task early. The expected appointment does not show up. You planned white space and did not have to use it. Many small tasks can be accomplished in these small bits of time. Catch up on phone calls or e-mails. Write that letter. Spend a few minutes in prayer. Call your spouse. Dream a bit.

In the average day, ministers will find many opportunities to redeem the time. Don't waste those minutes by surfing the Internet or checking Facebook or other social media. Make the most of each moment.

Every major event consists of a series of smaller activities. You may not have time to do all the activities at once, and likely should not try. By knowing what has to be done, and by when, you can utilize scores of these openings in each day to accomplish many of the smaller tasks that together make up the larger goals.

Compartmentalize Tasks, Intercompartmentalize Time

When managing multiple responsibilities, divide your tasks into compartments. Try to visualize the larger goals along with the individual tasks related to each. You may find it helpful to draw boxes on a larger sheet of paper or on the computer, with each box representing a major area of work or priority. Lay out various steps in the processes, not merely the immediate tasks. See the steps as cobblestones in a yellow brick road that leads to your goal.

Visualize your schedule as a chessboard. You likely will not take any single priority and stay with it from start to finish without a break. Plan your work concurrently, not consecutively. Most plans have a time and space sequence that allows for other intervening activities. By intercompartmentalizing your time schedule, weaving tasks back and forth between each other like pieces on a chessboard, you can accomplish several goals simultaneously.

Think Before Acting

As my carpenter grandfather reminded me, "Measure twice, cut once." Much time is wasted by acting without thinking through what must be done. Accurate understanding of the task and preparation for doing it well help insure the most efficient use of time.

Learn to Delegate

Someone has noted that when we do what someone else can do, we not only take time away from what only we can do, but we also deny that other person a blessing. Delegation helps develop other people's abilities and makes them feel valued. When delegating, be sure to discuss the results desired, allowing the delegatees freedom to accomplish the task their own ways. Make sure the persons doing the work understand what levels of authority they have for the project. Never doom people to failure by giving them jobs without adequate resourcing for success.

At the same time, never delegate simply to avoid unpleasant tasks. When Nehemiah was building the wall around Jerusalem, each person built near his home. However, no one lived near the Dung Gate, out of which the refuse of the city was carried. Instead of having someone too poor to say no to handle this unpleasant task, Malchiah the son of Rechab, the ruler of part of Bethhaccerem, took the responsibility of building the gate (Nehemiah 3:14). A true leader understands no one is too good for the dirty work. Leading by example means serving, even if it involves disagreeable jobs.

Learn to Say No

Many ministers have a psychological need to be needed. They may actually fear not being needed. Some fear disappointing others. In each case, they tend to say yes to every request, regardless of their priorities or available time. Focusing on God's agenda helps identify what one does and does not do. Saying no to activities that do not further God's priorities in your life and ministry frees you to say yes to those plans that do.

Focus

Focus on each task. Eliminate whatever distracts you from the details of your project. Turn the television off. Clean up your workspace. Close the door. If irrelevant thoughts intrude on your concentration, sit back a moment and refocus on your goal.

Simplicity, Simplicity, Simplicity

Excellence does not necessarily mean more complicated. Try to see the most direct route to your goal and avoid whatever creates detours to your day.

Avoid Wasting Time

Try to avoid interruptions to your productive time. How much time is spent in front of the TV, playing video games, doodling with the computer, or socializing with people who just want to hang out? Try to eliminate whatever keeps you from accomplishing the task at hand. At the same time, remember that people with genuine needs—even the need to relate—are never interruptions; they are why you're there!

Persevere

People who accomplish great tasks do not procrastinate or quit. They persevere. They keep on keeping on until the task is done, the goal reached, or the project finished.

When difficulties, roadblocks, and problems arise, allow the Holy Spirit to empower you. "And let us not be weary in well doing: for in due season we shall reap, if we faint not" (Galatians 6:9).

"To everything there is a season, and a time to every purpose under the heaven" (Ecclesiastes 3:1). Commitment to God's purposes causes us to value the time He gives us to fulfill His plans. If we are deliberate in our use of this nonrenewable resource, we avoid the regrets that so often accompany misused time. Making the most of the days God gives us results in a deep sense of satisfaction and anticipation of the Master's approval: "Well done, good and faithful servant."

Chapter 21

DEVELOPING A MINISTRY TEAM:
WORKING WITH MINISTRY STAFF AND LAYPERSONS

"For we are laborers together with God . . ." (1 Corinthians 3:9).

Paul's statement to the Corinthian Church was intended to end partisan divisions. His argument, however, has the secondary result of providing a basis for our working together in the church. Pastors, even in single-staff churches, are not the only ones doing ministry. We are always part of a group of people engaged in laboring together with the Lord.

Paul rarely went anywhere alone. He constantly brought other people to partner with him in the ministry. Barnabus, Silas, Luke, Timothy, Titus, Priscilla, Aquila, and others worked not only in support of Paul but in collegiality with him. Nearly every pastoral letter closes with lists of people who labored along with Paul in various places. Yet, Paul was simply using Jesus' pattern of leadership, which, while singularly individual in nature, involved others who could grow in their various roles of ministry.

Wise Next-Gen leaders follow the example of Jesus and Paul in developing ministry teams to work with them as they all labor together with God. You may be surprised to consider how many ministry teams you have in an average church: church staff teams, committees, various ministry leaders (youth/ student ministry, children's ministry, missions ministry, men's ministry, women's ministry), deacons, and others. Learning how to lead leaders will multiply your efforts and help you develop the effectiveness of other people in your congregation.

Working with Church Staff

Pastors of multistaff churches may think their paid coworkers are their only staff members. They should recognize they have many more ministry teams than those persons who get a paycheck from the church. At the same time, if you are the pastor of a single-staff church, you may be surprised to know you have a church staff. They may not be employed by the church, but they serve vital roles that complement your ministry and serve Christ's Body. How you work with each type of team should be customized based on several factors.

Ministry Roles

Ministerial: Ministerial staff includes those ministers who are ordained and other ministry leaders who are not ordained. The latter group may include women who direct children and preschool ministries. Also, larger churches may have various levels of ministerial staff. A Minister of Education (or Discipleship Pastor) could supervise several age-level ministers, including the Student Minister, the Senior Adult Minister, and the Children/Preschool Director. Staff meetings in larger churches may have all personnel involved for parts of the sessions, followed by separate meetings with senior ministerial staff.

A contemporary affectation is to label all ministerial personnel as a "pastor." While understanding the egalitarian and respectful nature of this trend, we need to recognize it has a potential for misunderstanding. For example, the Youth Minister may have the title "Pastor to Students." The young people may get the idea that the Student Pastor is their pastor while they expect the Senior Pastor to relate to the adults. Divisions, turf battles, and lack of coordination are just a few of the typical challenges churches may encounter if ministerial staff do not see themselves as part of the overall ministry of the church.

Support: I really don't like this term because it suggests these persons are not as important as ministerial staff. Administrative assistants, secretaries, bookkeepers, custodial staff, and other personnel sometimes feel like second-class citizens. While various types of workers function in different ways, each should be respected, appreciated, and supported. Often the church secretary has been tenured longer than some pastors, providing a valuable resource of institutional knowledge. At the same time, difficulties may arise when you apply correction to support personnel who have been at the church a long time or persons with families in the church. Wise pastors will recognize the value of each worker, including support personnel, and maximize their ministry for the good of the church.

Employment Status

Volunteer: All churches rely on scores of volunteers to work in the many organizations and ministries. In addition, most small churches rely on volunteers to fill what would otherwise be ministerial staff positions. Usually the music minister will be a layperson with some musical talent. Often this person will lack training in choral or instrumental conducting, although sometimes a school bandleader or choral teacher may be found to lead the music program. Also, the church likely will not have a paid minister of education but will have a volunteer serving as Sunday School Director. Similarly, the student (youth) ministry and the children ministry will probably be led by one or more volunteers who double as Sunday School teachers.

Work with volunteers the same way you would with paid personnel. In addition to the concepts mentioned later in this chapter related to working with volunteers, apply these principles to volunteers who serve in a ministerial capacity:

- Help them connect with experienced, professional staff persons in other churches who can help educate them about their ministries, give them tips on organization and other aspects of the work, and encourage them with prayer and friendship.

- Take them to training events hosted by your denomination's local association, state convention, or national agency. Quality training is available at little or no financial cost through these ministry partners.

- Involve them in regular staff meetings for prayer, planning, evaluation of events and ministry processes, and discussion of needs for the future.

- Hold them accountable, but remember they are volunteers. They are more likely to quit if they encounter too much conflict. When the need for correction arises, be firm but kind in the way you approach them. You may need to involve other appropriate lay leaders (deacon chairman or a committee chair) to prevent discipline from becoming a "me-versus-the-pastor" situation.

Part Time or Bivocational: A part-time staff minister is one who primarily is a layperson who has been given a small financial compensation to help with a church ministry. A bivocational staff member is someone who primarily is a minister who needs a second job to provide income for his/her family when the church cannot fully fund the position. You will find there is a major difference between these two kinds of ministers. The first is more volunteer than staff. The secular employment often takes preference over ministry needs. At the same time, both kinds of ministers are committed to the Lord, the church, and the pastor.

While having income separate from the church may make this minister a bit more independent, a wise pastor can build a strong relationship. You will lead more on the basis of shared vision and mutual commitment as opposed to hierarchical, positional leadership based on employment. Respect these co-laborers in ministry. Give them the support professionally and personally that they need to be effective in their various roles.

Fully Funded: When afforded the luxury of having one or more fully funded staff personnel, you may be tempted to build ministry around these co-laborers. Maintaining church office hours, they are generally more available than volunteers or part-time workers. Usually they have more training and experience, which may cause you to regard fully funded workers more highly than others. You may depend on this group more readily as you develop closer relationships, partly because of the regular interaction you experience in the office.

Be careful to give equal attention and respect to all the various co-laborers with whom you share ministry. Lead fully funded personnel to value volunteer and part-time/bivocational workers, to invest in their lives and ministries in training and support, and to show appreciation by integrating all groups into an effective ministry team.

Hired or Inherited?

Throughout your ministry, you will lead churches to hire (call) various persons in ministerial or support roles. Learn how to establish a position, develop a job description, determine skills and other qualification criteria, and follow a process to find and select the right person. However, as a new pastor, you may inherit some staff personnel from the previous minister.

If you've been called to a church that already has ministerial staff in place, do not make the mistake of thinking you should clean house and start all over. Take time to get acquainted with the ministerial staff and the support personnel. Don't just focus on job performance; get to know them as people. Learn their stories. What is their history? How did they come to be at this church? What have they been doing? How has the work progressed? How are their relationships in the church and with one another? What was their personal and professional relationship with the previous pastor? What are their expectations for working with you? What questions do they need answered about you and your story? Can you all discover a common vision that God will use to take the church forward? You probably discover that you have joined a solid team with committed individuals who can become just as connected to you as with the previous pastor.

On the other hand, you may find someone who needs to move on to another place of service. Several valid reasons may lead to asking the staff person to relocate. If the individual has proven to be incompetent, disloyal, divisive, corrupt, or otherwise unsuited for the ministry, work with your Personnel Committee to exercise appropriate discipline. Frankly, the committee and previous pastor should have handled the matter already. Unfortunately, the new pastor is often left to do the difficult work.

In other cases, some staff members may not be willing or able to make the transition to a different direction or vision. They are good-hearted and well-meaning but lack the skills or inclination for the kind of needs the church's new direction requires. In this situation, work with them to either change their hearts, equip them with new skills, or help them to relocate. Given time and kindness, these persons can usually make the appropriate change needed in such a way that saves the church and their families much distress and conflict.

Basic Principles for Hiring Personnel

Establish a Position

Determine what needs to be done and build a position around strategic need. Consider whether the job warrants a paid worker, a volunteer, or a part-time person. You may have several related functions that could be combined into a single position (such as a Minister of Music and Youth).

Rarely hire someone for a job that can be filled by a volunteer. Avoid hiring someone on a full-time basis for a position that can be served by a bivocational or part-time worker. At the same time, if you have a position that demands someone with a high level of skills and full-time availability, don't avoid hiring the best person just to save money. In fact, financial consideration is not key issue in any of these situations.

Many positions in the church can be well-served by volunteers. Willing and able church members not only can handle such nonministerial roles as custodial, lawn care, secretarial, and other positions, some can lead the music, educational, youth, and children's ministries. Developing church members maximizes their potentials as disciples and blesses them with the privilege of serving. Similarly, many bivocational and part-time workers can provide effective service in many positions.

Develop a Job Description

Potential workers need to know what they are expected to do. Details should include functions and responsibilities worded in precise enough language to understand the job without being so specific as to micromanage the worker. The job description should outline the qualifications, levels of authority, lines of accountability and supervision, compensation (if applicable), and methods of evaluation. Other issues, such as procedures for discipline and dismissal should be detailed, in the church's personnel policies. Require the worker to read the policies as well as the job description and sign a statement of agreement.

Follow Good Hiring Procedures

In many cases, advertise the position and seek the most highly qualified candidate. In some situations, pastors in larger churches may know gifted laypersons whom God might be calling into vocational Christian service. In either situation, obtain resumes and follow the procedures for interviewing outlined in the earlier chapter on dealing with Search Committees. Pray throughout the process that God will lead you to the right person. Be kind and fair; you are not merely hiring a worker, you are enlisting a co-laborer to share ministry in the House of God.

Basic Principles for Supervising Coworkers

Training

In some cases, the pastor may train workers personally, but more commonly he simply will ensure they get proper job education. Training may involve specialized skills for the position, but most church staff should already possess basic abilities. If you hire someone and later discover the individual lacks vital skills, you have two choices: dismiss the person and find someone else, or provide training to equip the worker. Often you will find the latter option is less expensive and definitely less disruptive.

Orientation

All workers, volunteer and paid, need orientation that includes where, when, and with whom the work will be done. Resources should be identified, including procedures for obtaining supplies or other materials needed for the job. Include a walk-about of the facilities, distribution of keys and computer codes, introduction to fellow workers, and instruction regarding computer networks and other equipment use.

Ongoing Supervision

Regular periodic meetings about upcoming plans, activities, and needs supplement daily assignments and function interaction. Some positions do not require constant supervision as do others. Results-oriented supervision always works better than having to micromanage people. Let people know what is expected and let them do their work, offering guidance, encouragement, and correction along the way. In all ways, follow the Golden Rule: "As ye would that men should do to you, do also to them likewise" (Luke 6:31).

Authority and Delegation

Make sure the worker and coworkers understand what level of authority each has in performing their jobs. Much confusion can be eliminated when everyone knows the lines of authority. Never delegate a function without giving the worker the authority to do the job. If you want someone to get permission before acting on a matter, make the expectations clear. However, having to watch over workers' shoulders demotivates them and unnecessarily consumes your time and effort. Try to place decision making as close to the level of action as possible.

Communicating

Workers not only need to know what is happening related to their areas of ministry, but they work best when they understand how their work interacts with others. Formal and informal channels of communication between all levels of work help insure smooth coordination of ministry. The section on communication provides good principles of accurate communication within the organization.

Reporting

Establish effective methods for reporting progress of work as it goes along, as well as when it is completed. Share feedback, including appreciation and correction as needed.

Evaluation

Few people enjoy evaluations. Usually they happen at the wrong time and in the wrong way. In his book, *Management: A Biblical Approach*, Myron Rush observes that having an annual evaluation is nearly worthless, since it gives no opportunity for correction during the year. In addition, he notes, typical evaluations are top-down. Rush suggests ongoing, two-way evaluations that empower workers to share with supervisors what they need to improve, as well as more frequent opportunities for supervisors to encourage and correct workers.[1]

Correction and Discipline

Nearly everyone needs correction from time to time. Correction is a good thing. Like small adjustments to the car's steering wheel, correction helps keep individuals and organizations out of the ditches. Wise people will respond well to correction offered with kind, but firm, words and good intent. ". . . Rebuke a wise man, and he will love thee" (Proverbs 9:8).

Still, few people enjoy being corrected, usually because it is often done in a way that belittles and demeans the individual. To help workers accept correction more readily, begin with acknowledgment of something done well and end with appreciation for the person. Be specific and timely when offering correction. If you speak in generalities or wait until the situation passes before offering correction, it lacks effectiveness.

If the worker refuses to accept efforts at constructive correction, the supervisor may have to initiate discipline. Personnel policies should detail procedures for employee discipline. Both attitudes and actions (or inactions) may invoke disciplinary steps, but supervisors should never use discipline improperly. Start with the lowest level of correction first; prayerfully, the worker will accept the admonition and improve. The person may not like discipline at the moment, but if responding correctly, the result can be very positive. ("Now no chastening for the present seems to be joyous, but grievous: nevertheless afterward it yields the peaceable fruit of righteousness unto them which are exercised thereby" (Hebrews 12:11).

Initial discipline should be done privately, preserving the subject's self-esteem. Maintain good documentation, not only of the causes of discipline but also of the steps taken in discipline. Involve witnesses if the initial correction does not work out. In everything, be kind and fair. Remember, all discipline should be intended to help, not punish. Your goal is to redeem the person and glorify God.

If termination becomes necessary, be sure to follow established procedures. The Personnel Committee should take the lead in handling the more severe levels of discipline, especially termination. Bring other leaders, especially deacons, into the process for information and support.

In some situations, termination will require the approval of the congregation. However, rarely can the church become involved without the issue becoming a matter of conflict in the wider congregation. Sometimes, you will benefit the individual and the church by leading the Personnel Committee to negotiate a resignation rather than having to go through a forced termination.

Rewarding

People appreciate appreciation. We all need to feel worthwhile and to believe what we do is significant, making a difference in people's lives. Simple acknowledgment and gratitude for a job well done provides strong motivation for continued well-doing. Obviously, people in ministry serve out of love for the Lord, but receiving sincere appreciation for their efforts is always helpful. People do not need to receive plaques and certificates, but a verbal pat on the back means much to someone who has put in extra effort to do a good job. Certainly, employees need financial compensation for cost of living increases as well as rewards for exceptional service. Still, the average person does not work for money alone. Without personal affirmation, most people will eventually feel devalued and lose motivation.

The apostle Paul urged the church at Thessalonica to encourage and edify one another (1 Thessalonians 5:11). The same should be true among contemporary churches toward servants of the Lord.

Minister to Your Staff and Their Families

Mac Brunson and James Bryant encourage ministers to pastor the staff.[2] Your staff and their families need your ministry. You are their pastor, not merely their boss. Love them. Pray with and for them. Be their intercessor and ask them to be the same for you. Begin meetings with time together with God.

Disciple them and help them be more like Jesus. When they are sick, visit them. Be constantly aware of their walk with God lest one should fall by the wayside morally or be stunted spiritually. Spend time with them individually as you talk about what God is doing in their lives. Encourage them to take time each day with the Lord.

Be sensitive to their personal needs, especially in case of financial difficulties. I served with a pastor once who became aware that my one suit had worn out, and I could not afford another. By the end of the week, I had a new suit without feeling ashamed over accepting the gift.

Help staff ministers balance their responsibilities to the church and to their families. Demonstrate love and concern personally for staff members' spouses and children. Let them know you are their pastor and their friend. If you ever have to discipline a staff minister, having a reputation for caring for the ministers and their families will help you get past emotional reactions and conflict.

Working with Lay Leaders (Committees, Ministries, Church Officers)

While the pastor is the overall spiritual leader of the flock, he is wise to work with the congregation to organize ministries and administrative functions around laypersons in the form of ministries, committees, and church officers. The deacons were formed to help the pastors with ministry administration so the ministers could focus on spiritual leadership. Similarly, committees and other lay ministries help accomplish many tasks in the church organization so the ministers are freer to do what only they can do.

At the same time, churches can have too many committees and too few ministries. Lead the church to evaluate its organizational structure to see if functions can be streamlined. Many tasks can be handled by a ministry of two or three persons instead of a committee of five to seven. Other functions can be combined into fewer groups. Since the average church has sixty-four persons on any given Sunday (including children!), the structure needs to maximize the human resources available without overloading individuals with multiple jobs.

Working with lay volunteers requires mutual respect, collaboration, and a servant spirit on everyone's part. Lay leaders should not view the ministerial staff as their employees; nor should the pastors consider laity to be mere cogs in the ecclesiastical machinery. Each group has interdependent responsibilities. God calls every believer to fulfill specific functions within the Body and blesses each with spiritual gifts, talents, abilities, and experience to accomplish the tasks.

Recognize the value of prayerful collaboration. Working with other people does not lessen pastoral authority; it defines how pastors use their authority. Scripture reminds us that "Where no counsel is, the people fall: but in the multitude of counsellors there is safety" (Proverbs 11:14).

Make friends with your lay leaders. See them as people who have jobs, families, and lives outside the church. When talking with them, don't always discuss church business only. Ask about their children, their work, and their hobbies. Use informal opportunities to build relationships and grow disciples. You will have many occasions to help lay leaders become more like Jesus as you engage them informally when you fish together, work on an old car together, or simply drink a cup of coffee at the local diner together.

Make sure lay leaders understand their functions. Written job descriptions for officers, ministries, and committees are helpful. Conduct an annual orientation at the beginning of the church year to insure each person understands what is expected of them, how they function as a committee, when their meetings will take place, how to put activities on the church calendar, how to access their line items in the budget, and how to report to the church through the staff and the business meetings.

Such orientations should also include a separate seminar for committee and ministry leaders to help them understand principles of group dynamics. They will benefit by an overview of how to recognize various personality types and how to help people work with one another in spite of differences. Also, teach leaders how to keep groups on task while, at the same time, making their work enjoyable and relational.

Don't surprise people. You may find unexpected resistance if you show up at a committee meeting with a new idea you have not discussed with the chairperson in advance. Having agendas for all committee meetings helps laypersons and ministerial staff stay on top of whatever decisions need to be made. Encourage the committees to give a copy of agendas to the church office, or you, in advance of meetings. Minutes of the meetings should be forwarded to the church office to be placed among permanent records for future reference.

You may use a church council to help ministries, committees, and staff coordinate and communicate regarding plans and activities. The church council often does not have any administrative authority but aids the interworking of various leaders. It usually is made up of the church staff, ministry leaders, and appropriate committee chairpersons, along with the leader of the deacons.

Like a good coach, give credit where credit is due, but avoid the blame game if something goes wrong. You never observe quality coaches blame the team when they lose, but they always recognize the efforts of the team when they win. Remember, loving people involved in the work is as important, if not more important, than the tasks they perform.

Principles for Working with Volunteers

A friend who managed the volunteer system for a major hospital shared with me her secret of success. When I asked her how she kept up with the hundreds of volunteers, she replied, "I treat them like employees." That's not a bad idea for working with volunteers in the church. Here are some basic principles that may help you engage volunteers for the Kingdom:

1. **Establish** a position based on need. Develop a clear job description, including expectations, chain of supervision, and accountability.

2. **Enlist** specific persons based on their SHAPE. Developed by leaders at Saddleback Community Church, SHAPE is a plan for identifying how to place people in various ministry positions. The acrostic represents the following: Spiritual gifts, Heart interests/commitments, Aptitudes/abilities, Personality types, Experience.

   Interview the volunteer as you would an employee, explaining the job's expectations and asking questions. Remember, the past is prologue. The quality of work in the past likely will be the quality of work in the future. Don't be afraid to turn down volunteers or redirect their interest to more suitable ministry positions. Just because people volunteer does not mean you have to accept their desire to work in a particular ministry. Not everyone is suited for certain jobs.

3. **Equip.** Train volunteers. Don't put people in positions and expect them to know automatically how to handle the job. For example, Sunday School teachers need instruction in how to study the Bible and the curriculum in order to prepare a lesson. They need to know how to handle their classes based on the developmental level and age of their members.

   Outline the job's functions and expectations and develop a training program combining classroom instruction and apprenticeships. Offer ongoing continuing education. Just because someone has held a job for several years does not mean that person does not need to gain new skills, discover additional knowledge, or improve in other ways.

4. **Empower.** Do not delegate without giving appropriate authority to act. Make sure the volunteers understand what levels of authority they have.

5. **Encourage.** Both volunteers and employees need an "attaboy" from time to time.

6. **Evaluate.** Hold periodic meetings to evaluate progress. Use Myron Rush's two-way evaluation—allow workers to share what they need from you before you offer your evaluation of their positives and negatives in performance. Evaluate attitudes as well as actions.

7. **Establish, Elevate, or Eliminate** as necessary. Some workers are at their best positions; establish them as long-term workers. Some workers show promise of performance at higher levels; elevate them. A few workers need to be removed based on problems with attitudes or performance. If you need to eliminate a person from a certain position, follow the same kind of procedural care, including documentation of problems, that you would with an employee.

Chapter 22

PLANNING FOR MINISTRY:
DISCOVERING AND IMPLEMENTING GOD'S VISION

"Where there is no vision, the people perish: . . ." (Proverbs 29:18).

Charlie had a specific vision when he assumed leadership of a mission group in North America. He had wrestled with his call for nearly two weeks before accepting the invitation to lead the work in this northeastern state. When he had a clear idea of what God wanted him to do, he yielded to the call and immersed himself in the work. After three years of nonstop labor, and some degree of conflict, Charlie was approaching burnout. He had accomplished his original goals. Week after week, he went to the office and supervised activities and workers but lacked the kind of enthusiasm he once felt for the job. Increasingly he wondered if he should go somewhere else and try something new. Only when he began to manage the stress in his life through prayer and Bible study did he gain a fresh vision of the next phase of ministry and a renewed commitment to the task.

What Is Vision?

What comes to mind when someone asks you about your vision for the church? Some young pastors launch into a description of what their churches can become. Others focus attention on what their ministries might accomplish. A few might discuss how their people express missional outreach to their world. However, Leonard Sweet teaches us:

> *"A vision is not about programs or objectives or scenarios or goals.*
> *A vision is about releasing energies.*
> *A vision is about life-giving spirit.*
> *A vision is about the excitement of shared possibilities.*
> *A vision is about seeing in such a way and communicating what you see that other people come to life with new enthusiasm and resolve."*[1]

Such a vision comes from God and focuses on God. True vision glorifies God. Fulfilling that vision exalts Him in the manner of its accomplishment as well as in the results. While we need to understand ourselves, our people, and our ministry context, godly vision relies on knowledge of God.

The Problem of Human Vision

Sometimes ministers begin work with a vision for what they want and a plan for how they intend to accomplish their goals. While this approach sounds admirable, it can be part of the problem. Vision is never ours; true vision belongs to and comes from God.

Human vision tends to be self-centered in orientation, limited in scope, and presumptuous in nature. It is self-centered because it originates from the heart and mind of the individual rather than from the Holy Spirit. It is limited in scope because it can only encompass human perspective rather than the knowledge and wisdom of God. It is presumptuous in nature because it assumes God will provide whatever resources and power is needed to accomplish the goal, even if God did not initiate the plan.

Human vision creates conflict and stress because each individual can claim the right to follow his or her dream, regardless of what others' vision may involve. If two or more leaders serve a common group of people, whose vision should determine what they will do? How they will go about it? In what areas can they cooperate? What results should they seek? Even if workers genuinely respect and care for one another, the pull of private visions can engender disagreement and disharmony.

Human vision can result in abuse of authority. Persons who occupy administrative positions over others may impose their ideas on people who are forced to accept the plan in order to keep their jobs. One leader called a meeting of seven workers under his supervision. He chastised them for a lack of progress in accomplishing various goals he had set for them based on his vision of the task. He said, "You are here for one purpose—to help me succeed." Not only did he misunderstand their purpose (or his, for that matter) but he failed to realize no one exists for someone else's goals. Just because a leader has the authority to impose his vision on others does not mean that he should.

The Benefits of God-Generated Vision

God-generated vision, on the other hand, brings people together. Harmony proceeds from having a shared purpose that is greater than oneself. When ministers set aside personal desires and commit to seek God's will, they will eventually receive a clearer picture of His vision, drawing people together instead of pulling them apart.

In one ministry setting, I had a leadership team composed of five persons with very different personalities. Each minister was passionate about helping churches reach people through his area of responsibility. This complex combination was ripe for conflict; however, the team was one of the most harmonious and productive groups I had ever known. One factor was a retreat in which we developed a common understanding of God's vision for our work. Our commitment to God's purpose motivated each of us to look past individual differences and work together for a common goal.

God-generated vision challenges His people with much greater possibilities than they could imagine from human perspectives. God showed Moses such an awesome vision that he could not take it in all at once. "And so terrible was the sight, that Moses said, 'I exceedingly fear and quake: . . .'" (Hebrews 12:21).

When ministers set aside personal desires and commit to seek God's will, they will eventually receive a clearer picture of His vision, drawing people together instead of pulling them apart.

Paul put it this way: "Eye has not seen, nor ear heard, neither has entered into the heart of man, the things which God has prepared for them that love him" (1 Corinthians 2:9). A group of leaders entered a retreat with the intention of learning new administrative skills. However, one presentation challenged the entire team to consider a radically different direction that would transform their strategy. After a lengthy meeting, they emerged convinced this vision was from the Lord. Committing to the new mandate, they restructured their plans for the next several years. The results were met with enthusiasm beyond their highest expectations.

God-generated vision guarantees divine provision for whatever is needed to accomplish God's purpose. When Nehemiah heard about the conditions in Jerusalem, he immediately felt a tremendous burden for his people. He held the influential position of cupbearer to King Artaxerxes of Persia, but he was still a slave. If he had acted on his burden rather than waiting for God, he would have failed, and likely would have been executed. Instead, by patiently seeking God's vision and timing, he went forth with the king's permission, accompanied by a strong military guard, and possessing a letter from the king giving him access to the resources to fulfill the task. When we trust God to give us His vision, we can trust Him for everything needed for its fulfillment.

Discovering God's Vision

Discovering God's Vision Takes Time. Nehemiah waited four months before God said, "Go." God gives some visions in shorter time frames; others take much longer. God rarely is pictured being in a hurry. We need to put ourselves on His timetable and wait patiently on Him. Abraham tried to accomplish God's will through human effort, producing generations of war between his descendants. Only when he surrendered to God's vision did he receive the fruition of God's plan. "And so, after he had patiently endured, he obtained the promise" (Hebrews 6:15).

Discovering God's Vision Requires Prayer. God does not change His will to conform to our prayers. We pray to discern God's will and surrender ourselves to it. God invites us to share our desires and our dreams, our pain and our praise. Yet, in the end, the servant awaits the Master's pleasure and follows His instruction. Twenty top leaders met for a retreat. A visiting speaker offered a powerful challenge to their organization's basic purpose. At first, they debated the issues among themselves. Finally, at nine o' clock in the evening, they ended the discussion and knelt in prayer, seeking God's direction. At three o'clock the next morning, they emerged from the prayer meeting with a mutual conviction that God was leading them in the new direction. United, they began to use God's vision to direct their plans, budgeting, personnel requests, and other activities.

Discovering God's Vision Requires Faith. "By faith . . ." Those two small words preface some of the most powerful expressions of faith-based vision found in Scripture. Hebrews 11 has been called Faith's Hall of Fame as it recounts the mighty acts of Abraham and other patriarchs, as well as the unsung and unnamed heroes who suffered and died in faithful pursuit of God's vision. God-sized vision cannot be comprehended, much less embraced, without confident trust that God will accomplish whatever He initiates. "Faithful is he that calls you, who also will do it" (1 Thessalonians 5:24). God's vision does not require great abilities in His servants; it merely requires faith and faithfulness. If we believe God, we can be faithful to follow wherever He leads.

Vision and Strategy Development

God draws people with a call and a vision. Each minister responds to the inner prompting of the Holy Spirit and a vision of varying clarity how he fits into God's plan. Paul had such a revelation during a dream-filled night in which he saw a man of Macedonia pleading for him to "Come over and help us" (Acts 16:6–10). Paul's original plan was to visit Asia. When the Holy Spirit vetoed that idea, Paul sought to visit Bithynia, but again the Spirit prevented him. At that point, God gave him a vision and a heart for Macedonia. If Paul had insisted on following his own plan and had not responded to God's calling, the church at Philippi might never have been born.

Vision is vital to every enterprise, especially for God's messengers. A familiar passage reminds us "where there is no vision, the people perish . . ." (Proverbs 29:18). Without a clear image of God's vision, people follow their individual desires, much like Israel before the days of kings when ". . . every man did that which was right in his own eyes" (Judges 17:6).

As long as people in an organization share a mutual vision and agree on how the vision should be accomplished, they function effectively and cooperatively. However, given the nature of human beings, they generally come to a divergence of opinions at some point. Having varying ideas is not bad. In fact, only an unhealthy organization demands everyone go along in order to get along. Creativity emerges as people share their different approaches. As long as they maintain respect for one another and remain committed to the overall vision and purpose of the mission, they should find common ground on which to proceed.

At the same time, sometimes God sends His people and they refuse to go. God had a clear vision—go into the Promised Land—but fear caused the people of Israel to reject the vision, resulting in their forty-year desert wandering. The leader must believe in what God is revealing in order to stand firm before the people and declare God's direction. At the same time, he must not be arrogant or self-centered. A godly leader maintains the humility that will allow input from God's people and other godly leaders. He is willing to adjust his understanding of the vision if his previously held beliefs about the specifics of a particular vision, or part of it, prove incorrect. At that point, you are ready to receive God's direction for the future.

Managing Change

Once you have led the church to discover God's vision, you likely will have a much more difficult task ahead—implementing changes. As mentioned elsewhere, no wise leader makes changes for change's sake. The church often is doing many things well. At the same time, if the church remains static in the midst of a changing environment, it may doom itself to decline, decay, and death as an institution. This assertion does not mean the church should adopt unbiblical habits of a godless culture. Instead, it involves following the positive direction God opens up before a people committed to His vision for the future.

Pray

The starting point for change, as with any aspect of ministry and life, is prayer. Only by getting in touch with the Lord through personal and corporate prayer can the pastor and the people prepare themselves to follow His direction. Prayer prepares the hearts of everyone involved to seek God's face, not just His plan. Each person must surrender personal preferences and prejudices in favor of God's perfect will. Change will surely produce conflict if participants have not yielded themselves to the One directing their paths.

Seek God's Will in God's Word

Along with prayer, the church seeks God's guidance through study of Scripture. God's will never comes at the expense of His Word. The Almighty is consistent—the same yesterday, today, and forever (Hebrews 13:8). Does that mean He never leads people to change? No. While He never changes, God constantly empowers His people to change.

However, the changes He initiates are never in contradiction to the principles found in the Bible. Before initiating change, be sure the new direction follows God's Word.

Understand the Situation

Change does not happen in a vacuum. The context of the church, the people as individuals and families, the community, and the larger culture affect the environment in which change occurs. Leaders of change need hard data on which to base plans. If the change involves an issue related to the church's location (either relocation, erecting additional buildings, or investing in renovations), have a group gather information regarding changes in housing, roads and infrastructure, community demographics, and location of current church members.

If the change affects worship services, talk with people of all age groups to determine if the new direction would truly help people worship more effectively. One pastor told his music minister to adopt a contemporary music style, only to discover the people both in the church and in the community preferred Southern gospel music. Another pastor tried to develop programs for a particular demographic group, but his church declined. He later discovered this group represented the smallest number of people in the community.

Comprehend the Values Affected by the Change

In its study of Empowering Kingdom Growth, the South Carolina Baptist Convention discovered if people's values did not support the pastor's vision, conflict would inevitably follow any changes based on that vision. Invest time with leaders and the average church member. Talk with them about what they consider to be important. Compare their values with Scripture. If the commonly held values contradict the Bible, take time to help people see matters from God's viewpoint through Scripture.

Base Change on Vision, Not Needs

Needs abound. If the church constantly changes its strategic direction based on all the perceived needs, it will never develop the stability of making a significant difference with any particular area. God leads some people to do one thing and other people to do something quite different. Make sure the idea is God's, not yours.

Work with Other Leaders

The church has invested trust in lay leaders as well as its ministers. Discover those persons worthy of trust, who can see with their spiritual sight (and not merely with 20/20 hindsight). Build a team of leaders whose walk with God, personal integrity, and investment in the congregation can couple with their abilities, wisdom, and knowledge to help guide the church through the change.

Do Not Get Distracted

One pastor had the perfect opportunity of a new congregation eager to build, resources to build, and a good plan for the building. However, he allowed peripheral issues to distract him at a critical juncture. The opportunity passed, conflict erupted, and the building was never constructed. Stay focused on the direction God is leading.

Sometimes distractions come in the way of opposition from inside the church or outside it. Like Nehemiah facing Sanballat outside Jerusalem and Tobiah inside the city, pastors will encounter naysayers who don't believe in the new direction, are opposed to the new direction, or simply do not like change of any type. Courageous leaders must have the confidence and faith that comes from assurance they are following God's direction in God's timing in God's manner. With that knowledge, you can find the strength to stand firm and move forward.

Get Everyone Involved

One key to implementing change relies on leading the people to develop ownership of the change. If people feel helpless in the midst of a change they do not understand, they probably will resist. On the other hand, if they feel they have a vital role and are invested in the success of the new direction, they not only will embrace the change but they will work diligently to make it work.

Listen and Adapt

You may have a great idea, but it may be improvable. Listen to other people. Keep an open heart so you do not dismiss other points of view without serious consideration. If you discover better ways of doing something, be humble enough to accept changes to your plan for change! Also, you may be able to accommodate input from other people by making reasonable adjustments that you may not feel are better than the previous idea but are not detrimental to the overall plan. Such accommodations may win support from segments of the church that may have opposed the ideas otherwise.

Recognize Each Small Success

Businesses employ benchmarks to gauge how they are progressing. Churches involved in change need to have several subgoals on the way to the larger result. Winning football teams understand the way to a winning score is to make touchdowns. The way to make touchdowns is to make first downs. The way to make first downs is to advance the ball on every play. Recognize the small successes along the way and help the people celebrate each one. They will be encouraged to keep moving forward and tackle the more difficult tasks ahead.

Get It Done

Nothing breeds success like success. Church members will be more likely to adopt future changes if they see evidence of accomplishment from past change. Stay with the task until the job is finished.

Praise God Before, During, and After

Certainly, you want to recognize the contribution of the various people involved in any project, but the focus of praise should be the Lord. Ultimately, anything of worth comes from His hand. Honor Him and glorify Him for His goodness. Be careful not to take credit either for other people's work or God's. Patricia Owens and Erma Davison wrote a song whose chorus reminds us: "Touch not the glory. Touch not the glory. Touch not the glory for it belongs to God."[2]

Chapter 23

ORGANIZING MINISTRY: BUDGET AND CALENDAR PREPARATION

"For which of you, intending to build a tower, sits not down first, and counts the cost, whether he has sufficient to finish it?" (Luke 14:28).

Budgets and Calendars

How does vision become reality? How do elaborate purpose statements and grand dreams become action? Many ministry leaders move congregations with glowing portrayals of growing futures but find themselves stymied when it comes to implementation. The difference in actualized visions and unrealized dreams is the ability to convert visions into specific plans, with the commitment and coordination of resources to make the plans happen. You must have the financial and human resources, time, facilities, and other tangible components needed to fulfill what God has laid before you.

The church budget and calendar reveal much about what a congregation really believes and, as importantly, what a congregation values. Unless you have unlimited resources, the church must decide how best to utilize its money, time, facilities, and people. Problems appear when we leap to our personal agenda rather than seeking to know God's plans. We are so busy organizing the church to accomplish our vision that we fail to discover God's desires.

A commitment to the will of God is foundational to discovering God's plans. As Jeremiah learned, God knows "the plans I have for you . . ." (Jeremiah 29:11). The problem is that we get ahead of God and make our own plans rather than seeking His direction.

Once we yield control of the situation to the Holy Spirit, we can discover the vision God has for our church. Lead your people to find God's vision together through prayer and Scripture.

"Thy Kingdom Come" (A spiritual planning process developed by the South Carolina Baptist Convention) emphasizes the vital relationships between vision, values, strengths, and results.[1] Once you can articulate God's vision, you need to study the values of the congregation and compare them to the vision and to Scripture. If all three do not align, you are only preparing yourself and the church for conflict. If the people's values are not in line with the vision, work with them through Bible study, prayer, discussions, and preaching. Be careful about moving forward until the church is ready to find and follow God's vision.

Next, outline the strengths on which the church can build its future. Every church has strengths. I spoke in a church in Siberia in 2005. One of the pastors responded to my comments about strengths by saying, "We only have four people in our church. We have no strengths." I asked him if his people were praying people. He said, "Yes." I asked if they were persevering. He said they had persevered in starting this church with nothing in the face of severe opposition. I pointed out that they indeed had at least two strengths on which to build. Don't focus on what you can't do but on what you can do.

Consider what results need to come from your plans. Too often, we think of budgets, calendars, events, and resources without a clear view as to the results desired. Without clear goals, you cannot make effective plans and, therefore, will have meaningless or counterproductive budgets, plans, and structures.

The planning form found below helps you put specific action plans into an organized, detailed outline. It begins with each ministry leader focusing on the overall purpose, or vision, statement of the church and the application of that vision to each specific ministry. It asks what is the observed need related to that purpose and demands a description of the strategy designed to accomplish the purpose and meet the need.

Ministry:			Date:		
Vision Statement:					
Observed Need:					
Strategy to fulfill vision and meet need:					
Target Group	Action Plan	Where/Place	When/Calendar	Who leads?	Materials needed? Cost?

At this point, the ministry planners consider their target groups. With whom are they actually going to do this ministry? For example, if the vision involves reaching a certain percentage of teenagers with the Gospel in an evangelistic presentation, you might think the target group comprises teenagers. While that may be true with some plans, others might focus on how you are going to reach the teens. One target group may be coaches of church athletic teams, or Sunday School teachers, or parents, or even teenagers who are church members. The activity for that target group may be a training event to help these groups learn and be motivated to reach lost teenagers. Naturally, you will establish a date, time, and place for the training, decide what materials and supplies you will need for the training, assign leaders to be responsible for carrying out the meeting, and arrive at a dollar amount the event will cost.

Now look back at your plan form, when you put all the dates of all the events from all the ministry plans together in chronological order, you have a calendar to propose to the church. Put all the list of places, with dates and times, together and you have your facilities schedule for the year. (Naturally, part of the process is to work together to resolve any date and place conflicts.) The list of leaders required gives you your Nominating Committee "need list" and training needs.

Finally, put all the dollar needs together, arranged by ministries, and you have your budget requests. If the overall budget requirement is too large for the reasonable, and faith-directed, expectations of income, there are several actions you can take.

The Budget Committee should not be the group to determine which activities ought to be done. A coordinated planning team, including the ministry leaders who compose a church council, should look at the plans. They might find areas that overlap and that could be combined. For example, a youth activity and a youth music activity may have similar goals and involve the same people. Those activities could be combined and the budget needs reduced. Such a decision should not be made by the Budget Committee but by the ministry leaders.

The church business sessions should include reports of ministry progress. As the ministry leaders share ministry results with the congregation, the church will see how their money is producing tangible benefits.

An equally important aspect of budgeting, and budget reporting, is an understanding of the seasonal nature of a church's budget. Certain times of the year produce larger offerings than other times. Senior adults usually tithe on monthly social security checks, which they receive at the first of the month. Farmers usually give the bulk of their tithe at the end of the year after they have sold their crops or livestock. Business people with investments may tithe on investments that produce income at the end or at the first of the year. Generally, November through January are the largest months for church income, while the summer months are the lowest (partially due to the absence of people who travel on vacations).

On the other hand, September to November and May through July may be the heaviest months for expenses. The quarterly purchase of Sunday School and other literature is heaviest in August, November, February, and May. Youth and other groups have trips, Vacation Bible School, summer camps, athletic teams, and other "high cost" activities at the same time that monthly income is lowest. Choirs purchase materials and supplies in early fall and winter for Christmas and Easter productions.

The wise administrator matches overall flow of income and expenses and ministry activities so the church will not get upset when certain months have more money going out than coming in. If the people understand how the church activities and budget money mesh together over the course of a year, they will be more supportive throughout the year.

Many budget managers advocate a zero-based budget for everything other than personnel, missions support, capital needs, and other entitlements. Too many churches simply look at the income and expenses of the previous year and add or subtract a percentage to all flexible budget items for the following year. Ministries become turf protective rather than purpose oriented, making it difficult to reduce unproductive budgets and increase activities with higher priorities.

On the other hand, with a long-range plan, you may have some years in which more money is budgeted for certain ministries and other years when budget money is moved to other ministries to accomplish the priorities as they change from year to year.

Developing Budget and Financial Processes

Work with the Stewardship Ministry (alias Committee) to develop a process. You might start with a large group meeting with all budgeted ministries to explain process and focus on purpose, strategies, and target groups. Over the coming weeks, host individual ministry meetings to help answer questions specific to that ministry and to brainstorm. Once individual ministries submit their plans, calendars, and budget requests, have another large group meeting to see how groups might work together and avoid overlapping budgets.

Use deadlines to advance the process:

- Date process begins, large group meeting, and forms distributed to leaders
- Dates small groups meet to make plans, consider costs
- Date large group meets for coordination
- Date budget requests are submitted to Stewardship Ministry
- Dates of Stewardship Ministry meetings
- Dates of submission to church for discussion, vote

Practical Suggestions

- Start with purpose and vision, strategies and goals, target groups and activities, resource needs, and finally financials.
- Help the people see the overall purpose.
- Focus on the needs to be met and the strategies designed to meet those needs.
- Help people to think about why they want to do something as much as what they want to do.

- Be people of faith, but not foolishness. If you are sure God is leading the church to stretch beyond its comfort zone, move forward, but do not presume God will fund what God has not initiated.
- Follow the appropriate process for changes. Inevitably, during the year some ministries will not follow through with some plans while, at the same time, unforeseen opportunities arise. Be flexible enough to adjust, but follow an established plan for making budget changes to help everyone understand the reasoning behind the changes. People will not support what they do not understand.
- If the total budget request ends up being too much, neither the pastor nor the Budget Committee should arbitrarily cut budgets. Work with the people involved in the ministries to see how plans can be accomplished in other, less expensive ways.

Establish Sound Financial Processes

As you implement your budget and plans, get professional legal and financial advice to establish sound processes for handling money. Simply because the church is the church does not mean it can ignore the law or mismanage the money. Work with the appropriate committees or ministries to write out processes for the following:

Collecting, Counting, and Depositing

How is money received? Who takes up the offering? Where does the money go once it has been put in the offering receptacle? What about money received during the week? Will the church set up electronic payment options via the Internet? Who counts the money? (Make sure more than one person counts all funds. Having a rotating committee helps prevent one or two persons from having too much knowledge about individuals' giving patterns.) When is the money deposited? What crosschecks are in place to prevent embezzlement or simple mistakes? Having good internal controls and annual audits can save churches much grief in the long run.

Purchases, Commitments, and Payments

Will the church require purchase orders to be preapproved before persons (lay members or staff) can make a purchase? Will purchases require a church check? Can the church credit card be used? By whom? For what? Will the church make reimbursements for purchases made by individuals? What are the state's laws regarding use of the sales tax exemption forms? (Individuals, including church staff, cannot use the church tax-exempt status for personal purchases!)

Reporting

What format will the treasurer use for reporting income and expenditures? A good report shows the budget for the year, the year-to-date, and the month, with actual expenditures for each period alongside. Beginning and ending balances sandwich income and expenses. Designated funds must be kept separately from general accounts.

Reports not only should be made to the church on a regular basis, but also to the various ranks of government. Some required reporting and tax payments include income tax and FICA/Social Security tax, W2 and W4 forms, I9 forms, payroll reporting, and more. Consult your certified public accountant for specific instructions. Another good source is Richard Hammer's *Church and Clergy Tax Guide*. Guidestone Financial Resources of the Southern Baptist Convention also has online guides for church and ministers.

Follow the Processes

Once you have established sound processes, follow them. Do not deviate from the plan without church approval, even with good intentions.

Avoid Even the Appearance of Evil (1 Thessalonians 5:22)

Do not make financial transactions that would cause anyone to question its validity. One of the most common problems involves use of the church credit card for personal purchases. Even when reimbursing the church for such use, it may be illegal and it certainly raises unnecessary questions.

Stay at "arm's length" of financial transactions. For example, if the church is selling equipment and an employee wants to buy it, have an open bid process so the purchase is available to anyone; then let the appropriate committee make the decision.

Ministers should not sign checks, especially checks made out to them. All checks should have two signatures; therefore, the church should have three or four persons designated for check signing.

Obey the Law

"And he said unto them, Whose is this image and superscription? They say unto him, Caesar's. Then said he unto them, Render therefore unto Caesar the things which are Caesar's; and unto God the things that are God's" (Matt 22:20–21). You may not agree with what the government requires you to do financially, but you have two choices: obey the law or challenge the law within legal procedures. You have processes by which you can legally appeal unjust or unconstitutional laws.

Teach Biblical Stewardship

The Biblical Principle of the Tithe

The principle of giving 10 percent of one's income to God's house is found in the Old and New Testaments. God spoke through the prophet Malachi, saying, "Bring ye all the tithes into the storehouse, that there may be meat in mine house, and prove me now herewith, says the LORD of hosts, if I will not open you the windows of heaven, and pour you out a blessing, that there shall not be room enough to receive it. And I will rebuke the devourer for your sakes, and he shall not destroy the fruits of your ground; neither shall your vine cast her fruit before the time in the field, says the LORD of hosts" (Study Malachi 3:8–12).

Jesus also taught the validity of the tithe. When he scolded the hypocritical religious leaders, he warned them about neglecting the weightier matters of God's Word. At the same time, he maintained they should do both—exercise justice, mercy, and faith while also giving their tithes. "Woe unto you, scribes and Pharisees, hypocrites! for ye pay tithe of mint and anise and cummin, and have omitted the weightier matters of the law, judgment, mercy, and faith: these ought ye to have done, *and not to leave the other undone*" (Matthew 23:23, emphasis added).

Even ministers are to tithe. "And in a sense Levi himself, who receives tithes, has paid tithes through Abraham, . . ." (Hebrews 7:9). You cannot teach or expect others to follow God's directions for giving if you do not do so yourself!

The Joy of Giving

Jesus, "looked up and saw the rich putting their gifts into the treasury. And He saw a poor widow putting in two small copper coins. And He said, 'Truly I say to you, this poor widow put in more than all of them; for they all out of their surplus put into the offering; but she out of her poverty put in all that she had to live on'" (Luke 21:1–4).

When people debate about whether they should tithe through their church or how much they should tithe, they reveal hearts that have not learned the joy of giving. People who love God do not rationalize to see how little they can give but rather they work to see how much they can give.

The Principle of Ownership (Matthew 25:14)

The prime principle of stewardship is that of ownership. The master in Jesus' parable delivers his goods into the hands of servants. God as Creator maintains the right of ownership to all things. He has placed creation into our hands as stewards. We must treat whatever God has given us (money, time, talents, or anything else) with a view to respecting His ownership.

We mistakenly think God only wants our tithes. Proverbs 3:9 reminds us to honor the Lord with ALL our substance, as well as the firstfruit of our increase.

The Principle of Use (Matthew 25:16–18)

Wise stewards used what the owner put into their hands to multiply the owner's wealth. If we understand that all we have belongs to God, we realize we have a responsibility to use that substance wisely. Money is mere paper and metal. It is only valuable insomuch as it can be exchanged for something else. Some people turn money into trash, wasting God's blessings on things that are worthless, or worse, harmful. Other people transform money into toys. Adults have their toys just as much as do children; the only difference is their toys are more expensive.

Wise stewards use substance (money as well as material matters such as homes, cars, clothing, businesses, etc.) to create treasure. True treasure is not gold, silver, or jewels; rather, true treasure is whatever draws our hearts toward God—whatever honors Him. If our treasure is in heavenly things, our heart will be there as well (Luke 12:24).

The Principle of Accountability (Matthew 25: 19–30)

Inevitably, the master returned to receive an accounting of his stewards. He rewarded faithful stewards and punished the unprofitable servant. God holds us responsible for our use of physical, as well as spiritual, resources. Just as God blesses proper profitable use of His creation, God also holds us accountable for our misuse of what He places into our care.

The principle of accountability should not be viewed as a sword of Damocles hanging over our heads but as a promise of reward and blessing to faithful stewards.

Chapter 24

GETTING ALONG WITH PEOPLE: PREVENTING AND RESOLVING CONFLICT[1]

"As much as it lies within you, live peaceably with all men" (Romans 12:18).

Conflict produces more stress than most other issues in our lives. No one likes conflict. Most people prefer positive, mutually encouraging relationships, but conflict tends to rise up in spite of our best intentions. Conflict may center on task issues—what to do and how to do it. Conflict arises from interactions between various personality types. However they start, conflicts tend to grow worse, not get better, if unattended.

The best way to resolve conflict is to avoid it. By demonstrating the fruit of the Spirit in our relationships, we are more likely to provoke positive responses. Generally, people will react well if we are loving instead of hateful, joyful rather than sour, peaceful rather than combative, patient rather than short-tempered, gentle rather than rough, good rather than evil, faithful rather than undependable, meek rather than arrogant, and temperate rather than self-indulgent (Galatians 5:16–23).

Scripture consistently urges people to live peaceably with one another. Note these proverbs:

- "Devise not evil against your neighbor" (Proverbs 3:29).
- "Hatred stirs up strife: but love covers all sins" (Proverbs 10:12).
- "He that is soon angry deals foolishly: and a man of wicked devices is hated" (Proverbs 14:17).
- "He that is slow to wrath is of great understanding: but he that is hasty of spirit exalts folly" (Proverbs 14:29).
- "The beginning of strife is as when one lets out water: therefore leave off contention, before it is meddled with" (Proverbs 17:14).
- "Go not forth hastily to strive, lest you know not what to do in the end, when your neighbor puts you to shame. Debate your cause with your neighbor himself; and discover not a secret to another: Lest he that hears it puts you to shame . . ." (Proverbs 25:8–10).

- "Where no wood is, there the fire goes out: so where there is no talebearer, the strife ceases" (Proverbs 26:20).

Unfortunately, conflict happens in churches because people are in churches. Even Christians can clash with one another, harming relationships and damaging the reputation of Christ and His church. What can a minister do to help resolve conflict? Most people go directly to Matthew 18, but this text is only one of several Scriptures offering wise counsel in resolving conflict.

Steps to Resolving Interpersonal Conflict

"And all things are of God, who has reconciled us to himself by Jesus Christ, and has given to us the ministry of reconciliation; To wit, that God was in Christ, reconciling the world unto Himself, not imputing their trespasses unto them; and has committed unto us the word of reconciliation. Now then we are ambassadors for Christ, as though God did beseech you by us: we pray you in Christ's stead, be reconciled to God" (2 Corinthians 5:18–20).

God Has Given Us the Ministry and Word of Reconciliation

Believers are the recipients of His gracious work of reconciliation, bringing us into a right relationship with Him through Jesus. As such, we have received a ministry of reconciliation. The foundation of the ministry of reconciliation is the word of reconciliation: ". . . that God was in Christ, reconciling the world unto Himself . . ." The basis by which we can help people resolve interpersonal conflict is God's atoning work in Christ.

Reconciliation Begins with Christ, Then One Another

Only Jesus can bring true peace within one's heart and between His people (John 14:27). Mediators who work with believers should begin by talking about their relationship with Christ. Jesus in one person cannot be in conflict with Jesus within another person. Where conflict exists, one or more of the parties have stepped away from a committed, submitted relationship to the Lord. Bringing each person closer to Christ results in their coming closer to one another. Jesus Himself provides the strongest common ground for people to experience reconciliation. ". . . as though God did beseech you by us: we pray you in Christ's stead, be reconciled to God."

Being Peacemakers Identifies Us as Children of God

Jesus is the Prince of Peace (Isaiah 9:6). We show ourselves to be His children and experience His blessing when we engage in making peace (Matthew 5:9). Disliking conflict, we may shy away from intervening into other people's conflicts, but such is the ministry He has given us. We cannot escape our responsibility to join Jesus in the ministry of peacemaking.

When conflict happens despite the best efforts, what can we do to resolve the disagreement and, in doing so, reduce the stress? Proverbs 20:3 reminds us, "It is honorable for a man to resolve a dispute, but any fool can get himself into a quarrel." So, what should you do if you find yourself in conflict?

1. Honestly examine yourself

Jesus said we should examine our hearts before we attempt to correct someone else. "And why do you behold the speck that is in thy brother's eye, but perceive not the beam that is in your own eye? Either how can you say to your brother, 'Brother, let me pull out the speck that is in your eye,' when you do not see the beam that is in your own eye? You hypocrite, cast out first the beam out of your own eye, and then you will see clearly to pull out the speck that is in your brother's eye" (Luke 6:41–42).

Honestly ask yourself if you are at fault in some way. Have you said or done something to provoke the dispute? Have you exhibited an attitude that offended the other person? Do you really love this person and want the best for him or her?

2. Lovingly consider the other person(s)

Do you understand what problems they may be dealing with at work, in the home, or personally? It may be that the conflict you are experiencing is actually fallout from conflict or difficulties in other places, producing stress that carries over into other relationships.

Could you be experiencing a personality conflict? As mentioned earlier, various personality types have difficulty understanding and relating to certain other types. Have you considered that each of you has approached an issue from your particular perspectives and you really need each other to gain a more complete understanding of the situation?

Have you wondered what this person wants from you and whether such expectations are legitimate? Does this person think you have not lived up to a perceived agreement? Or vice versa? What does this person really need from you?

Have you prayed about where this person is in relationship with the Lord? People who are not right with God will not be right with people. On the other hand, "When a man's ways please the LORD, he makes even his enemies to be at peace with him" (Proverbs 16:7).

3. Do not be quick to judge

Take time to listen and understand. Too often, we tend to jump to judgment. Instead of wisely listening to all sides of a dispute, we offer quick fixes that usually do more harm than good. "He who answers a matter before he hears it, It is folly and shame to him" (Proverbs 18:13). Peacemakers invest sufficient time to understand what is actually going on before trying to solve the problem.

Recognize your own liability. Don't be quick to judge because we all will be judged. "But why do you judge your brother? or why do you set at naught your brother? for we shall all stand before the judgment seat of Christ" (Romans 14:10).

Be fair. If we expect others to do what is right, we must be fair in handling all conflicts. We, too, have a Judge Who will apply whatever standard of judgment we have employed with others. "Judge not, that you be not judged. For with what judgment you judge, you shall be judged: and with what standard you measure, it shall be measured to you again" (Matthew 7:1–2).

Employ wise discernment. Avoiding being judgmental does not mean we cannot be discerning. Maintaining order in the Body of Christ requires us to use godly wisdom in determining the truth when fellow believers have disagreements. "Dare any of you, having a matter against another, go to law before the unjust, and not before the saints? Do you not know that the saints shall judge the world? And if the world shall be judged by you, are you unworthy to judge the smallest matters? Know you not that we shall judge angels? How much more things that pertain to this life?" (1 Corinthians 6:1–3).

Avoid a spirit of condemnation. Attitudes can make or break conflict resolution. If we approach others with a spirit of condemnation, we not only will fail to achieve reconciliation, but we also put ourselves in danger of judgment and condemnation. "Judge not, and you shall not be judged: condemn not, and you shall not be condemned: forgive, and you shall be forgiven" (Luke 6:37).

4. Wisely discern the real issues behind the conflict

Identify evidence of sin at the root of conflict. "From whence come wars and fighting among you? Come they not hence, even of your lusts that war in your members?" (James 4:1). Too often, people in conflict focus on assigning blame instead of resolving the problem. Everyone involved in a problem should humbly search their hearts to discern personal responsibility for sinful desires at the root of the fight. If the other person is at fault, love him or her enough to deal with the issue in a humble manner (Galatians 6:1).

<u>Is one of the parties to the conflict fearful of losing face (self-esteem)</u>? I counseled one minister who had become engaged in a terrible conflict with a church leader. The issue seemed so trivial I asked why he had not merely yielded for the sake of the relationship. He answered that he felt he would lose his place of leadership if he let the other person win. He would rather risk ruining a relationship and damaging the peace of the congregation rather than appear not to be in control. Granted, some situations require courageous stands against evil. However, this situation came down to one matter—pride.

<u>Some disagreements relate to generational perceptions and values</u>. Various age groups approach decisions differently. The environmental influences of their generations often develop values that differ greatly from other age groups. For example, the Builder Generation (older people, many of whom experienced the Great Depression) is fearful of debt and tends to be very frugal. The Baby Boomers grew up on credit and are only interested in whether they can make the payments. When a ministry decision relates to financial questions, these two generations will approach solutions from very different perspectives.

<u>Past experiences may shape a person's attitude</u>. The person in conflict with you may see in you some aspect of another person who offended them in the past. One church lay leader sought to change the church constitution and bylaws to eliminate much of the pastor's authority. When asked why he was so determined to make these drastic, conflict-causing changes, the leader related how a previous pastor had done something the layman felt was dishonest. He did not trust any pastor. In such cases, you have to help the person open up about previous conflicts and then show them you are not that person and this is not the same situation. Help them come to peace with their past so they might be at peace with their present.

<u>Pain also influences people's reactions to situations and other people that may have nothing to do with the pain</u>. One layman and his pastor experienced constant conflict in committee meetings. It seemed that no matter what the pastor did or said, the lay leader took the opposite position, often using strong emotion to insist on his point. Later, the pastor discovered that the layman was experiencing several painful situations. His employer was downsizing, creating fear he may lose his job. His son had become very rebellious and started using drugs. He was also suffering from a health problem that potentially could become life threatening. His personal pain did not excuse his behavior at church, but understanding it enabled the pastor to minister to the man with love and greater understanding.

<u>Some conflicts relate to task issues, while other problems are personal</u>. Understand whether the disagreement is over how to accomplish a particular task or if the conflict

has taken on a personal nature. People-oriented conflict is much more difficult to resolve and requires different approaches.

5. Try to limit the number of persons involved in the matter

Scripture advises anyone involved in conflict to approach the other person privately. "Moreover if your brother shall trespass against you, go and tell him his fault between you and him alone: if he shall hear you, you have gained your brother" (Matthew 18:15). The more people that are involved, the more difficult the resolution becomes. Pride rises. Sides are drawn. Advice starts flying from everyone at once, often without much wisdom, prayer, or seeking of scriptural guidance. In addition, peer pressure and the herd mentality are very real, creating an intractable situation.

6. Remember what is at stake

Who wins or loses is not as important as the honor and glory of God. When Christians fight, they dishonor the name of the One they claim as Lord. Jesus said, "By this shall all men know that you are my disciples, if you have love one for another" (John 13:35). In dealing with disagreements, both parties need to consider how the honor of the Lord is affected by the way they approach the problem and one another.

Also, lost people judge Christ on the basis of Christians' behavior. Does the community know you as people who love one another or as persons who cannot even be in right relationship with members of your own church?

In Shantung Province, China, prior to the Maoist revolution, a group of missionaries had labored for years with little fruit. A small Lutheran missionary lady, Marie Monsoon, entered the community and began asking each person she met, "Are you born again? Are you filled with the Spirit?" At first, other missionaries were offended at her questions. Then, one by one, they began to come under conviction for their attitudes toward one another. Missionaries from different denominational backgrounds, and even those within the same mission teams, had been unloving, envious, and, in some cases, hostile to each other. As God's Spirit humbled them, they began apologizing to each other and became reconciled to God and to one another. A great movement of God began with those missionaries, known today as the Shantung Revival. It swept first through the missionaries and then through the people of the land. Many Chinese came to Christ. Perhaps the only hindrance to evangelism and revival in some churches today lies in the hearts and relationships of God's workers.

7. Understand your part in the matter

<u>Are you a participant or a peacemaker?</u> Are you involved in the conflict or can you approach a problem as a third party whose only partiality is to the honor of God? If

you are party to the problem, you may need to be humble enough to seek a mediator to help resolve the situation. Jesus taught that if one cannot resolve an issue privately, then ". . . take with you one or two more, that in the mouth of two or three witnesses every word may be established" (Matthew 18:16). The witnesses are not simply people who will take one side against the other. Rather, they are able to view both points of view impartially and may be able to mediate a resolution. In any case, they can testify to what is actually said and done between the conflicted parties.

Avoid being drawn into someone else's fight. Some people will share a problem with you, expecting you to set the other person straight. Their battle becomes yours, and they often retire to the sidelines without responsibility for resolution or results, leaving you to suffer the scars that ensue. On the other hand, if you refuse to play their game, they may begin to perceive you as part of the problem and seek other people to take up their cause, often against you!

Realize that good shepherds protect the flock, even from themselves. Unfortunately, sheep bite! The shepherd who intervenes in conflict may discover painfully that some people will stop fighting each other long enough to attack you before going back to their battle. Still, good shepherds are willing to lay down their lives for the sheep. They do what is necessary to bring the sheep back to the Great Shepherd, Jesus, Who is the Prince of Peace. In doing so, they may hear His voice: "Blessed are the peacemakers: for they shall be called the children of God" (Matthew 5:9).

8. Take the initiative to seek a solution, regardless of who is at fault

People in conflict may be fearful of approaching others with whom they have conflict. Scripture reminds us that perfect love casts out fear. "There is no fear in love; but perfect love casts out fear: because fear hath torment. He that fears is not made perfect in love" (1 John 4:18). Prayerfully ask God to love the other person through you. When you come to the point of caring more for the other person than for your own pride or position, you are ready to initiate reconciliation and resolution.

Most people are willing to resolve conflict if the other person admits wrongdoing and asks forgiveness. Scripture does not give us the luxury of placing the responsibility for action on others. Regardless of who is at fault, we have the responsibility to go to the other person and initiate reconciliation.

If you are wrong. If you have harmed the other person, humbly admit the wrongdoing and ask for forgiveness. Confession may be difficult, particularly if the other party has also hurt you. Still, your responsibility is not what the other person may or may not do. You can only obey God's commandment for your actions. "Therefore if you bring your gift to the altar, and there remember that your brother has anything against you; Leave your gift before the altar, and go your way; first be reconciled to your brother, and then come and offer your gift" (Matthew 5:23–24).

If the other person is wrong. Don't wait until the person at fault comes to you. I was sharing with a godly friend about a Christian leader who had wronged me. I said, "If he would just come and admit his wrong, we could be reconciled." My friend replied, "You have just identified the spiritual one in this problem." He pointed out Galatians 6:1. "Brothers, if a man be overtaken in a fault, you which are spiritual, restore such an one in the spirit of meekness; considering yourself, lest you also be tempted" (Galatians 6:1). I knew immediately that I had to call the other person and initiate reconciliation.

9. Pray together

Put the matter in God's hand and seek to know the mind of Christ. It is hard to be angry with someone as you pray with them.

10. Act

Do not delay. Several practical reasons suggest you should take action as soon as the conflict becomes known:

- As time goes by, anger turns to bitterness, making resolution much more difficult.
- When caught early, most adversaries have not reached inflexible positions.
- If allowed to go unchecked, conflict draws other people like flies to trash, creating a much more complex situation.
- Conflict is like an infection; it rarely heals itself but only gets worse. Scripture also commands believers to move quickly to resolve disagreements.
- "Agree with your adversary quickly, while you are in the way with him; lest at any time the adversary delivers you to the judge, and the judge delivers you to the officer, and you are cast into prison" (Matthew 5:25). Whether the other person is at fault, or we are wrong, the principle remains: work quickly to resolve the issue. Delayed reconciliation leads to escalation of the conflict, always causing more harm than the original problem.
- "Be ye angry, and sin not: let not the sun go down upon your wrath: Neither give place to the devil" (Ephesians 4:26–27). Delaying reconciliation prevents anger from being resolved. Allowed to go on unchecked, anger develops into bitterness. When we refuse to

deal with our anger, we give the devil a platform within our hearts to attack our relationship with God and other people.

11. Remain calm and speak gently

"A soft answer turns away wrath: but grievous words stir up anger" (Proverbs 15:1). Replacing anger with godly, Spirit-generated love allows you to respond to others with a humble heart. Instead of speaking with raised voice and strident spirit, you can speak in such a manner as to reduce the other person's anger. Once, a fellow minister angrily approached me about a matter. He stood up, raised his voice, and gestured threateningly. Having grown up constantly fighting, my base nature was to also stand and respond in kind. However, God gave grace, enabling me to remain seated, speaking in a low voice. The louder he got, the softer I spoke—not in fear but following the Spirit's leading. Soon, the man realized his anger was inappropriate. He sat down, lowered his voice, and allowed us to enter a genuine discussion of the issue. Reconciliation ended with both of us praying, thanking God for His grace.

> *Replacing anger with godly, Spirit-generated love allows you to respond to others with a humble heart.*

12. Lovingly rebuke wrongdoing

Going to other people does not mean you ignore their wrongdoing. "Take heed to yourselves: If thy brother trespass against thee, rebuke him; and if he repent, forgive him" (Luke 17:3). The word translated *rebuke* is *epitimaō*. The sense of the passage does not suggest a harsh accusation but a firm admonishment. You may express strong disapproval, yet do so in a loving and gentle manner, remembering your own shortcomings (Galatians 6:1).

13. Beware of holding grudges

Some personalities get mad easily but get over anger quickly. Others take time to boil over, yet retain anger much longer. Unfortunately, too many people blame their personality type for their unwillingness to reconcile. They use the "Popeye" defense: "I am what I am and that's all that I am." Many people justify their bitterness by pointing out others' wrongdoing.

Believers have no excuse. We are more than the sum of our personalities because the Holy Spirit lives within us. We are responsible to submit to the scriptural admonition: "Grudge not one against another, brethren, lest you be condemned: behold, the judge stands before the door" (James 5:9).

14. Forgive and ask forgiveness

Scripture admonishes us to rebuke offenders, but it equally commands us to forgive (Luke 17:3). Interestingly, many people in ministry speak much about forgiveness, but in personal practice are among the most reluctant to forgive. Throughout the New Testament, believers are admonished to forgive.

Consider these passages: "Forbearing one another, and forgiving one another, if any man has a quarrel against any: even as Christ forgave you, so also do you" (Colossians 3:13). Christ has forgiven us such heinous sins that only His blood on the cross could make atonement. If He has forgiven us such great wrong, how can we refuse to forgive others? "And be kind one to another, tenderhearted, forgiving one another, even as God for Christ's sake hath forgiven you" (Ephesians 4:32).

Sometimes we forgive, only to have the other person continue to harm us. At what point do we stop "turning the other cheek?" Jesus gives us the answer through His lesson to Peter: "Then came Peter to him, and said, Lord, how often shall my brother sin against me, and I forgive him? Till seven times? Jesus said unto him, I say not unto you, Until seven times: but, Until seventy times seven" (Matthew 18:21–22). Jesus then told a parable of a man who owed much and was forgiven, only to be unforgiving toward a fellow servant who owed him a small amount. When other servants told the king, the unforgiving man was thrown into prison and his forgiven debt reissued. Jesus warned His followers, "So likewise shall my heavenly Father do also unto you, if you from your hearts forgive not everyone his brother their trespasses" (Matthew 18:35). The key phrase is "from your hearts." We cannot give lip service to forgiveness; it must be totally genuine, without reservation.

The only commentary Jesus offered about his Model Prayer was the phrase about forgiveness: "And forgive us our debts, as we forgive our debtors." Following the prayer, Jesus told His followers, "For if ye forgive men their trespasses, your heavenly Father will also forgive you: But if ye forgive not men their trespasses, neither will your Father forgive your trespasses" (Matthew 6:12–15). We may be uncomfortable with the idea that our forgiveness is tied to our willingness to forgive. Yet, Scripture offers this same admonishment not once but several times.

> *"And when you stand praying, forgive, if you have anything against any: that your Father also which is in heaven may forgive you your trespasses. But if you do not forgive, neither will your Father which is in heaven forgive your trespasses" (Mark 11:25–26).*

> *"Judge not, and you shall not be judged: condemn not, and you shall not be condemned: forgive, and you shall be forgiven" (Luke 6:37).*

If you are wrong, admit it. Confess your faults not only to the Lord but to the person(s) you have offended. Scripture links confession to healing (James 5:16). Refusing to admit wrongdoing and resisting asking forgiveness increases internal stress. The other persons become a source of stress because they remind us of our guilt. Since we dislike the discomfort stress produces, we tend to avoid those people who are parties to our conflict.

Scripture admonishes us to realize that denying our sin places us in the position of calling God a liar (1 John 1:10), but if we confess our sin, "He is faithful and just to forgive us our sin and cleanse us from all unrighteousness" (1 John 1:9). Just as confession and repentance are keys to reconciliation and forgiveness from God, we need to humble ourselves to seek forgiveness from people we have offended (Matthew 5:23–24).

15. Emphasize God's honor

It's not about us. When dealing with conflict, people tend to focus on themselves and their problems. They forget how believers' behavior reflects on the name and reputation of God. Remind everyone involved that God's honor is at stake. Ultimately, the most important outcome lies not in who wins or in who gets his or her way but whether God is glorified. Keeping the Lord's image in the forefront of the discussion motivates everyone to speak more kindly and to open themselves up to God's solution.

16. Find common ground

During marriage counseling, I rarely begin by discussing the couple's problems. Talking about disagreements does not build a basis for healing wounded relationships. Instead, we talk about their relationship with Christ because they cannot draw closer to Him without getting closer to one another. We also talk about what attracted them to one another to begin with. As they recall good times and positive experiences, they recover common ground of the past on which to resolve current conflicts.

Common ground may involve agreement about issues. Before focusing on points of divergence, help each person to discover areas of agreement. At the famous Jerusalem Conference, the two sides came to the common agreement that God had brought salvation to the Gentiles just as He had to the Jews. The conditions of acceptance were agreeable to both parties. Peace was made and God was glorified (Acts 15).

Working with a church that was divided 60/40 on nearly all issues, I spent several weeks teaching about the importance of glorifying God in all things, including decisions about the church's future. In a series of meetings, we placed people around tables by random selection to force various parties to work together who had not been on speaking terms. Tasking each table with deciding on five priorities for the church's future, but requiring unanimity before reporting to other groups, we left them to find common ground among themselves. After three weeks, each group shared their results. They discovered that they agreed on similar directions for the church after all. Having the first unanimous vote in years on those priorities led to a period of joy and growth. Conflict disappeared as the people committed themselves to one another and to the glory of God.

17. Discuss issues and solutions honestly and respectfully

Instead of imposing solutions on others, invite all parties to share their viewpoints. Sometimes, the basic problem relates to a misunderstanding of how each one perceives the situation. Encourage people to ask questions to address any confusion as to what someone meant by various statements. Discourage attacks on personalities by keeping the attention focused on the issues.

During the discussion, ensure a fair hearing by everyone. Often people will go along with different ideas if they feel others are giving them a genuine opportunity to present their positions. As participants debate the problem and possible solutions, work to keep communication flowing. Once people stop talking honestly and freely, resolutions become nearly impossible.

18. Commit the situation and solutions to the Lord

Sincerely seek God's direction, surrendering personal desires. The best resolution may be totally different than any of those proposed by participants. Search the Scriptures for principles that may apply to the current problem. While specifics of the situation may be difficult to identify from biblical accounts, the Bible contains spiritual principles applied to every human dilemma.

Seek agreement in which people do not identify who wins or loses, but rather they achieve a decision that glorifies Christ and, consequently, benefits His children. Such a result allows everyone to feel positively about the outcome and commit themselves to the ensuing direction.

What Do We Do If Conflict Is Not Resolved?

Jesus was the most Spirit-filled person ever to live; yet He constantly encountered opposition. In some situations, He resolved the conflict. In other places, He was rejected. In all cases, He loved the people involved, even when He rebuked them for their sin. Sometimes conflict is unavoidable. You cannot control other people; you can only choose to behave in a peaceful, Christlike manner. Paul advised, "As much as it lies within you, live peaceably with all men" (Romans 12:18).

Give It Time

Some personalities get over personal pain quickly; others take much longer. The deeper and more emotional the hurt, the more time is required for healing. The old saying, "time heals all wounds" is not exactly correct because time alone does not heal. Still, over a period of time, people become more open to healing and reconciliation. Give God time to work in your heart and in the lives of others involved in conflict. The Lord can heal and reconcile in an instant; however, people have to yield to His Spirit. Prayerfully and patiently wait for God's healing touch, opening your heart so, at least for your part, God can bring freedom.

Trust the Lord

When we swallow our pride and initiate actions to produce reconciliation, we expect action. We look for results immediately. If others do not respond quickly, we wonder if we have wasted our time; we are tempted to doubt God's willingness to work. Don't give up. Trust the Lord to fulfill His promises. He wants His children to live in harmony. Trust His willingness and His ability to work reconciliation in His timing.

Love in Spite of the Conflict

Do not fail in letting God's grace continue to work. Avoid letting bitterness build a foothold in your life. Instead, love the other person as Jesus has loved you. "A new commandment I give unto you, That ye love one another; as I have loved you, that ye also love one another" (John 13:34). Jesus did not wait to love us until we responded to His grace. "But God commends his love toward us, in that, while we were yet sinners, Christ died for us" (Romans 5:8).

What if the other person does not respond positively to your advances toward reconciliation? Jesus teaches us by precept and example to love people, even when they maintain hatred toward us. "But I say unto you, Love your enemies, bless them that curse you, do good to them that hate you, and pray for them which despitefully use you, and persecute you; That ye may be the children of your Father which is in heaven: for He makes his sun to rise on the evil and on the good, and sends rain on the just and on the unjust" (Matthew 5:44–45).

Some Conflicts Will Not Be Resolved. Accept It and Move On

Paul and Barnabus fell into such contention over John Mark and the second missionary journey that the disagreement could not be resolved. Both were godly men but were not able to reconcile their different commitments. The argument could be made that Paul was arrogant, demanding total allegiance to him and the task, while

Barnabus wanted his nephew to have a second chance to be used by God on the mission field. In any case, their positions were irreconcilable and they agreed to move forward separately. Paul took Silas and Barnabus left with Mark. The positive end of the story resulted in Paul's realizing John Mark's worthiness and asking Timothy to bring Mark with him, "For he is profitable to me for the ministry" (2 Timothy 4:11).

What about Church Discipline?

Yes, Matthew 18 teaches that the church should become involved in adjudicating a matter when someone refuses to deal with wrongdoing after private and, then, mediated admonishment. However, the purpose remains reconciliation. A prime example lies in the situation in the church at Corinth. Paul rebuked the church for not disciplining a man who was having an immoral relationship.

Between First Corinthians and Second Corinthians, the sense of Scripture shows that the church disciplined the person and put him out of the fellowship. The man repented and Paul instructed the church to receive him back into the fellowship. "Sufficient to such a man is this punishment, which was inflicted of many. So that contrariwise you ought rather to forgive him, and comfort him, lest perhaps such a one should be swallowed up with overmuch sorrow. Wherefore I beseech you that you would confirm your love toward him. For to this end also did I write, that I might know the proof of you, whether you be obedient in all things. To whom you forgive anything, I forgive also: for if I forgave anything, to whom I forgave it, for your sakes forgave I it in the person of Christ; Lest Satan should get an advantage of us: for we are not ignorant of his devices" (2 Corinthians 2:6–11).

Chapter 25

PRINCIPLES OF ORGANIZATIONAL COMMUNICATION

"And the LORD answered me, and said, Write the vision, and make it plain upon tables, that he may run that reads it" (Habakkuk 2:2).

A deacon once told me, "An informed Baptist is a happy Baptist." He was right. Most church members will support leaders who trust them with the truth. Remember the old adage: trust the Lord and tell the people. If we trust the Lord and if we trust the people, we will be open with information, sharing with people what is going on and what is going to be going on so they feel a part of it.

Somewhere in the middle of these two is the leader who is not necessarily afraid of people having information; he is just not very competent in getting information to the people. He thinks that an announcement from the pulpit on Sunday morning, or placed in the church bulletin or the newsletter, is enough. When people express surprise about a meeting or an initiative, the poorly communicating pastor responds, "Well, we put it in the bulletin!"

Who Owns the Responsibility for Communication?

While everyone has some responsibility, the leader is ultimately responsible for using the best principles of communication to insure that the people are able to function well and harmoniously.

The Bible uses the analogy of the church as the Body of Christ, with each person serving as a different functioning member. Have you ever seen someone who is paralyzed? The brain is functioning, but messages are not getting to the various limbs properly. The result is similar to what happens in a church when communication does not happen correctly.

Effective ministers are committed to good communication. Here are several principles you can utilize for better communication:

1. Be deliberate

Do not assume communication takes place. Build into the systems of the church methods and channels for information gathering and sharing. Examine your church's methods of information sharing. Are they effective in making sure everyone knows what they need to know? Do they feel the freedom to share their own information with others?

2. Use multiple channels of communication

Do not rely on just one or two methods of communication. Use print media (bulletins, newsletters, special mail-outs, posters, handouts, etc.). Use electronic media (e-mails, websites, text messaging, podcasts, weblogs, etc.) Use visuals (PowerPoint, videos, dramas, object lessons, etc.). Use forums (small groups, committee meetings, Sunday School class, department meetings, etc.) Use dialog sessions in large and small group formats. As people get the message through multiple channels, they are more likely to understand, retain, and respond to the information.

3. Be accurate and specific

When you communicate, check your facts. Make sure the information is accurate and specific. Do not say, "The youth committee will meet next Monday." Some people will think you mean the Monday following the announcement, while others will believe you intend the Monday after the Monday following the announcement.

4. Make sure people are sharing information between organizational units

Does the music ministry know what the youth ministry is planning? Does the Nominating Committee know why the committee on committees passed over a particular person for a leadership position? Does the treasurer know that the building committee is going to need a certain amount of available cash to pay for repairs on the roof before he puts that extra $20,000 into Certificates of Deposit?

5. Encourage open reporting

People like to know what is happening in the church. Committees, ministries, and staff can have written reports for business meetings highlighting their activities (failures as well as accomplishments) and plans for activities ahead. These events offer good opportunities for testimonies of God's blessings.

6. Create a nonthreatening atmosphere

If people are afraid, they will cover up or minimize problems or failures. If people do not know there is a problem, they can't pray or help correct the problem. Help staff, committees, ministry leaders, and others know that it is okay not to succeed every time. If they succeed 100 percent of the time, they are not stretching very far. Extraordinary success comes from people who reach beyond their grasp, winning sometimes and losing sometimes, but always trying their best.

7. Model communication

Not only share with people openly and freely, but elicit their input deliberately and consistently. If people believe you really want to hear from them, they will not only share their true thoughts with you but they will listen to you in return.

8. Keep records

When communication is verbal, it lasts only as long as everyone's memory. Sooner or later, someone is going to remember things differently from someone else and disagreement and conflict will result. Keep minutes of meetings, with enough specific information that when examined months (or years) later, people can understand what the agreements and decisions were and on what basis they were made. Maintain a good cross-reference file so leaders can find information from past meetings quickly and effectively.

9. Use technology to improve communication.[1]

Telephones are no longer telephones but mobile multimedia devices supporting e-mail, phone service, text messaging, Internet browsing, and PDA applications (address book, calendar, lists, notes). People watch movies, catch up with social media, take pictures, and make videos. Who wants to place a phone call when you can watch TV shows, check the stock market and make trades, listen to favorite music downloads, and participate in virtual sports, all on your lunch hour? With hands-free microphone/receivers that fit around one's ear wirelessly connected to the phone on one's hip, they go anywhere.

Technology involves much more than information, transforming manufacturing, social services, health industries, education, and, yes, religious life. Higher education and continuing education have decentralized with online education becoming the standard, incorporating advanced technologies into learning systems as well as using the web to make education available to people anywhere in the world.

Audio technology allows the best in vocal quality at reasonable costs (people will not believe what they cannot hear). Video enhancements of PowerPoint, Media

Shout, or video clips help people combine visual senses with auditory senses as the congregation takes in the emotional as well as the cognitive content.

In ministry, pastors who may have been to seminary, or not, can access biblical research, commentaries, sermonic helps, leadership advice, programs for all ages, and much more. Podcasts and webcasts allow us to share the sermon with thousands of people outside the church at negligible costs. Blogging the sermon also increases interest in the message. Streaming video allows online visitors to the church's website to participate in worship regardless of their location around the world.

Chat rooms and other websites can be used to witness to millions of people who are not accessible to the Gospel message in any other way. E-mail, IM, phone trees, and other innovations allow churches to maintain pastoral contacts more regularly and efficiently. Databases allow church leaders to keep up with membership needs and contact information efficiently.

Availability of inexpensive computers, printers, and on-demand printing software allow churches to publish high-quality, full-color brochures, visitors' information materials, and other printed promotional needs.

At the same time, do not depend on technology to replace the personal touch in ministry. As mentioned before, important issues such as conflict resolution are best handled face-to-face. Mass communication cannot substitute for individual attention.

Ministers have never faced such raw temptation as technology offers. Thousands of ministers confess to accessing Internet pornography, using sermons from preaching websites as if they were their own, and participating in flirtatious virtual affairs in Internet chat rooms. Some ministers have lost power in the pulpit because they no longer wrestle with the biblical text or spend time with God in prayer. They justify plagiarizing other ministers' sermons by pointing to the example of others and to their own busy schedules.

Technology can enhance your ministry and maximize effective communication, but be careful to control the technology rather than allow it to control you.

10. Make sure information is available to organizational leaders

Growing churches, like growing businesses, understand that if information is only available to the people "at the top," it is basically useless. Sunday School teachers need access to information about their class members. Ministry budget directors need to know how their individual budgets and the overall church budget are doing. Open-book management has proven that an informed Christian is not only a happy Christian but also makes a more effective Christian.

Church information systems are available that can be integrated with church websites to enhance information availability. Sunday School teachers and other leaders may have password-protected web access to their members' attendance data and other information vital to their ministries. Offer orientation sessions at the beginning of each year to help new workers understand how best to access and use information.

Information overload is one of the hobgoblins of the IT age. With so much material available just a click away, churches may ignore it altogether and focus on the tried and true. You may not like the idea of shifting through huge amounts of extraneous material to gain the few nuggets that could make a difference in your church. However, facing unprecedented opportunity, the church must embrace the tools God has placed in its hands to reach this world on a global scale.

Chapter 26

MANAGING LEGAL AND BUSINESS ISSUES

"They say unto him, Caesar's. Then said he unto them, Render therefore unto Caesar the things which are Caesar's; and unto God the things that are God's" (Matthew 22:21).

I am not a lawyer or the son of a lawyer, so please do not read the following as if you are receiving legal advice. You're not. Still, every pastor needs to be aware of legal issues related to the church. What follows will give you some ideas about what questions to ask. This information is offered for educational purposes only. Before making legal decisions, always consult a qualified Christian attorney who understands church legal matters.

Church Incorporation

While most churches are incorporated, many are not. Some congregations may have the mistaken idea that incorporation makes them somewhat less of a church. Such is not the truth. The primary issue regarding incorporation is legal status. Basically, incorporation establishes a legal entity. Unincorporated churches, like other unincorporated groups, are associations of people. Their legal status may simply be is as individuals, rather than the group. The legal status of the church may affect these issues:

- **Owning property:** Being a legal entity, an incorporated church can own, buy, and sell property. Usually transactions are signed by church trustees who act on instructions of the congregation. Unincorporated churches may also own property but do so through action of the trustees. Depending on state law, the unincorporated church may have some difficulty in property transactions.
- **Lawsuits:** Lawsuits against incorporated churches involve legal entities. The members of the church usually are shielded from personal liability unless they have acted improperly as individuals. Unincorporated churches, not being legal entities, face a more difficult situation. Often, lawsuits will name members of the church

as defendants. Again, state law defines how churches respond to lawsuits. Some states prohibit church incorporation, but treat churches as if they were incorporated.

Incorporation usually occurs by applying to the Secretary of State of the state in which the church exists. An attorney can help the congregation with the process of application. Leaders should take care to insure the articles of incorporation match the church's constitution and bylaws, especially regarding officers and business matters.

Federal and State Identification Numbers

Churches need a tax identification number in order to open bank accounts, pay employees, handle tax payments, and other needs. An attorney can help make application for the numbers from the federal government and the state. Care should be made to insure the proper name of the church is used in all legal applications, as this name becomes the legal identifier in association with the tax identification number.

Tax Exemption

Are churches exempt from taxation? Yes and no. You should consult your attorney and CPA for specific advice. Churches generally enjoy exemption from paying property and income tax, and in some cases state sales tax. However, some property may be taxed, as in property that is not used for religious purposes and that generates non-church-related income (such as rental property). Similarly, church purchases may be exempt from state and local sales tax, provided a sales tax exemption has been obtained and the procedures have been followed for use of such an exemption.

Churches are generally liable for various payroll taxes, including paying the employer's half of Social Security/FICA taxes for nonexempt (unordained) employees. The church treasurer must also collect the nonexempt employees' portion of taxes (both income and Social Security/FICA) and pass it along to the appropriate governmental agency (IRS). Exempt (ordained) ministers are usually responsible for paying their own taxes, although the church must report income to the government. Ministers may elect to have the church withhold certain funds and pay taxes on their behalf through regular payroll deductions.

People who make donations to churches may receive deductions on their personal income taxes. Churches generally are automatically exempt, but applying for 501c3 status may be a good idea. At the end of each year, the church must give donors a written receipt indicating donations and whether they were for "non-tangible religious benefits only." Some limitations apply.

Again, anytime you handle legal and tax issues, you should seek the advice of a qualified consultant—an attorney and/or a certified public accountant.

Developing a Constitution and Bylaws

Many Next-Gen ministers are church planters. Their missional hearts beat faster with the idea of starting a new congregation. Sometimes, however, building relationships, evangelizing a community, handling logistical issues, and other demands can distract leaders from basic legal matters regarding establishing the new church. One of the first matters involves developing an effective constitution and bylaws.

The Church Constitution

The church constitution basically defines who the church is. It should include the following:

Name: Include the legal, formal name of the congregation, and, usually, its location. If the location changes, the constitution should be changed. An attorney can advise how the document may be worded so the church, especially a new one, may have greater flexibility for relocation.

Purpose: The purpose or missions statement should be more than a mere slogan and less than a comprehensive inclusion of all the church ministries. The statement basically says, "Here is who we are and why we exist."

Church Covenant: The constitution often includes a statement of the covenant members establish between themselves. Baptists usually use a standardized covenant that has been in use for many years, although Next-Gen ministers may prefer customized statements.

Articles of Faith: The church may detail various statements of faith. If the congregation is in agreement with an established set of doctrinal beliefs (such as the Baptist Faith and Message of the Southern Baptist Convention), a shorter route may be to simply include a statement that the church is in agreement with that statement of faith.

Church Government: Include a general statement about how the church is governed. If it is a Baptist or other congregational-oriented form of government, this statement often will state that the church's authority rests with the congregation and is not under the administration of other ecclesiastical bodies. At the same time, it might specify certain organizations (local association of churches, state or national conventions) with which the church may voluntarily cooperate. If the church is part of a hierarchical denomination (such as Methodist or Episcopalian), ownership of property and external control of certain aspects of church government become an issue.

Membership: Define how persons become members and how they may be removed from membership. Specify what rights and responsibilities members have.

Adoption and Amendments: Specify how the document will be adopted by the church and how it may be amended. Be careful to be specific about voting and quorum requirements. If you simply say, "80 percent of members must approve . . . ," then 80 percent of *total members* must vote to approve. Total members include nonresident and inactive members, and few churches reach that level of participation. The constitution should read: "80 percent of members present and voting must approve . . ." Generally, the document should require at least one or two weeks of notice in writing to the membership for changes to the constitution. You do not want this document changed by a small group of dissidents showing up at a random business meeting without advance notice.

As you can see, the constitution is not very long and contains only basic "who we are" kinds of information. The church should not put matters into the constitution that will be changed very often. It is a basic, foundational document. General rules for church organizations and making decisions are not found in the constitution but in the bylaws (a separate document often associated with the constitution).

The Bylaws

As the constitution describes "who we are," the bylaws detail "how we function." This document should not contain every administrative function, staff position, or policy. Those kinds of issues should be included in an administrative manual, separate from the constitution and bylaws. An administrative manual can easily be changed to accommodate changing policies, personnel configurations, and other administrative matters. The bylaws document outlines basic information about how the church is organized and how it will operate.

Space will not allow a detailed explanation of everything typical bylaws will contain, but here are a few:

- **Meetings**: When will the church have business meetings, both regular and special meetings? How can special meetings be called? What constitutes a quorum? Who will moderate? What records will be kept?

- **Officers**: Who will be considered church officers? What are their qualifications? How will they be selected? What will be their duties? How can they be removed from office? Typical officers include the pastor, deacons, treasurer, trustees, and clerk. Staff ministers other than the pastor are best listed in the administrative manual. You don't want to change your bylaws every time you change your staff structure. A general statement about how ministerial staff other than the pastor should be selected, how they will be administered, and how they can be terminated may be listed in the bylaws or the administrative manual.

- **Organizations and Committees**: Do not try to list every organization or committee. The Administrative Manual will suffice for most groups. The bylaws should only include the most basic organizations, such as the Sunday School or Bible teaching ministry, the men's and women's ministries, and the missions ministries. Similarly, the bylaws should include details for basic standing committees, such as the Nominating Committee, the Finance/ Stewardship Committee, and the Personnel Committee. Listings should include duties, composition, qualifications, and procedure for removal of members. Other committees and groups may be placed in the Administrative Manual.

- **Church Discipline**: The bylaws should specify how church discipline may be exercised. This detail may be included in the membership section of the constitution, within the listings of each officer, committee, and organization, or in a separate section. You would be wise to have a clear policy that follows Scripture, maintains order in the congregation, and provides secure legal means of handling removal of members or dismissal of leaders. Most courts will not interfere with a church as long as it follows its policies with due process. You may want an attorney to look over this section, as well as the entire documents. However, do not get caught up in such technical legal language that people do not understand their own policies.

- **Licensure to Preach and Ordination**: The church should have specific procedures for licensing qualified men to preach the Gospel and for ordination to the Gospel Ministry. This section should also detail how such license and ordination might be revoked if necessary.

- **Adoption, Amendment, or Repeal**: A final section of the bylaws should indicate how the document will be adopted, how it can be amended, and how it may be repealed. As with the constitution, care should be given to be specific in details regarding quorum and percentage of members "present and voting" necessary for action.

Administrative Manual

In addition to the constitution and bylaws, which are foundational documents that rarely change, the church needs an Administrative Manual, which contains those matters that may need adjustment from time to time. Included may be organizations and committees not specified in the bylaws. The manual should also list policies for personnel administration, weddings, funerals, facility use, nursery, and other policies. This document also details financial procedures such as budget development, counting, deposits, reporting, purchase orders, credit card use, check writing, audits, and other matters.

Leading Church Business Meetings

Few people enjoy business meetings, usually because conflict often associates with decision making. It does not have to be that way. Conducting business is a basic function of any organization. The church is not excluded. Sometimes decisions relate to doctrine, as at the conference in Jerusalem to decide whether the Gentile Christians should be required to submit to circumcision (Acts 15). However, most business meetings involve everyday matters regarding *property* (building, repairing, furnishing, maintaining), *personnel* (hiring, firing, supervising), *procedures and policies*, *plans* (events, ministries), or *finances*. Generally, meetings include reports from ministries, committees, organizations, and other groups.

> *Business meetings ought to be as spiritual as any other meeting or function of the church.*

Business meetings can be a wonderful opportunity for church members to learn more about what God is doing through various ministries. Reports, usually in written form, may be accompanied by testimonials of God's blessings. For example, a monthly or quarterly financial report could be laced with stories of how various events, ministries, and programs impacted people's lives.

Prayer

Business meetings ought to be as spiritual as any other meeting or function of the church. Prayer should not be merely tacked on to the beginning and end of the meeting. The pastor can lead members in approaching God's throne in worship and supplication, invoking His guidance so the attitudes displayed and decisions reached might honor Him. If issues become disputed or emotions raised, prayer draws people back to their spiritual focus.

Moderator

The key to making business meetings a positive experience involves the attitudes of the participants and the skill of the moderator. Often, the pastor may serve as the moderator of business meetings. While this role enables the minister to maintain some level of control over the tone and atmosphere of the meeting, it also can tie him to controversial issues and put him in a lose-lose situation. Some churches specify that a neutral individual should be elected by the church annually to serve as moderator.

Parliamentary Procedures

Whoever serves as moderator should be well educated in how to lead formal meetings. A good knowledge of *Roberts Rules of Order* is helpful, since this book is widely accepted as a manual of procedures. Parliamentary rules guide an orderly process for meetings. They help groups make decisions in a fair, systematic manner. At the same time, some people can misuse procedures to get their own way. Moderators should understand that the purpose of rules is to help the church make wise, biblical decisions. They should resist any attempt to use procedures to keep the congregation from information it needs and decisions it desires.

Discussion

Sometimes, choices do not involve right and wrong decisions but legitimate differences of opinion by good people. Issues should not come before the congregation if they have not been properly vetted by appropriate committees or ministries in advance of the business meeting. Still, people may need additional information before voting about a matter. If possible, accommodate requests for more data, even if it means delaying the decision. If the matter cannot be postponed, allow people the opportunity to share their opinions in a respectful, kind manner. No one should be allowed the platform of a business meeting to vent anger or make personal remarks that offend others.

Agenda

Having a printed agenda available before meetings helps people know what is to be discussed. The church could reasonably request (or require) matters for business sessions to be submitted to the church office at least a week in advance, unless approved by appropriate groups—whether the pastoral staff, a committee, deacons, or other group.

Voting

Rarely call for a vote unless you have already developed an informal consensus before the meeting. In many cases, votes only solidify decisions that have already been made. Work with committees and ministries ahead of meetings so their recommendations and requests are biblical, well considered, and have the support of leaders.

Some votes will require only a majority vote. However, only a foolish leader proceeds with a slim majority. Work to build a win-win situation so that decisions have the support of the congregation. You may not have unanimous votes, but seek to keep dissension at a minimum. Determine the nature of disagreement. Do people need more time or information? Do they simply need to voice different points of view and have their ideas respected? Are they experiencing personality clashes? Is a turf war happening in the background? Discovering the real issue is the beginning of resolving conflict and helping the congregation advance in harmony.

In a few cases, if the matter is important enough and dissension is based on nonbiblical issues, you may have to proceed without a strong majority. If so, be prepared for lingering conflict. Decide if this is a hill worth dying on. Work with your leaders to make sure you don't just win a battle only to lose the war. The bottom line is not whether you get your way but whether God's will is accomplished in such a way that He is glorified.

Records

Usually the church clerk will keep the records of proceedings. All motions should be written down verbatim, along with notations as to the results of voting. After the meeting, the clerk, or someone tasked with keeping records, compiles all of the matters from the meeting. The clerk may keep a personal copy of business minutes, but the church office will also need a copy for permanent archives. Without good records, you are dependent on fallible human memories and condemn the church to inevitable conflict over who said what and when.

Conclude business meetings with a positive expression of thanksgiving to God for His blessings. Praise Him for how He has worked through the various ministries. Draw the people's focus toward the Most High at the beginning of the meeting, throughout the meeting, and at the end of the meeting. In all things, glorify Him!

Chapter 27

COOPERATING WITH YOUR DENOMINATION

Many pastors miss a wonderful blessing by not working with other ministers, especially in cooperation with their church's denomination. God will gift you with other ministers in your local association and in your community, as well as your denomination at large. They can be sources of knowledge and support as you serve your congregation. To paraphrase an old adage: no church is an island, nor is any pastor a Lone Ranger!

Granted, some ministers who struggle in their churches seek satisfaction and affirmation by spending too much time in denominational or ministerial association business. God's primary call is to serve your local church. If you have difficulty finding enough time to visit your members, study for your preaching, or managing the business of your congregation, then you do not have time to be involved with other groups. However, more often, being part of the larger ministry can help you be more productive in your primary work at the church.

Pastors can find help for themselves and their churches through interaction with other ministers and the resources of their denomination. Following are examples of levels of cooperation and resourcing in a typical denomination. I use the Southern Baptist model as the ongoing example since I'm most familiar with it and have been blessed by it for many years.

The Local Association

The local association of churches within a denominational structure is the oldest and most widespread level of cooperation among congregational churches. Churches within a geographical region (usually one or two counties or parishes) voluntarily associate to offer mutual encouragement, missions endeavors, training opportunities, and resources. Most associations have several ways you might be served and in which you can serve others.

The Associational Director of Missions

The associational missions director often serves as a pastor to the pastors. You can draw on his experience and knowledge to help you with many aspects of church ministry. He can be a mentor as you learn how to lead your church in its various ministries. He can be a friend to encourage you when you are downhearted. He can be a mediator if you need help resolving conflict. He can be a resource for training and materials to help your church's ministries excel. While you are new to the community, the Director of Missions likely has had experience with your church for several years and can offer valuable insights into the church's history, leadership, problems, and possibilities.

The Pastors' Conference

On Monday morning, you may feel depressed from something that happened on Sunday. Having lunch at your associational pastor's meeting gives you the opportunity to share and pray with other ministers who can encourage you. You may find wise counsel and willing ears from your peers around the table. Prayer and preaching, along with a generous supply of good humor, can become a regular source of spiritual revitalization.

Ministries and Organizations

The average association sponsors various ministries to the local community through the cooperative efforts of member churches. Many associations have food pantries, clothes closets, and other ways to aid local people who have financial needs. Having a single point of service can be more effective than having needy families go from church to church for handouts.

Many associations and state conventions have disaster-relief teams composed of church volunteers. Such teams help during natural disasters that occur locally, regionally, and nationally. Mud-out units, chain saw teams, feeding units, and other specialized groups have trained and committed members ready to help when the need arises.

Associational ministries may include training opportunities for Sunday School, Discipleship, Evangelism, Music, Children and Student Ministries, Bible Drill Teams, and others. The association usually will offer events at which your laypersons can find the latest resources and training for their local church ministries.

Missions

Since the average church has only sixty-two persons on a Sunday, few congregations can be involved in mission work by themselves. The local association provides ways local churches can work together. They may sponsor new church plants in the local area or elsewhere. Often the association will organize mission trips to other parts of the United

States or internationally. Ministers and laity can find great satisfaction in being part of a cooperative effort to reach people for Christ.

Support

The local association is supported by the voluntary financial gifts and the voluntary work of the churches that make up its membership. Most churches put the association in their budgets and give regularly either on the basis of a percentage of income or a flat sum. Some associations receive additional support from their state conventions.

The State Convention

In Baptist life, churches within a state (or within two or more contiguous states) voluntarily associate together in a state convention of churches. Like the association, the state convention does not have any authority over the churches but is a vehicle for channeling ministry and mission efforts on behalf of the churches.

Governance

State conventions are operated under the direction of messengers sent by member churches to an annual meeting. Between annual meetings, an Executive Board or a State Board of Missions oversees the work of the state convention. Its members are elected by the messengers from the churches at the annual meeting. The Board elects Ministry Staff who serve under an administrative leader (usually called the Executive Director).

Ministry Staff

The number and kinds of ministry staff vary according to need and availability of support. Obviously, larger state conventions can afford more personnel and are able to provide a greater variety of ministries to the churches. In smaller conventions, individual ministers may wear many hats and have multiple responsibilities. These state missionaries exist to help the churches and their pastors. Feel free to contact various state convention staff to help you with the different ministries of the church.

Institutions

In older, more established conventions, educational and benevolence institutions are part of the overall ministry. In most cases, trustees for these institutions are elected by the messengers from the churches at the annual convention meeting.

Resources

Tremendous resources are available to your church in cooperation with your state convention. Highly skilled specialists will offer training events for ministers and lay leaders related to nearly every type of ministry found in the average church. In addition, most state convention leaders are available for individual consultations. Materials also may be available for needy churches to aid in their ministries. Regardless of the size of his church, every pastor will find state workers ready and eager to lend their assistance.

Missions

State conventions work with churches, associations, and missions agencies for national and international work. New church plants and other missions ministries can find training, guidance, and financial support through the state missions office, usually in cooperation with other groups. Partnership missions also enable churches to work together in mission trips and mission support for work in other parts of the United States and overseas. Associational missionaries partner with state missions personnel for work in local areas.

Funding

In Southern Baptist life, state conventions are supported primarily through the Cooperative Program. Established in 1925, the Cooperative Program enables every member church to support missionary, educational, and benevolence ministries across each state and around the world. Each church voluntarily contributes a percentage of its undesignated income to the Cooperative Program. Part of the donations remain in the state convention for statewide ministries; the remainder goes to the national Southern Baptist Convention for support of national and international missions, seminaries, and other ministries. What a wonderful blessing! The smallest church who participates in the Cooperative Program has part in the work of ten thousand missionaries worldwide, provides seminary training for thousands of ministers, and contributes to ministries across the state and around the world!

National Denominations

Ministries

Different denominations have various ministries. Following our ongoing example, Southern Baptists sponsor the North American Mission Board, the International Mission Board, six seminaries, a publishing house (LifeWay Christian Resources), an annuity and insurance agency (Guidestone Financial Resources), and an agency related to ethics and religious liberty.

Governance

National denominations operate differently depending on history, organization, and polity. Hierarchical denominations are more directly involved in educating, certifying, and appointing pastors to church positions. Congregationalist churches, like Baptists, reverse the authority structure, placing control of the national organization into the hands of the local churches. Messengers from local churches come to an annual meeting at which the policies, ministries, and budgets of the various agencies are approved.

Funding

Again, each denomination has its own funding program. The national organization of Southern Baptists is primarily funded through the Cooperative Program (described above). In addition, the missions agencies have annual giving emphases in which churches may give specifically to their missionaries' support. Seminaries and other agencies may also have individuals who help provide financial support for scholarships and operations.

Resources

Each agency has many resources available to the local church. Pastors and lay members can access materials and training through the various agencies' websites, as well as in connection with agency missionaries and staff leaders. Curriculum for Sunday School or Connect Groups is published by LifeWay Christian Resources, which uses highly trained writers and insures doctrinal fidelity for every publication. Materials related to evangelism, church planting, music and worship, preaching, and every other aspect of church ministry can be obtained through the various agencies.

You may be in a larger church that has plenty of resources. You could be like the pastor I met who said, "I really don't need the convention. My church is doing fine on its own." That may be true of your church. You may not think you need the denomination, but your denomination and its churches need you. You might be the blessing to some other minister in a small, struggling church. Your church's contribution may mean the difference in more missionaries going to the neediest of fields or having to come home for lack of funds. Your participation in serving at various levels of denominational work may open the door for vistas of ministry that will touch thousands.

Remember, "we are laborers together with God" (1 Corinthians 3:9).

Chapter 28

ENDING WELL

Very few pastors spend their entire ministries in one church. The national average for tenure is around twenty-four months, although this number is affected by some hierarchical denominations that move ministers around more often. In contrast, growing churches usually have pastors who stay for a long time. However long your tenure may be in a given location, how do you know when it is time to go?

False Indications

Too many ministers suffer from short terms of service because they leave too soon. They misread the signs in themselves and their churches. Fearful they might overstay their welcome, such pastors put themselves, their families, and the churches through the trauma of ending a ministry. What are some wrong reasons for leaving a place of service? D. L. Lowrie observed that many pastors make a vocational change for the wrong reasons.[1]

Call

Certainly, responding to God's call is a good thing. On the other hand, some ministers leave one church simply because another church is willing to call them. Not every open door is an indication God is calling. Sometimes a Search Committee will approach a prospective minister with absolute determination that he is to become their pastor. Usually flattered by the attention, the minister may entertain their invitation without really praying about whether God is calling him away from his current location. Through the years, I've been blessed by turning down some opportunities, even though other people were convinced they knew God's will and I should come. In hindsight, it proved that each situation would have been disastrous had I moved too soon. Remember, no one but you can determine God's will for your life.

Conflict

Perhaps the number one cause of premature ending of a ministry is conflict or fear of conflict. Most pastors are peaceable people. Like the average person, they prefer everyone just get along. Unfortunately, because human nature still suffers from the Fall, people inevitably experience problems with one another. Instead of working through conflict, too many ministers run from difficulties instead of resolving them. Developing a pattern of fleeing problems not only breeds weak character, but it leaves the church to deal with the mess left behind.

Culture

God often calls ministers to leave the environment of their youth and work among people in a culture vastly different from what they have known. At first, the uniqueness of a new place seems quaint and interesting. Over time, if the minister and his family cannot adapt to their adopted home, wrestling with different cultures can produce intolerable stress. In many cases, the minister may do better than his family in managing culture shift. His work keeps him engaged with people. His wife and children, however, may have difficulty making friends with people who view them as outsiders. Building a life in a strange environment may produce so much pressure that the easiest choice is to move back home.

Confusion

Arriving on a new church field is always exciting. New possibilities, new vision, and new beginnings provide a bright new vista of opportunity. With time, possibilities fade into realities, goals may be unmet, and the fresh patina of the glossy new job dulls into the daily routine. Just as many men experience midlife crises, so ministers go through periods when their lives seem drab, boring, unchallenging, and unfruitful. They may start looking for other opportunities simply because they lack the spiritual and personal energy to revitalize their ministry.

Sometimes the pastor's confusion results from external circumstances. If the church experiences a growth plateau or begins to decline, he may believe it is time to move on and let someone else have a shot at turning things around. Should the local community begin changing and his church field no longer has the demographics to sustain the church, he may leave rather than face the uphill battle required to help the congregation transition with its neighborhood. In either case, the pastor demonstrates he is a hireling that leaves when the enemy approaches rather than laying down his life for the flock of God (John 10:11–13).

The Cares of Life

Unmanaged stress drains people of energy, resilience, and hope. Ministers and their families experience personal burnout as often, if not more so, than any other profession. Ironic, isn't it? The men who preach and teach other people how to find strength in God lose their way on their own pilgrimage. Stress and strain from caring for other people and their problems can be debilitating. Unless pastors and their families develop the ability to recognize the cause of their stress and master ways of managing it, they may throw hands up in surrender and end their ministries.

Legitimate Reasons for Moving

While pastors should not pull the trigger too quickly when it comes to relocation, they ought to be careful not to ignore legitimate indications it is time to move on. Lowrie outlined several signs ministers should not ignore when praying about God's leadership in moving to a new ministry.[2]

Conclusion

In many ministries, a pastor knows when his work is finished. In some cases, God may call a man to a particular place for a specific task. When that goal is accomplished, the Lord moves him to the next venue for a new job. Pastors should be careful first to pray about whether God is finished with them where they are or if they need to receive His next assignment in their current location.

Call

As mentioned previously, a call from a Search Committee may not be an indication God wants you to move. At the same time, the same conviction of divine call that brought you to your current place of service may lead you to your next one. Rarely should a pastor leave a church without having a call to a new ministry. Unless you have disqualified yourself for service, the Lord has a plan and purpose for your ministry. Be sensitive to the ways the Holy Spirit works to show you His direction for the future.

Conflict

Do not leave merely because you are experiencing conflict, but recognize when the conflict is not resolvable. Don't give up too quickly. Use every resource, including mediators, to find a solution. Still, if you have lost your ability to shepherd the people, whether because of conflict or some other reason, it may be time to consider God's next assignment.

Wrapping It Up

Once you determine God is calling you to a different ministry, conclude your work in such a way that honors the Lord and benefits the church.

Be Nice

D. L. Lowrie's book is entitled *A Glad Beginning, A Gracious Ending*. He was right. We should close our ministries graciously. You may have had harsh thoughts toward certain people and lacked the courage to speak them until now. Remember, only a coward takes a cheap shot as he walks out the door. Do your best to resolve conflict and restore relationships as you conclude your ministry. How you leave likely sets the stage for how the next pastor arrives.

Be Honest

Maintain high integrity regarding finances, obligations, and possessions. Scripture reminds us to "Owe no man anything, but to love one another: . . ." (Romans 13:8). Lowrie warns about leaving town with unpaid debts.[3] Skipping out on debts not only leaves you with a bad credit score but it leaves a bad taste with merchants toward ministers in general. Lowrie also advises pastors to be sure to leave behind whatever does not belong to them, whether books, supplies, or equipment.

Be Helpful

Offer your successor the blessing of your knowledge. You may have lists of new members, prospects for evangelism, officers, and workers, and other groups that the next pastor needs to know. Leave a packet of information about the church and community that may help him get a jump-start to a successful ministry.

Be a Blessing

Bless your people as you leave. Many of them, particularly those who love you the most, may not understand why you choose to depart. They may even feel betrayed, or think you no longer love them. Assure them of your continuing affection. Let them know they are not the reason you are leaving but that you are following God's leadership. Prepare them spiritually and emotionally to release you and your family so they might embrace their future pastor and his family.

Surviving Forced Termination[4]

[This part of the chapter is an article by Jere Phillips that first appeared in *Preaching* magazine, May-June, 2013. © 2013, *Preaching* magazine. Used by permission.]

Preacher, You're Fired!

When uttered on a pseudo-reality show by a billionaire, "You're fired" produces smirks and brisk discussions about which celebrity should have been dismissed. However, when addressed to a minister (or anyone else for that matter), these two words evoke raw emotions. Like most people, a preacher who loses his job immediately enters the first stage of grief—shock and disbelief. Questions flood his mind: "Why?" "What did I do?" "What now?" "Can I find another church?" "How will I provide for my family?" "What will people think?" "How do I tell my family?"

Part of the uniqueness of termination for preachers involves our identity. Like many other people, we tend to meld who we are with what we do. Stripped of the pulpit, we can find many vocational means for earning a living, but heralds of God immediately feel lessened when denied the opportunity to preach. In addition, our self-image involves speaking for the Most High. Ministers believe they are bringing a Word from God to their congregations. Termination makes them think either the church leaders are desperately wicked and have made their decisions outside of God's will, or the preachers themselves have been judged by God and found wanting.

None of these drastic evaluations need be true, although in some cases both are accurate. When confronted with the forced separation from a ministry one loves, a preacher can take several steps to avoid personal despair and professional disaster.

Reboot

Take a deep breath. Few good decisions are made by people whose emotions drive their decisions. Anger is a natural part of grief, but, in the heat of the moment, rash statements and unconsidered actions can make a bad situation worse. Instead of responding immediately, take time to think through the situation.

Remind yourself that God still loves you. You haven't been kicked out of the divine family. Not only is your salvation secure but your heavenly Father cares deeply about you and your earthly family.

Rest a bit. Emotional stress begets physical weariness, and tired people have difficulty thinking clearly about next steps. Someone once said that sometimes the most spiritual thing you can do is take a nap! Without giving in to depression and the escape of sleep, you need physical, emotional, mental, and spiritual respite.

Reinforce

Both you and your family need encouragement. How you respond to the situation will influence your family's reaction. Many ministers' wives and children become bitter toward churches in general and church people in particular because of the pain experienced during forced termination. Their lives have suddenly been turned upside down. You face the loss of a home (especially if you live in a church-owned parsonage). Your spouse may worry about facing friends and relatives with the undeserved, but genuinely felt, shame of one's spouse being fired.

Children, especially teenagers, may resist going back to school because they fear what other kids might say to them. Since their peers belong to families in the church, young people's emotions and relationships can be especially traumatized.

The preacher cannot simply offer a stiff upper lip. Your pain is real. To be authentic, you need to share your family's ache, but it needs to be accompanied by the spiritual reinforcement of knowing God has not abandoned you. Reinforce your faith and set the example for your family. Pray together. Honestly express yourself to the Father while affirming your trust in His love and care. Allow your family to pray, "casting all your care on Him, for He cares for you" (1 Peter 5:7).

Reflect

Understanding why the termination occurred is vital to recovery and to making good decisions about the future. Perhaps conflict has been occurring for months. Why has it culminated now? What was the precipitating factor? Before casting blame on the church, its leaders, or others, a healthy approach involves considering the beam in our own eyes. Have we done something wrong? What should we have done differently? Self-reflection does not mean that termination is the minister's fault. However, before we can fairly evaluate others' roles in the problem, we must begin in our own hearts and histories. If needed, now is a good time ask forgiveness, admit a shortcoming, or address a skill deficiency.

On the other hand, self-reflection can reaffirm God's calling. Trace His handiwork through your ministry, see the good things that have happened, as well as the difficult. Remember people whose lives God has allowed you to touch in many positive ways. People have been led to Christ. Marriages have been made and saved. The bereaved have been comforted. Lives have been transformed. Good things have happened. Allow yourself the blessing of seeing how God has worked through your ministry. Remember, too, that He is not finished with you yet. "He who began a good work in you will perform it unto the day of Christ Jesus" (Philippians 1:6).

Reexamine

A wise preacher will make an appointment with one or two individuals to help him reexamine why the leaders believed termination was necessary. All of us have blind spots. If we authentically seek help opening the window of self-awareness, even our enemies may be willing to work with us. In some occasions, antagonists can be won over if approached with a sincere desire to understand their points of view.

If you discover flaws in character or competency on your part, take appropriate steps to make amends. If others are at fault, forgive as God for Christ's sake has forgiven you (Ephesians 4:32). Calmly share your point of view. They need the opportunity to recognize their wrongdoing and, possibly, seek your forgiveness. Your honesty may prevent a future minister from suffering similar problems.

In either case, renew your ministry of reconciliation so that, as much as lies within you, you can live at peace with all parties (Romans 12:18). As you move on to a new place, you don't want to look over your shoulder with animosity between you and these people.

Once you make it past the immediate shock and anger of the termination, you may be tempted to enter another common stage of grief—bargaining. You might try bargaining with God or even attempt engagement with the church to save your job. God does not want our bargains; He simply desires our trust. As for the church, sometimes one may well be able to talk calmly through the issues and negotiate a peace treaty with the powers that be. Indeed, some pastors can work through situations that could have ended their ministries and have come out better, with stronger positions, on the other side.

Restructure

A terminated minister's life has been thrown into chaos. Without deliberate action, he and his family can be swept away by the perfect storm of emotional, financial, and vocational forces. Work with your wife and children to restructure your life. Immediate concerns, once you've addressed the emotional wounds, include financial security and, if living in a church-owned house, providing a home for your family.

Unless the separation from the church has been very acrimonious, most terminated ministers can negotiate some level of compensation, including some transition occupancy of the parsonage. Most reasonable congregations will offer a minister from one to three months of support.

One key need involves continuation of health insurance. Federal health insurance rules may or may not apply to this church. Still, your health insurance company likely offers some type of portability. An early call to your provider may save you difficulties down the road.

Restructuring your budget will help you gain some level of control over your financial stability. If your family has significant debt, you may benefit from consultations with a financial or credit counselor. Many creditors will work with you to adjust interest rates or make other concessions provided the debtor responds responsibly.

Beyond financial issues, work to restructure your lifestyle. Your life has been built around a work schedule determined by office hours, hospital visitation, committee meetings, sermon preparation, and other demands. Suddenly, your time is your own. Too many terminated ministers fall into a depressive state with little motivation to seek a new place of service, or even to handle his family's needs. Develop self-motivated discipline. Set a work schedule that will help you take those proactive steps necessary to secure your family and seek God's direction for the future. Get up in the morning, bathe, dress for work, and begin your transition.

Make time with God a priority in your schedule. Your greatest need is intimacy with the Lord. His Spirit will comfort and guide you. His love will embrace and heal you. His power will refresh you and give you the ability to rise to the challenge.

Spend time in Bible study and prayer. You will find God speaking through your devotional reading. Pour out your heart to the Lord. Allow yourself to commune with your Lord. You may find God opening passages of Scripture with new light.

Keep developing sermons. You may not have a regular place to preach, but be ready "in season and out." You will maintain your homiletical skills and, at the same time, be prepared for opportunities to preach as a supply speaker or interim pastor. In addition, by having sermons at the ready, you won't be scrambling for a message when the next church contacts you.

Reengage

Terminated ministers may feel uncomfortable reengaging in ministry settings, such as returning to the local pastors' conference meetings. However, your peers understand your situation better than anyone else. They can encourage you and possibly help with referrals to churches needing a supply preacher or permanent pastor. Networking with denominational leaders, seminary contacts, and others also opens possibilities and provides important reinforcement personally as well as professionally.

Reengage in service. You do not have to be paid to have a ministry. Opportunities abound for the preacher who has a servant's heart. Hospital chaplains may welcome a volunteer assistant. Nursing homes invite ministers to provide a Sunday or mid-week service. Fire stations need persons willing to lead Bible studies or worship on Sundays.

Join a church. You need a place to worship, a pastor to minister to you and your family, and a church family to care for you. You also would benefit by investing your time and skills in a congregation. Find God's will for the kind of place you need right now. It may be a larger church where your children and teenagers can find friends and activities that minister to their need for belonging. It may be a smaller church that needs your skills as a volunteer teacher. In both cases, spend some time with the pastor to insure you and he understand your new role and needs.

Restart

In His timing, God will likely call you to a new place of ministry. You may be hesitant at first to reenter a vocation associated with difficulties and dislocation. However, if God guides you to a church, prayerfully trust His leadership. Your Lord wants what is best for you and for His Church. Don't allow the pain of the past to prevent your welcoming God's plan for your future.

As you restart your ministry, consider what you learned through this process. Applying the education you received from the school of hard knocks can help you avoid repeating former errors. In addition, you have a lifetime of positive ministry experiences to help you do a great job in a new position. Draw on both sets of skills to begin afresh.

Proceed with the confidence that God loves you and your family. Move forward into a bright new day of ministry. Preach the Word! Fulfill your ministry!

BENEDICTION

"Now the God of peace, that brought again from the dead our Lord Jesus, that great shepherd of the sheep, through the blood of the everlasting covenant, Make you perfect in every good work to do his will, working in you that which is well pleasing in his sight, through Jesus Christ; to whom be glory for ever and ever. Amen" (Hebrews 13:20–21).

ENDNOTES

Chapter 1

1. Ed Stetzer, Richie Stanley, and Jason Hayes, *Lost and Found: The Younger Unchurched and the Churches That Reach Them* (Nashville: B&H Publishing, © 2009), 200.
2. Stephen Furtick: "Radicalis 2011: Three things this generation demands." http://www.stevenfurtick.com/leadership/bonus-tracks-3-things-this-generation-demands/)
3. Charles Swindoll, interview with Michael Duduit, *Preaching* magazine; http://www.preaching.com/resources/articles/11629161/page-6/)
4. Brett McCracken, "The Dangerous Pursuit of Cool," http://www.outofur.com/archives/2010/09/the_dangerous_p_2.html)
5. Ed Stetzer, *Comeback Churches* (Nashville: B&H Publishing, © 2007), 7.
6. Some aspects of this subchapter first appeared in Dr. Phillips' article entitled "Trans-generational Preaching," published in *Preaching* magazine, © 2005, used here by permission of the publisher.
7. Voddie Baucham Jr., *Family Driven Faith: Doing What It Takes to Raise Sons and Daughters Who Walk with God* (Wheaton, IL: Crossway Books, © 2011).
8. Reggie Joiner, *Think Orange* (Colorado Springs: David C. Cook Publishers, © 2009), 26.

Chapter 3

1. George Barna, *A Fish Out of Water* (Ventura, CA: used by permission by The Barna Group, © 2002).
2. Lyman Abbott, *The Christian Ministry* (Boston: Houghton Mifflin and Company, © 1905), 202–203.
3. William Taylor, *The Ministry of the Word* (New York: Anson D. Randolph and Co., © 1876), 25.
4. Francis Chan, *Crazy Love: Overwhelmed by a Relentless God* is published by David C. Cook © 2013. Used by permission. All rights reserved. Publisher's permission required to reproduce. pp. 35–36.
5. E. M. Bounds, *The Preacher and Prayer* (Publishing House of the M. E. Church, South, © 1907), 37.

Chapter 4

1. The above section on the value of the call is also found in *The Missionary Family: Managing Stress Successfully*, by Jere Phillips, © 2013 Innovo Publishing.
2. H. B. London and Neil B. Wiseman, *The Heart of a Great Pastor* (Ventura, CA: Regal Books, © 1994), 20.

Chapter 5

1. Conner, R. Dwayne, *Called to Stay* (Nashville: Convention Press, © 1987, reprinted and used by permission), 30.
2. A good list of potential questions can be found in the *Pastor and Staff Search Committee* resource kit by Don Mathis and Donna Gandy. While a bit dated, this list can be very helpful. Don Mathis and Donna Gandy *Pastor and Staff Search Committee Resource Kit* (Nashville: Convention Press, ©1998).

Chapter 7

1. James Means, *Leadership in Christian Ministry* (Grand Rapids: Baker Book House, © 1989), 41.
2. Tom Peters and Robert Waterman, Jr., *In Search of Excellence* (New York: Warner Books, © 1982), 279.

Chapter 8

1. D. L. Lowrie, *A Glad Beginning, A Gracious Ending* (Nashville: Broadman Press, ©1988), 22–24.
2. Ibid.

Chapter 10

1. "Training Deacons to Minister to the Bereaved," Doctor of Ministry Project Report by Dr. Kenny Bruce; Southwestern Baptist Theological Seminary, 1989. Copyright by Dr. Kenny Bruce, used by permission. (The outline of this section belongs to Dr. Bruce. Comments are by Jere Phillips.)

Chapter 11

1. David Benner, *Strategic Pastoral Counseling* (Grand Rapids: Baker Academic, © 2003), 31.
2. Jay Adams, *Christian Counselor's Manual* (Grand Rapids: Zondervan, © 1973), 433.
3. Jay Adams, *How to Help People Change* (Grand Rapids: Zondervan, © 1986), 149.
4. Jay Adams, *The Christian Counselor's Manual* (Grand Rapids: Zondervan, © 1973), 176.
5. Charles Solomon, *Counseling with the Mind of Christ* (Fleming Revell, © 1977).

Chapter 12

1. David Kim, *20 and Something* (Grand Rapids: Zondervan, © 2013), 25.

2. Ibid, 67.

3. Norman H. Wright, *Premarital Counseling Handbook* (Chicago: Moody Press, © 1992).

4. The DISC (Discernment) Personality Profile is available online from various vendors. Counselors should receive training before using it. Ministers should not employ any inventory without proper preparation and certification.

Chapter 13

1 "The Broken Matzah," accessed June 4, 2014, http://www.chaim.org/afikomen.htm

2. Chabad.org "The Silent Cup," accessed June 4, 2014, http://www.chabad.org/library/article_cdo/aid/117141/jewish/The-Silent-Cup.htm

Chapter 14

1. John R. Stott, *Between Two Worlds* (Grand Rapids: Eerdmans, ©1982), 15, 50–51.

2. James S. Stewart, *Heralds of God* (Grand Rapids: Baker Books, ©1972), 12, 27.

3. Bryan Chapell, *Christ-Centered Preaching* (Grand Rapids: Baker Books, © 1994). 257.

4. Jerry Vines, *Power in the Pulpit* (Chicago: Moody Press, © 1999), 64.

5. Haddon Robinson, *Biblical Preaching* (Grand Rapids: Baker, © 2001), 26; for original source, see William A. Quayle, *The Pastor-Preacher* (Grand Rapids: Baker Book House, ©1979), 27.

6. Bill Hybels, Haddon Robinson, Stuart Briscoe, *Mastering Contemporary Preaching* (Portland: Multnomah Press, © 1989), 146. Used by permission of Stuart Briscoe.

7. Andrew Blackwood, *The Preparation of Sermons* (Nashville: Abingdon, © 1948 by Stone and Pierce), 39.

8. Sidney Greidanus, *The Modern Preacher and the Ancient Text* (Grand Rapids: Eerdman's, © 1989), 15.

9. Haddon Robinson, *Biblical Preaching* (Grand Rapids: Baker Academic, © 2001), 20.

10. Sidney Greidanus, *The Modern Preacher and the Ancient Text: Interpreting and Preaching Biblical Literature* (Grand Rapids: Eerdman's Publishing, © 1989), 2.

11. Stephen Olford and David Olford, *Anointed Expository Preaching* (Nashville: B&H Publishing, © 1998), 69.

12. Harold Bryson, *Expository Preaching* (Nashville: B&H Publishers, © 1995), 112. Used by permission of the author.

13. Dr. Robert Pitman, unpublished manuscript, copyright © 2005 Dr. Bob Pitman, used by permission.

14. Haddon Robinson, *Biblical Preaching* (Grand Rapids: Baker, © 2001), 54.

15. Part of this section originally appeared in *Preaching* magazine under the title "The

Curious Case of the Illusive Illustration." Copyright 2009. *Preaching*. The content was written by Dr. Jere Phillips. Used by permission.

16. Robert E. Coleman, "Introduction" to R. Alan Street, *The Effective Invitation* (New Jersey: Fleming Revell, © 1984), 15.

17. Derek J. Prime and Alistair Begg. *On Being a Pastor: Understanding Our Calling and Work* (Chicago: Moody Press, 2013).

Chapter 15

1. Desiring God Foundation, "Worship Is an End in Itself," accessed June 10, 2014, copyright 2014 by John Piper, used by permission, http://www.desiringgod.org/sermons/worship-is-an-end-in-itself

2. Ed Stetzer, *Comeback Churches*, pp. 81–84.

Chapter 16

1. This section comes from an article by the author entitled "Evangelism Methods that Grow Churches." It first appeared in *The Journal of Evangelism and Missions*, Mid-America Baptist Theological Seminary, © 2011. Used by permission.

2. W. A. Criswell, *Criswell's Guidebook for Pastors* (Nashville: Broadman Press, (xc) 1980), 136–137.

Chapter 17

1. John Mark Terry, *Church Evangelism* (Nashville: B&H Publishers, © 1997), 195.

Chapter 19

1. Henry Blackaby, *Spiritual Leadership* (Nashville: B&H Publishers, © 2011).

Chapter 20

1. Steven Covey, statement made in a seminar based on his book, *Seven Habits of Highly Effective People*.

2. Hyrum Smith, *10 Natural Laws of Successful Time and Life Management* (New York: Warner Books, ©1994), 65.

3. Richard Swenson, *Margin* (Colorado Springs: NavPress, © 2004).

4. Peter M. Senge, *The Fifth Discipline: The Art & Practice of The Learning Organization* (New York: Doubleday, © 2006).

Chapter 21

1. Myron Rush, *Management; A Biblical Approach* (Wheaton, IL: Victor Books, © 1984), 185ff.
2. James Bryant and Mac Brunson, *The New Guidebook for Pastors* (Nashville: B&H Publishing, © 2007), 91.

Chapter 22

1. Leonard I. Sweet, *AquaChurch: Essential Leadership Arts for Piloting Your Church in Today's Fluid Culture* (Loveland, CO: Group Publishing, 1999). Used by permission of the author.
2. "Touch Not the Glory," Words by Erma Davison, Music by Patricia Owens, Copyright © 1993 by Ron and Patricia Owens, Used by Permission.

Chapter 23

1. *Thy Kingdom Come* is a spiritual planning process developed by the South Carolina Baptist Convention, (Copyright © 1998, South Carolina Baptist Convention).

Chapter 24

1. This chapter originally appeared in *The Missionary Family: Managing Stress Effectively*, by Jere Phillips, (Collierville, TN: Innovo Publishing, © 2013.)

Chapter 25

1. Originally published as part of the article "The Stewardship of Technology" by Jere Phillips in *The Messenger*, Mid-America Baptist Theological Seminary, © 2007.

Chapter 28

1. D. L. Lowrie, *A Glad Beginning, A Gracious Ending* (Nashville: Broadman Press, ©1988), 65. Used by permission of the author.
2. Ibid., 69.
3. Ibid., p. 92.
4. This part of the chapter is an article by Jere Phillips. It first appeared in *Preaching* magazine, May–June, Copyright © 2013. Used by permission.

CPSIA information can be obtained
at www.ICGtesting.com
Printed in the USA
BVHW011911250320
575981BV00007B/165